The Book of Job

The Book of Job

A Modern Translation and Commentary

LEONARD S. KRAVITZ
and
KERRY M. OLITZKY

WIPF & STOCK · Eugene, Oregon

THE BOOK OF JOB
A Modern Translation and Commentary

Copyright © 2017 Leonard S. Kravitz and Kerry M. Olitzky. All rights reserved. Except for brief quotations in critical publications or reviews, no part of this book may be reproduced in any manner without prior written permission from the publisher. Write: Permissions, Wipf and Stock Publishers, 199 W. 8th Ave., Suite 3, Eugene, OR 97401.

Wipf & Stock
An Imprint of Wipf and Stock Publishers
199 W. 8th Ave., Suite 3
Eugene, OR 97401

www.wipfandstock.com

PAPERBACK ISBN: 978-1-5326-3604-2
HARDCOVER ISBN: 978-1-5326-3606-6
EBOOK ISBN: 978-1-5326-3605-9

Manufactured in the U.S.A.   NOVEMBER 3, 2017

The authors gratefully acknowledge the following for permission to reprint previously published material:

Leonard Kravitz and Kerry Olitzky, *Kohelet: A Modern Commentary on Ecclesiastes*. New York: UAHC Press, 2003, p. 20, 41. © Behrman House, Inc., included with permission. www.behrmanhouse.com.

Leonard S. Kravitz and Kerry M. Olitzky, *Mishlei: A Modern Commentary on Proverbs*. New York: UAHC Press, 2002, p. 13, 55, 106, 204, 243. © Behrman House, Inc., included with permission. www.behrmanhouse.com.

Leonard Kravitz and Kerry Olitzky, *Pirke Avot: A Modern Commentary on Jewish Ethics*. New York: UAHC Press, 1993, p. 9. © Behrman House, Inc., included with permission. www.behrmanhouse.com.

To Hanna, for everything,
as ever!
—LSK

For Lee Livingston,
and his unconditional friendship and support.
—KMO

Contents

Acknowledgments | ix

Introduction | xi

Chapter 1 | 1

Chapter 2 | 8

Chapter 3 | 14

Chapter 4 | 21

Chapter 5 | 27

Chapter 6 | 34

Chapter 7 | 41

Chapter 8 | 48

Chapter 9 | 54

Chapter 10 | 60

Chapter 11 | 66

Chapter 12 | 72

Chapter 13 | 78

Chapter 14 | 85

Chapter 15 | 91

Chapter 16 | 98

Chapter 17 | 103

Chapter 18 | 108

Chapter 19 | 114

Chapter 20 | 121

Chapter 21 | 127

Chapter 22 | 134
Chapter 23 | 141
Chapter 24 | 145
Chapter 25 | 151
Chapter 26 | 154
Chapter 27 | 157
Chapter 28 | 163
Chapter 29 | 168
Chapter 30 | 174
Chapter 31 | 180
Chapter 32 | 188
Chapter 33 | 194
Chapter 34 | 200
Chapter 35 | 207
Chapter 36 | 212
Chapter 37 | 219
Chapter 38 | 224
Chapter 39 | 233
Chapter 40 | 239
Chapter 41 | 245
Chapter 42 | 250

For Further Reading | *255*

Acknowledgments

WE HAVE BEEN COLLEAGUES and friends for nearly forty years. Together, we have cultivated many ideas, constantly striving to provide access to the sacred texts of the Jewish tradition to a growing number of people. And we have struggled with many sacred texts in which the inherent theology of the text does not immediately resonate with our own beliefs. This is by far the most difficult aspect of our work, never more so than with this book. For the book of Job forces us to confront the basic claims of Jewish theology and faith.

Even as we are mindful of the people whom we knew who lived righteous lives and yet were not rewarded with long life, we remain resolute in our commitment to Jewish faith and practice.

We are exceptionally appreciative of all those who have contributed of their own talents to turn the idea of this volume into a reality, particularly Ben Denckla and Rabbi Gail Diamond, the latter of whom served as a content editor. Both have been amazingly supportive partners and gentle critics throughout the process, making sure that the book speaks to those who yearn to listen. We also thank our new friends at Wipf and Stock who believe in the power of this sacred text as much as we do, especially Jim Tedrick.

We also thank our many former students and colleagues at Hebrew Union College-Jewish Institute of Religion and Big Tent Judaism who allowed us to probe the text with them and to teach Torah to others through a variety of means.

More than anything else, we express our deep appreciation to our families for supporting us on this and other journeys of the spirit that we have taken over the course of our lifetimes and our work together. It is their unconditional love that gives a depth of meaning to any of the words contained within the pages of this book. And we thank God daily for the opportunity and ability to continue to work in such vineyards so that others too may enjoy the sweet fruits of our labors.

Leonard S. Kravitz
Kerry M. Olitzky

Introduction

BECAUSE OF THE BURDEN of evil that riddles its pages, Job is probably the most difficult book in the Bible to read. Like some noxious plant that spreads its tendrils to poison anything it touches, evil emerges in its manifold and variegated forms throughout the book of Job. And the reader, whose experience of the world mirrors various aspects of the life of Job, is forced to confront the role of a good God in the midst of such evil. The characters in the book of Job, whether they are human or superhuman, with the possible exception of Job, manifest various forms of this evil. Thus, the image of God that is depicted in the book of Job presents the reader with more than just an abstract notion of theodicy, that is, the relation of evil to a God of goodness. Rather, the God who is portrayed in Job is a viciously playful deity who, in order to win a wager from Satan, is willing to cause a devout person (Job) to suffer. Even the wager itself is consummate evil.

Thus, the one who proposes or accepts it is evil. This makes the challenge to understand and relate to the God of the book of Job even more difficult since God, as portrayed, accepted Satan's challenge. Such an understanding could potentially distance us from such a God when the study of sacred text is supposed to bring us into a closer relationship with the Divine, to close the chasm that may naturally exist between humanity and divinity. Satan is devilishly clever. He threatens God's image by asking about Job's motivation: Is God so loveable that Job is willing to serve the Divine out of love or is God not so loveable that Job is only prepared to be of service because he receives something priceless in return? The reader might imagine Satan's sneer: "You are so marvelous that the only reason anyone would love You is because you pay!" Satan's comment reflects our own struggle when our faith is challenged by the rabbinic system of reward and punishment that the book of Job exposes as riddled with difficulties. This is why the Rabbis' commentaries are important to explore before coming to our own conclusions about the religious message of the book of Job.

Job is a virtuous, wealthy man who lives in Uz. God permits Satan to attack Job's property, his family, and then his person. But human beings look no better than do the supernatural in Job. Job's wife, in a moment of rage, assuming that God will punish Job for so doing, tells her husband to curse God and die. Her anger counsels his suicide.

Job's so-called comforters and friends are no better. These friends come to visit him in his misfortune: Eliphaz the Temanite, Bildad the Shuhite, and Zophar the Naamatite.

A fourth, Elihu the Buzite, begins speaking in chapter 32, but his arrival is not explained.

They spend a week with Job sitting on the ground, a sign of profound empathy, but they don't speak until Job breaks the silence—a practice that has been institutionalized among other Jewish mourning principles derived from the book of Job. Because their belief in God does not waiver, a position that we consider unrealistic and not reflective of the contemporary life of the spirit, Job's friends are convinced that punishment deserves sin. Job must have done something wrong; otherwise he would not be forced to suffer. They cling to their belief that God rewards good and punishes evil. So they convict Job without analyzing his situation. Like too many other humans, they seem to enjoy seeing Job in distress. They luxuriate in Job's misery so that they can rise above it and explain to him why his actions have not found favor with God. Job's behaviors prove to them that Job was not the righteous person he professed to be. What happened to Job "proves" that he was a fake. His punishment demonstrates that he was fooling everyone with his righteous acting. Finally, the truth has emerged. Perhaps this is one of the reasons that the reading of the book of Job appeals to so many of us. We too wonder: although we may attempt to lead righteous lives, and we may try to say the right things, perhaps we too are fakes and deserving of some of the things we are forced to endure in our own lives.

Job refuses to accept the reasoning of these first three friends. But he also refuses to curse God. Then Elihu speaks. Elihu mediates for Job and in a scene that has become depicted in art throughout history: God responds in the whirlwind of a cloud. God condemns Job's friends, because they spoke incorrectly of God's motives and directs them to offer sacrifices for Job and to pray for their welfare. As we review the arguments made by Job's friends, along with his own rebuttal, we are being invited as readers to enter the text, to become the individual characters. And when we leave our study, we take the text with us. It has become part of who we are, indelibly written into our soul. At the same time, we leave a little of ourselves in the text. As a result, we become changed—as does the text itself. This is why these sacred texts retain their dynamism but only when we are willing to enter them fully and engage them.

Our treatment of the book of Job in this volume is no simple read with commentary, although such an approach can be an important tool in understanding Job. Rather, this volume uses the classic approach of calling on the understanding of former rabbinic commentaries before coming to our own conclusions about how to understand the theology of the book and attempt to answer some of the basic answers of human existence posed by religion: Why is there evil? Why do the good suffer? Why do those who do evil seem to go unpunished? Are acts of goodness rewarded?

Let's begin by discussing the first question that the book of Job asks, whose definition will be required to understand the entire book: what is evil? Evil is admittedly quite complex. The book of Job tries to present a simple definition of evil by demonstrating that the intentional actions of Satan—who attempts to force disaster on Job—are not deserved. Thus, evil is more than the absence of good. Rather, evil is that which emerges when good is not permitted to surface. We name the very act which prohibits good—and disallows a system of good to operate—as evil, however it is personified.

The evils presented in the book of Job are the intentional actions of Satan and the compliance of God with such actions which afflict Job with suffering and pain. Evil has yet another aspect in this book. Job is being accused of being an evildoer himself. Since biblical theology reflected the idea that God punished evil, Job's suffering was taken as proof that he was being punished and hence was a doer of evil. Job's maintenance of his position as being innocent threatened the belief in a just God. If Job were innocent, then one could say God was guilty. Such a blasphemous notion was never made explicit in the book of Job, but it would explain the motivations of Job's comforters.

The suffering of Job is considered evil, because it is unmerited and caused by the One who is supposed to be on the side of good and not the perpetrator of Job's suffering.

Such an image of God—as portrayed in the beginning of Job—conflicts with the general notion of God as we know it in most religious sources. After all, a God who acts badly to win a bet is hardly the model of rectitude which individuals should imitate. Moreover, a God who is moved to such an immoral act by Satan, a lesser being, would hardly be a model for the resistance to temptation that any of us would care to emulate. Although we may not resonate with the stand that Job takes and are often taught in the postmodern world to take a stand against injustice, Job serves as a religious exemplar in the rabbinic minds, because he does not complain about what has happened to him. "Shall we receive good from God and not evil?" (Job 2:10) is the profound question he puts to his wife. One wonders if any human could really be motivated to make such a statement, especially in the face of what Job endures. That Job serves God out of love and not for reward does not adequately explain his response. One may act out of love but in response to what the Rabbis call *yissurim shel ahava* (the suffering of love), one would still expect the natural human response of a person to complain when suffering is unwarranted. Job responds to his suffering by rending his clothes, falling down and uttering a claim which has become a familiar phrase later associated with Jewish mourning and bereavement, "I came naked from my mother's womb. And naked shall I return. Adonai gave. Adonai takes away. Praised be the name of the Lord" (Job 1:21). In the biblical context Job is not prepared to teach us what some postmodern theologians want us to learn, that God is beyond the question of good and evil, that some actions occur in the natural course of events in the world. As a result, we cannot take seriously the proposition that God would respond to the challenges of a Satan, were such a being even to exist. Nevertheless, the message that transcends the book is that a religious life is to be lived; it is a reward unto itself.

We also have to recognize that even if this book comes from two different sources, as noted above, it has been bequeathed to us as a unit. It is, therefore, incumbent on us to ascertain the message of the editor when presenting us with the book as a whole. To help us fully understand the positions taken by the author of the book of Job, it is important to understand its literary and structural design. The book of Job may be considered a didactic poem—one whose purpose is to teach a lesson—that is set in the frame of a prose narrative. The introductory and concluding sections serve as a frame for the middle of the book, which chapters together form the poem.

Some date the book as written during the Babylonian exile (586–538 BCE). Secular scholars claim that the form of Job was fixed by the fourth century BCE although the book is familiar to the seventh-/sixth-century BCE prophet Ezekiel (14:14). Fragments of the book are contained in the Dead Sea Scrolls.

Because the traditional understanding of the book of Job is important to the contemporary reader as he or she struggles with its meaning, we use the prism of various commentators through which to view the text. We selected those who might best be described as classical commentators, representing the traditional spectrum of Jewish religious and philosophical life. These commentators sought to view such texts through the lens of their own time and understanding. By each generation attempting to understand a particular text, it provides a foundation for the succeeding generation to do the same. We do the same in our time, as reflected in the entire volume, as well as our specific comments on individual selections of text. These classical commentaries include the *Targum*, the Aramaic translation of the text from the third century of the Common Era in the land of Israel which is as much commentary as it is translation.

We will also see what Abraham Ibn Ezra (1098–1164 CE) has to say about the text from the perspective of one who was born in Spain; lived in Mantua, Rome and London; and was model for Robert Browning's poem "Rabbi Ben Ezra." This commentary reflects the impact of philosophy on Judaism.

Rashi (the acronym for RAbbi SHlomo Itzchaki) who lived in Troyes from 1040–1105 CE is considered Judaism's commentator par excellence because of his encyclopedic sweep of classic Jewish text and tradition. As a result, his commentary reflects the notions of Rabbinic Judaism more than most others.

Our final commentator, Rabbi Levi ben Gerson (1288–1344, otherwise known as Gersonides or by the acronym Ralbag) reflects the high point of philosophical involvement in Judaism. Just as Rashi read the rabbinic tradition into the text, Gersonides read philosophy into the text. Neither Ibn Ezra nor Gersonides follow classical Jewish tradition's view that Job deserved his suffering as punishment for his failings. Only Rashi maintains this position.

We have also added mini-essays at the end of some chapters to further elucidate various ideas that emerge in the commentary. Unless specifically noted, all translations and English renderings are by the authors of this volume. At times, the authors have used quotation marks to indicate what Job or another character in the text might have said or was trying to say, even when it is not an exact rendering of the verse.

Chapter 1

> 1:1 There was once a man from the land of Uz whose name was Job; that man was honest and upright, fearing God and keeping far from evil.

THE AUTHOR OF THIS text is quite clear: Job was upright and honest. Not only was he a good man, but he also kept himself far from evil. Undaunted, Rashi claimed that Job's virtue was forced. He comes to this conclusion by understanding the verb *v'haya* "(and) was" to mean "became." So the remainder of the verse, suggests Rashi, implies that because Job was afraid of God (and not because Job loved God) Job kept himself far from evil. Ibn Ezra rejects Rashi's explanation and supports the author's claim of Job's righteousness.

According to Gersonides, Job had been successful in acquiring possessions that were illusory, like those of money and children. They ultimately had no real value. While we might accept his position about the former, few parents would accept his opinion about the latter. Gersonides argued that Job's children were well-behaved in terms of political behavior, blending desire and love as evinced by their continual eating together so as to intensify their feelings of community. Job would seek to consecrate them from one period to the next. Every seven days he would offer sacrifices with the assumption that somehow one of them might have sinned and condemned God because of the temptations offered by their wealth and their easy life.

> 1:2 Seven sons and three daughters were born to him.

This is a straightforward verse. Job had seven sons and three daughters.

> 1:3 He owned seven thousand sheep, three thousand camels, five hundred yoke of oxen, and five hundred female donkeys, and a great household as well. He was the most important person of all of the people of the east.

While this verse may be read as a way for the author to further introduce the reader to Job, its real purpose is to describe the extent of Job's wealth and influence.

> 1:4 His sons took turns holding feasts in their homes and they invited their sisters to eat and drink with them.

In order to get a better sense of the duration of the feasts, or perhaps to define them in terms of time, the Targum suggests that each feast lasted seven days. Rashi too wants the reader to understand the nature of these feasts. He reports that each brother held a feast in his own home.

> 1:5 When the cycle of feasting was finished, Job would send for his sons and daughters and sanctify them. Arising early in the morning, he would offer burnt offerings for each one, thinking [to himself], "What if my children have sinned by cursing God in their thoughts?" [so] Job kept doing this.

It is clear that Job, like most parents, worried about his children and tried to protect them. He offered sacrifices as a prophylactic measure. The sacrifices served to sanctify Job's children. Although the text says, "Job would send," it does not indicate for whom he sent. Following Rashi's suggestion, we have added "his sons and daughters" to our translation. Thus, we translated *banai* (literally, "my sons") as "my children."

> 1:6 One certain day the angels of God came to present themselves before Adonai and Satan came along with them.

This verse echoes an earlier time in which an anthropomorphic notion of God was more prevalent. Satan's presence among them comes as no surprise to the reader to whom a power of evil was manifest in the world as a reasonable conclusion to the events he or she endured.

> 1:7 Adonai said to Satan, "Where are you coming from?" Satan thus answered Adonai, "From roaming around the earth and from walking up and down in it."

In this verse, Satan is not very responsive to God. The Targum suggests that when he is "roaming around the earth" Satan is examining the deeds of humans. Similarly, Rashi argues that Satan is looking for those who are good and those who are evil. Satan is disappointed that he has not found anyone to match Abraham.

> 1:8 Adonai said to Satan, "Have you noticed my servant Job? No one is like him in all the earth. Perfect and upright, he fears God and keeps far from evil."

God is familiar with Job. He is a good person and God knows it. Rashi thinks that the question is posed as God's way of asking Satan whether Satan wants to accuse such a person of transgression and misdeeds.

1:9 Satan answered God, "Does Job revere God for nothing?"

While the sense of the verse is clear, it is difficult to translate into a contemporary American English idiom. The interrogative *hay* introduces "for free, for naught, for no reason, for nothing."

> 1:10 "Haven't you set up a [protective] hedge around him, around his family, and around everything that he has? You have blessed him so that his flocks have spread out throughout the land."

This verse continues Satan's statement from the previous verse. He is asking whether there is piety for its own sake, without reward—does Job not get something for his faith? We are caught up again with the Torah and rabbinic statements that promise reward and threaten punishment. On the other hand, the author of the book of Job places such statements in the mouth of Satan which suggest that there can be disinterested piety.

The Targum wants the reader to understand the power of Jewish observance, specifically following the words of Torah. It translates the verse as "Has not Your word screened him, protecting him, his family, and all that he has? You have blessed the work of his hands. His flocks increased throughout the land." The verse seems to imply an actual hedge whereas the Targum translates it more as a metaphor or even a spiritual screen of some sort.

> 1:11 Just stretch out your hand and touch whatever he has and he will curse you right to your face.

This continues Satan's dialogue with God. Satan is convinced that all God has to do is undermine Job and Job will immediately be transformed from a person of faith into one who curses the Almighty. Satan is attempting to demonstrate the superficiality of Job's faith—that it is solely dependent on his well-being. As soon as his fortunes change, so will his faith, claims Satan. In an attempt to mitigate the message of Satan slightly and avoid any possible anthropomorphism, the Targum changes "You" (as in ". . . he will curse You") to "Your word." This means that Job would curse the word of God rather than the Divine self.

> 1:12 Adonai said to Satan, "All right, you have power over all he has, but don't touch the man himself." Satan then left the presence of Adonai.

Although the sense of the verse is clear, it is difficult to translate the words themselves into idiomatic English. God has given control over Job's possessions to Satan as a way of proving that Job does not serve God only while he appears to derive benefits from his faith. While the text never tells us that he gained his wealth because of his faith, it can be presumed in a system of reward and punishment.

> 1:13 It happened on a day when the sons and daughters of Job were dining and drinking wine in the home of the oldest brother.

This verse introduces the action that will take place in the next verses. The Targum reminds us that this "day" is the beginning of the seven-day cycle of feasting that each of the sons of Job carried out. (See the Targum on Job 1:4 above.)

> 1:14 A messenger came to Job and said, "The oxen were plowing and the asses were grazing near them."

The meaning of this verse is straightforward.

> 1:15 "The Sabeans made a raid, taking them [the animals] and killing the servants by the sword. I am the only one who got away to tell you!"

Given the context provided by the previous verse, we have translated the word "them" as "the animals." Having taken the animals, the raiders had no need to kill the servants; yet they did. The report given by the sole survivor adds horror to what took place.

> 1:16 While this messenger was still speaking, another came and said, "A fire of God came down from heaven and totally burnt up the sheep and the shepherds and I am the only one that got away to tell you this!"

Another tragedy for Job to absorb. Unlike the previous assault, this one was due to some kind of natural (or divine) occurrence. It was not the result of human action. Gersonides explains, however, that this is an example of the negative effect of chance events.

> 1:17 Yet another messenger came while he was still speaking and said, "Arrayed in three groups, the Chaldeans spread out around the camels and snatched them away. With swords, they killed the guards. I am the only one that got away to tell you this!"

Still more tragedy. Two tragedies are a result of surrounding peoples—the Sabeans and the Chaldeans—and one is due to an unexplained natural event. No matter the details, the results are quite clear. A group of marauders came, killed the shepherds and stole the animals.

> 1:18 The last was still speaking when another messenger came and said, "Your sons and daughters were dining and drinking wine in the oldest brother's home."

Although this verse follows the pattern of the messengers' previous announcements, the author creates suspense by dividing the action into two verses. The use of the participle *medaber* (speaking) and *ochlim v'shotim* (were dining and drinking) present the reader with the immediacy of the situation.

Rashi contends that the messengers who brought Job the bad news were agents of Satan determined to provoke Job into sinning by presenting a graduated set of losses beginning with that which was comparatively negligible, the loss of cattle and their keepers, and ending with what is horrific, the apparent loss of Job's children.

> 1:19 "All of a sudden, from deep in the wilderness, an enormous wind blew in, smashing the four corners of the house, collapsing it on the young people, killing all of them. I am the only one who got away to tell you this."

While this seems like a simple reporting of events, there is no way to describe the deep pain implicit in this verse. All of Job's children have been killed by an unexplained and unanticipated natural force. Most of the commentators wisely do not try to interpret this verse and simply allow it to stand in all of its ugliness. They do, however, try to understand the location of *eyver ha-midbar*, which we have translated as "from deep in the wilderness."

> 1:20 Job got up, tore his garment, shaved his head, fell on the ground and prostrated himself.

Job's pain could not be articulated in words. He knew not what to do. So he responded silently. But the reader can hear the pain screaming out from his silence.

Understandably, Job collapses on the ground. Yet, the Targum feels compelled to translate *v'y'ishtachu* (prostrated himself) as *segeed* (worshipped). It therefore suggests that Job's reaction was to worship God—a highly improbable reaction. On the other hand, Rashi's interpretation of *vayagoz* (shaved his head) is probably more accurate: "he tore out his hair."

> 1:21 Job said, "Naked came I from my mother's womb and naked will I return there. Adonai has given and Adonai has taken away. Praised be the name of Adonai!"

This is a well-known verse. The last phrase has entered into the liturgy for Jewish funerals. This stoic and faithful response seems not to be in accord with the reaction described in the previous verse. Perhaps some time transpired between Job's actions in 1:20 and what he says in 1:21.

In his commentary, Gersonides reminds us that even with this terrible trial, Job maintained his integrity and his faith, directing us to the verse that follows. Job did not sin. Rather, he continued to praise God.

Anyone would have expected Job's reaction to be one of outrage and anger. For the believer, however, one might have expected a response such as "There must be some divine purpose in all of this" or "We cannot know why God so acts." For most of us, his reaction is not a Jewish reaction; we would not expect a Jewish person to resign oneself to whatever one receives in life. Rather, one expects him to cry out, to lash out. The reaction of Job is not one with which we are familiar nor to which we can relate, even among the faithful.

> 1:22 With all of this, Job did not sin nor did he say anything bad about God.

This is what we have learned about Job. He experiences the worst things imaginable and accepts it all. We assume that his faith was unshaken. For the book of Job's logic to work, Job had to maintain his belief in God. Job does not express his discontent by rejecting God nor by behaving the way someone who does not acknowledge God might behave. Rather, he continues to lead a good life and presumably continues to praise God, maintaining the same life of faith as he had before his family was taken from him.

SATAN

Unlike in popular culture (which is informed by Christian religion), in the Hebrew Bible, Satan is not used as a proper name nor is it a reference to a demonic antagonist to God (except for its usage in 1 Chronicles 21:1). Instead, Satan is an adversary—sometimes even human—who opposes and obstructs. We have chosen to use Satan as a proper noun nonetheless in this translation. The term is used in another form in the rabbinic imagination of the heavenly court of judgment referring to the prosecutor and the role of the antagonist in general. In Job, Satan is clearly subordinate to God and a member of the celestial court.

Satan is given a much more prominent role in the Talmud and midrash. He is even identified as the *yetzer harah* (evil inclination) and the Angel of Death (Babylonian Talmud, *Bava Batra* 16a). He appears as the tempter, but his role is more clearly defined by the Rabbis as the accuser. References to Satan in the liturgy are sparse, although Satan is mentioned in the *Hashkiveinu* prayer of the evening service and the morning blessings that precede *P'sukei D'zimra* (verses of song).

Chapter 2

> 2:1 It was on another day that the angels of God came to present themselves before Adonai. Satan also came along to present himself to Adonai.

A SCENE SIMILAR TO the one about which we read in 1:6 opens chapter 2. The author writes the verse to suggest that the scene is rather routine. The angels regularly present themselves before God and Satan is apparently included among them. *B'nai elohim* figure as the progenitors of *giborim* (mighty men) in Genesis 6:4. That those at Sinai (Exodus 20:2) were warned against *elohim achareyim* (others gods) suggests that monotheism proceeded first out of monolatry. *B'nai elohim* as a kind of congress of deities does not seem to faze the writer of the book of Job.

For Gersonides, the mention of Satan in this verse indicates a connection between the last and worst of the evils that befell Job. For Gersonides, evil doesn't exist independently. Gersonides notes that unlike the previous verse (1:6) which also described the "children of God" who presented themselves before God with Satan in their midst, this verse tells us that Satan presented himself alone. For Gersonides, this is an allusion to that portion of the human soul to which advice may be directed, that is, for the service of the human intellect so that it may achieve perfection. So for Gersonides, the book of Job is a parable about imagination's role in moving us toward what is impermanent and away from what is permanent.

> 2:2 Adonai said to Satan, "Where are you coming from?" Satan answered Adonai, "From wandering around the earth and walking back and forth through it."

As in 1:7, the Targum adds that Satan's movements were to *mivdsak b'ovdai bnai nesha*, to "examine the deeds of humans."

> 2:3 Adonai said to Satan, "Have you paid attention to my servant Job? Nobody on earth is like him. Upright and honest, revering God and turning away from evil, he remains without blame,

even though you have incited me against him to batter him for no reason."

God shows Satan that Job didn't react as Satan had expected. Rather than react with anger to what befell him, Job continued to lead a life of blessing.

> 2:4 Satan answered, "Skin for skin. For one's own life, a person will give up everything he [or she] owns."

Many families have their own insights that reflect the folk wisdom of this verse. The phrase "skin for skin" appears to be a proverb of some kind. To help understand it, the Targum translates the proverb as "limb for limb."

Rashi thus understands the phrase: Were one to see a sword about to strike one's head, one would raise one's arm to protect oneself. How much the more, he adds, would one use one's entire fortune to protect oneself.

> 2:5 Just stretch out your hand and touch his bone and flesh and he will surely curse you right to your face.

Satan remains dissatisfied and wants to continue his abuse of Job. What had taken place to this point was apparently insufficient. Satan assumes that eventually Job will reach his breaking point and curse God as a result. So now he argues that if Satan causes him physical pain, rather than the psychic pain of his losing his family, then Job would strike out against God.

Gersonides offers us philosophical insight on this verse. Satan thought that Job might curse God as a result of Job's apparent misunderstanding of divine providence. Job thought that God did not afford that providence to lower beings. Had he conceptualized the matter correctly, he would never have been moved. Job's confusion was due to the lack of proper philosophical investigation in the matter of perfection, so says Gersonides, which protects a person from what will turn out to be imaginary evils.

For Gersonides, what we read of the terrible things that happened to Job is only a parable: with God's permission, Satan had attempted to harm Job's body in every possible way. However, Satan was forbidden to harm Job's soul. That soul could have ruled over Satan had it wished to do so. It was given over to Satan at one point because of Job's imperfect reverence for God and Job's loss of faith on being tested. This is the meaning of the statement "And touch his bone . . . [*atzmo*, which Gersonides takes to mean his essence, that is, his soul]."

> 2:6 Adonai then said, "Alright, he is in your hands. But spare his life."

In this verse, God is again portrayed badly. God does not try to protect or defend Job. Instead, God allows Satan to continue to play with Job—asking only that his life not be taken. God seems to be wagering on Job's virtue. As a result, God is willing to allow Job to suffer. And in this case, even if it is not apparent at other times, God seems to be able to intervene in order to prevent Job's suffering from taking place. Job has become a pawn in a game of chess between Satan and God with no value at all.

Rashi surmises that God's demand presents a problem for Satan. How can Satan afflict Job badly but not kill him? Rashi reminds us of the midrash (Yalkut Shimoni II: 893:2) in which the rabbis make the comparison of Satan to a person being told to smash a wine barrel filled with wine and still preserve the wine for drinking.

> 2:7 No sooner had Satan left God's presence that he afflicted Job with painful blisters from the soles of his feet to the top of his head.

Satan couldn't wait to do his dirty work on Job, especially now that Satan had God's permission once again to do so. The author uses the same word—*shecheen* (blisters)—that the Torah uses to refer to one of the plagues afflicting the Egyptians. This is really to emphasize the severity of the affliction. However, the specific description of the ailment is not clear. They are some kind of boils or sores. Since it seems that the intent was to cause Job excruciating pain, we have translated *ra* (evil) to mean "painful."

> 2:8 Job took a potsherd with which to scrape himself and sat in the ashes.

Job's discomfort is palpable. So Job grabs whatever he can in order to try to relieve himself of his pain. Perhaps the choice of a "potsherd," something broken and discarded, is symbolic of Job's condition. Sitting in ashes or dust is symbolic of his mourning.

> 2:9 His wife said to him, "Still without blame? Curse God and die!"

While the comments of Job's wife are certainly not sympathetic, they are understandable. She is looking for something that might explain her predicament, as well. She has also grown impatient with Job for his refusal to confront or curse God. In Job 2:3, we translated *machazeek b'tumato* as "remains without blame," instead of other possible translations. We chose this particular translation of *odecha machazeek b'tumatatcha*, "still without blame," because the English words suggest something which, although not as explicit in the Hebrew, seems to stand behind Job's wife's bitter statement:

"You don't blame God? You should! Curse God for what God has done to you, even if it means that you will die!"

Since Job's wife is not identified by name, the Targum attempts to identify her. It suggests that she is Dina, Leah's daughter, who brazenly fell in love with Shechem, the son of Hamor (Genesis 34:1–3). Perhaps the implication is that it is not Job who is to blame. It is Job's wife—and her actions—that are to blame. That would change the dynamic of the story considerably. As Gersonides notes, Job still holds on to his virtue even in response to his wife's words.

> 2:10 Job answered her, "You are talking like one of the foolish women! Should we be willing to [only] receive the good from God and not accept the bad?" In all of this, Job did not sin with his lips.

As in all attempts to translate idiomatically, there are challenges implicit in our translation of the verse. The plural noun *ha-n'valot* (foolish women) has a moral dimension to it. Looking at the context, "foolish" could be an epithet that a spouse, even one as sorely tried as Job, might direct at his wife.

Our rendition of Job's question to his wife seeks to take it from the abstract and make it real. Hence, we have added "willing" to our translation of *nekabel* "we shall receive, get," and "things" to the translation of *tov* (good) and *rah* (bad).

> 2:11 When the three friends of Job—Eliphaz the Temanite, Bildad the Shuchite, and Zophar the Naamatite—heard about the calamity that had befallen him, each one left where he was, met together, and agreed to visit Job to console and comfort him.

The author presents these three friends of Job coming from a distance and after a period of time "to console and comfort him." It is not clear how far away they are or how much time has elapsed. It is possible that the author intends to imply that both a physical and a metaphysical distance separate Job from his friends.

As a response to the implicit question as to what impelled Job's friends to visit, especially at this particular time, the Targum tells us that they saw the trees in their orchards wither, the bread served at their meals became raw meat, and the wine served turned into blood. Because of their act of kindness, they were delivered from the place in Gehinnom that had been reserved for them.

Gersonides tells us that while Job's three friends saw how upset he was, none of them were able to offer any words of consolation (as indicated in

2:13). Gersonides contends that had they been accomplished thinkers, they together with Job would have been able to conduct a philosophical investigation that might have led to a religious solution and would have avoided the contention that follows.

> 2:12 When they saw him from afar, they almost did not recognize him. Sobbing loudly, each one ripped his coat and threw dust upon his head.

While this verse is made up of familiar words, it is still difficult to render into idiomatic English. The verse begins with the familiar biblical idiom "and they lifted their eyes from a distance," that is, when they first saw him. Because of his suffering, Job had changed so much that they didn't recognize him—*lo heekeeruhu*. But the Hebrew that follows implies that Job's friends did recognize him. That is why we have rendered the phrase as "they almost did not recognize him."

The verse continues *vayisoo et kolam vayvkooi*, "and they lifted up their voices and wept," which we translated as "sobbing loudly." The last Hebrew clause (*va'yizrkoo afar al rosheyhem ha-shammamah*—they threw dust heavenward upon their heads) suggests some kind of mourning ritual in which dust is thrown in the air in order to fall on the heads of mourners. It may simply mean that they sprinkled themselves with ashes.

> 2:13 The three sat with him on the ground for seven days and seven nights. Seeing how great was his pain, no one said anything to him.

Job's friends sat with him on the ground to share his pain. As noted in 2:11, Gersonides sees their act as a shortcoming rather than an expression of empathy. Nevertheless, it is the Jewish custom not to speak to mourners when visiting them during their period of mourning until they have spoken to you. The text does not report any initial exchange between Job and his friends, even when they first approached him. So it is really not known if the author's intent is to imply that no words were spoken at all or, to use an English idiom, that "they had nothing to say to him." In other words, Job's condition was so bad that they didn't possess any words that could provide any measure of solace and, as a result, remained silent.

> 2:14 Then Job opened his mouth and cursed the day of his birth.

In some editions this verse is 3:1. By placing it in 2:14 it serves to bridge the gap between chapter 2 and chapters 3 through 41. We have followed the critical manuscripts and included it here. Regardless of where it is placed, in this verse, Job finally expresses the pain that has been bubbling under the surface of this text since the beginning of his misfortunes. How could he not express himself in such a way given what he has experienced? One would expect no less. It is the reason why a mourner is exempt from certain religious obligations during the initial days of mourning. The Rabbis understood the position of someone who has suffered a loss of such magnitude. Perhaps the silence of his friends provoked Job to speak out at that moment. It might have been a reaction to the bitter words of Job's wife—following his reflection on them. While the author uses the word *yomo* (literally, his day) at the end of the verse, we translated it as "the day of his birth," following the suggestion of Ibn Ezra (and as implied in 3:2).

GEHINNOM

The Jewish version of hell, Gehinnom, also called Sheol, literally refers to a valley south of Jerusalem on one of the borders between the territories of Judah and Benjamin. (Compare Joshua 15:8; 18:16.) During the time of the monarchy it was a site associated with a cult that burned children. Jeremiah condemned the practice. In the rabbinic period, the name is used to refer to the place of torment after death reserved for the wicked. It stands in contradistinction to *Gan Eden*, the "Garden of Eden," which, in rabbinic literature, became known as the place of reward for the righteous. In the Bible, these two names never connote the abode of souls after death. Yet, in rabbinic literature, such references abound: in *Pesachim* 54a, Gehinnom and Gan Eden existed even before the world was created; Gehinnom is at the left hand of God and Gan Eden at God's right in the midrash to Psalms 50:12.[1]

PROVIDENCE

Sometimes referred to as "divine providence," it is the notion that God can enter into people's lives and history and exercise control. To better understand the notion, it might be called divine supervision of the individual. It includes the opportunity for God to intervene in nature "miraculously" as needed.

---

1. Kravitz and Olitzky, *Pirke Avot*, 91.

Chapter 3

> 3:1 Job then said,

THIS SIMPLE PHRASE IS formulaic. When the Bible uses the phrase *v'yaan . . . va'yamar* (literally, "he answered . . . and said") it means that a declaration is being made. (See Deuteronomy 21:7; 27:14 and Jeremiah 11:5.) Rashi's understanding of the idiom, taking a lead from Deuteronomy 27:14, is that Job shouted loudly. Ibn Ezra takes his cue from the phrase as it is used in Deuteronomy 26:5. He thinks that the use suggests that a person so described is responding to a question. After three days of sitting in silence, Job's three friends finally asked him how he was feeling. This verse, therefore, introduces his response.

> 3:2 Would that the day I was to be born had disappeared, the night when it was said, "a boy was conceived!"

Job is so disgusted with his life that he wished that he had never been born (the day) and never conceived (the night). We find a similar sentiment in Ecclesiaste 6:3 ". . . a still birth would be better off."

> 3:3 Let that day be dark. Let God on high never search for it. And let no light shine on it.

This is a curse. Like other forms of proverbs, they are often presented in patterns. In this verse, the author heaps up notions that are introduced in the preceding verse. Darkness, which is the salient element of the curse, is presented in three ways in the verse, all reflecting the oblivion for which Job currently yearns.

> 3:4 May darkness and gloom pollute it. May a cloud take residence above it. May those who can make a day terrible make it that way [or even worse].

This verse is Job's attempt to dig even deeper into the darkness of the curse as an expression of his state of mind. He is grasping at words and images that will express how he feels and his perspective on the world. It is dark and depressing and he is wallowing in the darkness. The sense is that the day should become ritually impure: may it be plunged in darkness even at daytime (the cloud). May the day terrify all within it. In many languages, darkness is linked to suffering and pain. Thus, the Yiddish curse *a finstere fire af im* (a dark fire should envelop him / Go to hell).

> 3:5 As for that night, may deep darkness take it. May it never be connected to any day of the year. May it never enter the cycle of months.

Job continues to express his anguish. He wants the day never to be repeated. It stands alone in its misery and no one else should have to suffer by it. He is asking that it be taken out of history so that it should not be given the dignity of acknowledging that it ever even existed.

> 3:6 May that night be desolate. May no joyous sound ever come into it.

Job continues the expression of his innermost feelings of despair. For Rashi, Job will be bereft of contact with human or animal. And for Gersonides, it indicates that the night is so dangerous that people wouldn't even go out in groups since they are so concerned about personal safety.

> 3:7 May those who curse the day, [go ahead and] curse it. Indeed, even those who are ready to stir up Leviathan [may do so].

This verse seems to be an echo of a prebiblical pagan world replete with other deities. Nevertheless, the author has Job continuing to direct his imprecations at the moment of his conception and the moment of his birth with the help of gods so powerful that they have no fear of Leviathan, the so-called god of the sea.

For Ibn Ezra, the last phrase of the verse is like a statement made by those onboard a ship about to flounder. They might curse the day that they boarded the ship since they are now destined to be eaten by Leviathan (which he understands simply as a large fish).

> 3:8 May its morning stars be dark. May it hope for light and not find it. May it not see the rays of the morning light.

The images continue to be bleak. Perhaps the verse refers to a day in which dawn does not yield much light even as it might be anticipated.

> 3:9 Because it did not lock the gates of my [mother's] womb nor conceal trouble from my eyes.

Job continues to decry the day of his birth. His deep-seated cry of agony frames an entire experience of life as "Why was I born to suffer?"

Rashi adds insight to our understanding of this verse by suggesting that the antecedent of "it" refers to the one who has power to do so—either God or the angel appointed to watch over childbirth. Had that Being/being done so, Job would never have known the suffering he would endure; it would have been "concealed from [his] eyes."

> 3:10 Why did I not die at birth? Why did I not croak as I came out of the womb?

This verse continues Job's lament. It suggests that Job was prepared to die immediately upon birth, as soon as he came out of the womb in order to avoid what he eventually experienced.

> 3:11 Why were there knees to receive me? Why were there breasts that I might suckle?

Job continues his dirge with a more graphic description of his birth. The knees are, of course, the knees of his mother, which both catch the child at birth and later provide a place of support and comfort. Rashi tells us that Job complained because it was determined that he was to be born into a life of pain and suffering but that his mother would nurse him.

> 3:12 For now I would be lying still. I would be asleep and at rest

> 3:13 together with the sovereign rulers and the counselors of the earth who built those places now in ruins

Because of Job's pain, he cannot be consoled. He yearns only for the sleep of death; it is only there where he will find any respite for his pain. In this poetic frame, Job acknowledges that death is the way of the world, even for those who are as powerful as kings. They end in ruin, as do the areas over which they rule—even the buildings that they erected to celebrate their greatness. But in this interesting turn of events, Job seems to hope that just as these rulers have made a mark on the world, perhaps his death will do the same.

> 3:14 or with nobles who had gold and who filled their houses with silver.

This is clearly a continuation of the preceding verse. The Targum wants to make sure that we realize that such "houses" as the author designates are really their storehouses or their treasure houses.

> 3:15 Or would that I would have been like a still birth hidden away or like babies who had never seen the light?

It seems like the author, as confirmed by the Targum's translation of the verse, is suggesting that the baby was hidden away in the womb and thereby died as a fetus *in utero*. The light to which the author refers is probably the simple "light of day." Such a sentiment is insufficient for the Targum and argues that such light is "the light of Torah."

> 3:16 The wicked cease their agitation there and the weary can rest.

Everything ends in the grave. Trouble and troublers are no more. Pain and suffering cease.

The Targum provides some hope to those who are wicked. If they repent, the pain of Gehinnom will be taken from them. Death promises reward to the righteous. Those students who have become "weary" in mastering their Torah studies will find rest.

Rashi explains how "the wicked cease." They are prevented from doing beneath the earth what they wouldn't stop doing above the earth. Ibn Ezra suggests that "the wicked cease" moving about in the grave and so cease provoking the people with whom in life they came into contact. Gersonides offers a straightforward insight from life. After the death of "the wicked," no one has to be afraid of them.

> 3:17 Prisoners can relax together; they do not have to pay attention to the taskmaster's voice.

In the grave, even prisoners driven to toil are now at ease. They could not relax for a moment while they were still alive. They were unable to relate to one another. Every moment included pain. They had to listen to their jailors. Only death brought them to oblivion.

> 3:18 There are great and small. And the slave is free from one's master.

While there are social distinctions in life, there are no such distinctions in death. All are equal in the grave. As in previous verses, the Targum changes the tone of the verse by referring to the Patriarchs: in the grave is Jacob (called a young lad) and Abraham (called the old man) and Isaac (called Servant of Adonai) who went free from the captivity of his master.

For Rashi, the verse means that the distinctions that are made in life remain in death. The "great" are still great and the "small" are all small.

> 3:19 Why does God give light to those who must toil and life to those who are ever embittered

While it is not clear who is the subject of the verse, it is quite probable that the author intends Job to make reference to God. This is the position that Rashi takes. Thus, we have translated it gender neutral. The author has Job ask, "Why did God not kill them when they were born?" Verses 19-21 are one complete statement or rhetorical question.

> 3:20 who long for death, but it does not come; who search for it more than for a hidden treasure,

For some, life has become such a burden that death is preferable. For Rashi, those "who long for death" are those "bitter of soul" (from the previous verse). They yearn to die and complain when they don't. More than any amount of wealth, they search for death.

> 3:21 who are exceedingly happy, and indeed rejoice when they find the grave?

It is a sad state of affairs when the ultimate expression of happiness is only found with death. But this is Job's theme throughout this section of the book. For him, death seems to be the only antidote for life. But it is really life—and living it to its fullest—that can be the only response to death.

> 3:22 To a person whose way is hidden and whom God has hedged in,

This verse is connected to 3:23. Obviously, the way that is hidden is hidden to the person seeking his or her path in the world. To make clear the meaning, the Targum adds some words in its translation of the verse: all that is bitter [to the person . . .]. Rashi has a different sense of what is hidden. He suggests that all the good that a person has done is hidden from God. But the "hedging in" is related to the verb used in Hosea 2:8 (*vayaasech*), which is more like "putting a screen in front of that person to lock the person in." For Ibn Ezra, it is indeed God who has locked the person in. Attributing his explanation to Saadya Gaon (late ninth-, early tenth-century philosopher/rabbi who was head of the academy in Sura), Ibn Ezra argues that the "way is hidden" means that a person receives no pleasure from anything, not even from eating. Gersonides is even more direct and claims that God has fenced off the way this person would go so that the person can attain none of his [or her] desires.

> 3:23 my sighing comes before my food. My screams gush out like water.

The author presents the reader with a picture of anguish, of one imprisoned by one's circumstances. Before Job can eat, he must sigh and reflect on his suffering. As he thinks about his situation, a scream erupts from the depths of his soul. But there is no one to hear his cries or to help. As Gersonides notes, Job's suffering—like water that continues to flow downward—was continuous.

> 3:24 What I feared has happened to me, what I was afraid of, came upon me.

Job's suffering was intensified by the anticipation and then the realization of his worst fears. Rashi tells us that Job was afraid that something terrible would happen to him, a fear that consumed him throughout his entire life. He feared that something had already been decreed. Perhaps Rashi used his insights as a father when he said that Job was afraid that somehow his children had offended the Deity.

> 3:25 I wasn't at ease. I wasn't quiet. I wasn't at rest. Yet trouble came.

Readers can feel Job's anxiety in this verse—even if he has the right to be anxious because of what he suffered. It is as if Job knew the statement of Rabbi Aha (Genesis Rabbah 84:1) who quotes the verse that when the righteous wish to be at ease in this world, Satan accuses and "trouble" comes. Although Job was not at ease, still "trouble came" upon him. Rashi thinks that the author is trying to tell the reader that Job could simply not stop worrying about everything.

LEVIATHAN

The Leviathan is a sea monster of sorts, as also noted in Psalm 74:13–14 and Isaiah 47:1. According to Rashi (in his commentary on Genesis 1:21), God created the Leviathan. As a result, this monster is subject to God's direction and control. Some suggest that it was created on the fifth day of creation. This monster, interpreted in various ways, appears in a variety of contexts in rabbinic literature.

SAADYA GAON

Saadya ben Joseph (882–942), from Fayyum in Egypt, is considered by most to be the father of medieval Jewish philosophy. He was the first to develop the notions of Islamic theology and philosophy in a Judaic manner. Similarly, he was the first to develop a philosophic justification for Judaism. He received his training in Egypt, where he lived the first thirty years of his life.

He subsequently lived in the land of Israel, Syria, and Babylonia. In 928, he became the gaon (head) of the well-known rabbinical academy in Sura, Babylonia.

Saadya was also a pioneer in Hebrew philology. He translated the Bible into Arabic, and his commentaries on it laid the foundation for a scientific interpretation of the Bible. Much of his extensive literary output focused on polemics against Karaism. (The Karaites were a Jewish sect that accepted the biblical text, *kara* in Aramaic, alone, and rejected all rabbinic interpretation of oral law.) Saadya's entire system of philosophy can be found in his book *Beliefs and Opinions*. His doctrine concerning the relationship between reason and revelation—which was accepted by most subsequent Jewish philosophers—provided the methodological foundation for his religious philosophy. For him, religious truth, a distinct form of truth, is found in revelation. Reason provides the common foundation for all religions.[1]

---

1. Kravitz and Olitzky, *Mishlei*, 243.

Chapter 4

4:1 Then Eliphaz the Temanite replied,

As readers of the book of Job have already learned (2:11), Eliphaz was one of Job's friends. There was no real question asked, but Eliphaz is responding to Job's predicament and anguished cries. In contemporary usage, the Hebrew place *Tayman* is identified with Yemen. The Targum translates the Hebrew *v'yaanan . . . va-yomer* (literally, he answered . . . and said), the Aramaic formula of response put into the mouth of Laban (Genesis 31:43) which we have translated as "replied" by rendering the first verb as *v'aytiv* (he replied) and the second verb as *v'amar* (and he said).

Amos Hacham, an Israeli Bible expert primarily of the twentieth century, claimed that the bulk of the book of Job consists of "*ma'anot*," a Hebrew term which is taken from this language of reply that is used in the introduction to each new section.

Rashi wants to clarify Eliphaz's bona fides. So he comments that Eliphaz was the son of Esau but he had grown up under the influence of Jacob. As a result, he was worthy of the Divine Presence resting upon him (and therefore being able to explain to Job what had taken place).

> 4:2 If someone tries to say something to you, will you be too weary [to hear]? But who can refrain from speaking?

As a friend, Eliphaz feels bound to speak. He simply wonders whether Job has the inner strength to listen to him after all that Job has experienced.

Rashi understands Job's experience as a test. Thus, he reads the verse as "Has one test by your Creator so wearied you? Henceforth, control your speech, for who can respond to you?" This is not Ibn Ezra's understanding at all. For Ibn Ezra the phrase means "How shall we bear a word to you?" In other words, "How can we convince you?"

> 4:3 Look, you have instructed many and strengthened weak hands.

Our translation as "you have instructed" assumes what is taught is moral instruction. Rashi understands it as "with many words you have reproved and chastised." Thus, the hands that have been strengthened are those belonging to those who fear retribution. Job had told such persons that God would judge them with the application of God's attribute of justice.

> 4:4 Your words have supported the one [who is] about to fall.
> You have strengthened buckling knees.

This verse continues Eliphaz's words of support to Job, explaining to him—and for the benefit of others—all the good that Job has done in his life, especially in supporting others when they are in dire straits. The Targum tells us that a person might fall because of sin. Similarly, one's knees might buckle because of transgression.

> 4:5 Now trouble has come to you and you are exhausted. It has touched you and you are astounded.

Eliphaz makes the point that American slang would make clear: Job has talked the talk but can he now walk the walk?

> 4:6 Are you not confident in your piety? Should you not depend on the perfection of your ways?

It seems that Eliphaz is putting questions to Job. On the one hand, "Shouldn't you believe that somehow you will be delivered from your suffering because of what you believe and what you practice?" On the other hand, "Perhaps you really don't believe that what you thought you believed and what you practiced will indeed bring you deliverance from your tragedy?"

As Rashi explains the verse, Job's faith at this point suggests something about his initial belief. His piety was not well-based at all. It was folly.

Gersonides presents his understanding of the verse as "'Perhaps,' Job is being asked, 'your reverence for God was so that your possessions would be protected. Now that you have seen your possessions destroyed, that reverence has departed.'"

> 4:7 Note well: who being innocent was ever punished? Who being upright was ever destroyed?

Because of the statements that precede this verse, it seems to reflect more of the speaker's sense of unyielding faith rather than intentional irony that might be inferred should the verse have stood alone. We have all witnessed the perishing of the innocent and the destruction of the upright as we struggle to retain a belief in justice. Perhaps it is a statement of hope or prophetic vision for the future.

> 4:8 What I have seen is that those who plow iniquity and sow trouble [will] reap it.

By implication, Job's suffering proves his guilt. Perhaps Eliphaz's experience was limited in scope. Perhaps it was a position that the author of Job crafted in order to make a statement or to later undermine it. Or maybe this is Eliphaz's hope for the world—even in the midst of Job's tragedy, which seems to counter it. Sometimes evil is requited and virtue is rewarded but it is not frequent enough for such a statement to be offered unconditionally.

The Targum struggles with the theology of the verse by suggesting that it is not a reference to an individual. Rather, it is referring to an entire generation: "the generation that is sunk in false deeds and that serves vanity will receive a similar recompense."

Rashi explains that just as those who would plant seeds must first plow the land, so those who would devise evil must first think it through in order to bring it into action. Even so, such malefactors will find that they will harvest the evil intended for others.

> 4:9 They are destroyed with one breath by God. They are consumed by a snort of Divine anger.

If it was unclear in Eliphaz's previous statements whether God was the implied source of such reward and punishment, he makes it explicit in this statement. The author of Job, through the statement of Eliphaz, makes a conventional presentation that is buoyed by a standard hoped for result: vice will be defeated and virtue will be defended.

In order for Rashi to reconcile the theology of the verse with what he experiences in daily living, he contends that "consumed" means to be "totally consumed," making reference to the generation of the flood.

> 4:10 Old lions may roar and young lions may howl, yet the teeth of the cubs will be broken.

Even those who are among the fiercest of creatures are sometimes unable to protect their young. Whether this is a metaphor, poetry or simple illustration from nature, the theology seems at odds with preceding verses. For the Targum, this verse contains a statement about the people of Israel rather than an individual. It renders it as "Seir (Rome) is comparable to a ravaging lion whose cry resounds like a raging bear which terrifies [people] by its violence and whose officials are like lions ranging out to find prey." Rashi understands the words as describing the different sizes of lions, as a metaphor for the various ranks of those in power in Rome, the kings, officials, and servants of Rome who will be destroyed as enemies of Israel.

> 4:11 Lacking prey, a lion perishes. Scattered are the cubs of the lioness.

Without food, even a lion dies. So its offspring are scattered, forced to seek food that once was provided by the parents. Eliphaz is arguing that there is no arbitrary pattern to the world. If Job now suffers, he did something to deserve that suffering.

> 4:12 A word came to me in secret. My ear picked up a trace of it.

With this verse, Eliphaz changes the subject. Rather than relying on what he has observed in the world, the focus of his previous statements, he now offers a different source for the information he wants to share with Job. Rashi understands that Eliphaz has returned to the posture of reproach from 4:7. Now he claims that he has received insight by way of prophecy on Job's behalf.

> 4:13 In troubling thoughts set up by dreams of the night when deep sleep falls on humans.

This is a continuation of the sentiments expressed in the previous verse. Eliphaz has received this communication in the night, probably in a dream or in those few moments of confusion when one first awakes after a dream.

> 4:14 I was seized by trembling fear and all my bones began to shake.

This verse serves as the author's introduction to the feelings of a night terror. Often this phrase is translated as "fear and trembling," the same phrase in English used by the philosopher Soren Kirkegaard to describe the suspension of the ethical during Abraham's journey to sacrifice his son Isaac known as the *akedah* (literally, binding). Eliphaz is clearly terrified by what he has experienced.

> 4:15 A spirit slithered past my face and all my hair stood on end.

Eliphaz's sentiment—as expressed by the author—is quite clear. Eliphaz is scared and uncomfortable. To use a more colloquial expression that reflects the image of hair standing on end: it has him "freaked out."

> 4:16 Although it stood still, I could not make out what it was. There was something in front of me. There was silence and then I heard a voice.

Just reading Eliphaz's description is scary. You can feel his fear. He experienced something in his dream or as a result of his dream. The intent of the author—whether to tell us that the terror was evoked by a nightmare or something that happened to Eliphaz when he awoke—is unclear. Something moved past Eliphaz, either a wind or a spirit. Then it stopped in front of him. He could not tell what it was even though it stopped in front of him, literally, "in front of his eyes." Then out of the silence came a voice. The phrase resonates, as Ibn Ezra points out, with the verse from 1 Kings 19:12, *kol demama dakah* (a still small voice)—which announces that a kind of prophecy will follow.

> 4:17 Can a human be more righteous than God? Can one be more than one's maker?

Apparently, these questions emerged from the voice in the previous verse. While these questions are to be read as statements, Rashi sees them as real questions. And since his answer to both questions is "no," he sees no value in complaining.

> 4:18 Behold God does not trust the divine servants and charges the angels with error.

This argument is strained. What does God's mistrust and impugning of heavenly beings have to do with Job's suffering? Job is a human being. No one has asked him to be more than human. Others may sin. Others may fail. But what does this have to do with Job? The author is making the argument: if divine servants and angels can't be trusted not to sin, then how can a mere mortal like Job claim that he has not sinned?

While most readers will assume that God's mistrust of the angels is negative—perhaps they were responsible for carrying out God's instructions to destroy Job's life—Rashi offers us a more positive perspective. He claims that the angels are righteous. Knowing that they are human and might sin—an insight into Rashi's perspective on angels from which we might learn—God takes them from this life before their time so that they cannot sin.

> 4:19 How much the more for those who live in clay houses, whose foundations are in the dust, who can be crushed easier than a moth.

The author makes a point in the form of a logic syllogism: if those close to God—either servants or semidivine beings—are not worthy of God's concern, how much less worthy can mere mortals be? At a time when authority of whatever kind could not be questioned, such an argument might have made sense to the reader. It makes little sense in our time when the way we think and what we have experienced have made many people question authority of any kind. Even as it is presented here, the argument is problematic. We humans as mortals are indeed limited in knowledge and lifespan. But we can still ask, if we are not worthy of God's concern, why would such a Deity be worthy of our concern? What kind of Deity would place us on this earth and have no regard for us?

> 4:20 They are crushed between morning and evening [but] no one cares. They disappear forever.

This echo from Ecclesiastes reflects the life and death of many people—even in our own time. For those whose lives are "crushed," no one notices that they are gone. They are forgotten. For Rashi, this "crushing" is important. It takes place within one day. Those who are crushed don't even care enough to return to their Maker.

> 4:21 Has not their thread of life been pulled out? They shall die without wisdom.

Perhaps we are dealing with an idiom in this verse that might have made sense to tent-dwellers and their descendants but did not fit the city world in which the book of Job is played out.

Ibn Ezra tells us that this verse is about the money that people will lose at the time of their deaths. He contends that these people will die without wisdom, because they thought that they should amass wealth rather than knowledge, forgetting that humans were created to acquire wisdom.

GOD'S ATTRIBUTE OF JUSTICE

According to rabbinic tradition, God's attribute of justice (called *midat hadin*) is held in balance by God's attribute of compassion (called *midat harachamim*). These are God's two primary attributes. This notion is consistent with the rabbinic idea of opposing categories and the search for the Golden Mean at their center. The goal of prayer is to move God from the state of *hadin* to the implementation of *harachamim*. According to the Rabbis, God's own prayer is "May my attribute of compassion overcome my attribute of justice." We live in a relationship with God that is contextualized by the tension between these two attributes.

Chapter 5

> 5:1 Call out now. Who will answer you? To which of the holy ones will you turn?

Eliphaz continues his presentation from the previous chapter. By using Eliphaz to raise these questions, the author has raised others. Job has suffered. Does he expect his suffering to be justified? Does he expect to be saved from his present difficulty by a miraculous intervention? Moreover, does anyone who suffers expect to be justified? Can anyone expect divine intervention?

> 5:2 Anger will kill a fool and jealousy will slay the simple.

While it is difficult to discern the relationship of this verse to Job's situation, the author is clearly quoting some sort of proverb or truism. Perhaps he is simply telling Job that anger—however deserved—will not help him to resolve his predicament. Only a fool would think that the expression of anger can make a difference. Jealousy of good fortune comes from looking at others without seeing deeply inside of the individual and his or her situation. Those who were jealous of Job were jealous when he was well-off. They ceased being jealous once they discerned his later predicament.

> 5:3 Although I saw such a fool put down roots, suddenly I cursed the fool's home.

Why would Eliphaz curse the fool's home? Perhaps Eliphaz is suggesting that the fool's actions bring a curse to the home in which the fool lives—or to the fool's family that lives in the fool's home. That would mean that Eliphaz is implying that Job brought the curse to his family (read: his home).

> 5:4 The fool's children will be far from any help. Wronged in court, they will be without a defender.

Eliphaz considers Job to be a simple fool. As a result, Job, like others like him, pass down their punishment to their children. Even in a court of law, presumed to be sensitive to children who are at a disadvantage, no one will help them. The "court" for Ibn Ezra (*b'shaar*, literally, the gate) is simply "in public."

> 5:5 The hungry eat what the fool harvested. Picking out the thorns, the thirsty pant after what the fool has.

This verse has to be translated in the context of the previous verses. The first clause of this verse suggests that the fool cannot even control his or her own property. As a result, someone who is hungry can just come and eat. And even the harvest is of poor quality since it is full of "thorns." Whatever the specifics, this is clearly a continuation of Eliphaz's attack against his so-called friend Job.

> 5:6 Disaster does not come from the dust nor does trouble sprout out of the ground.

Quoting some sort of a proverb or idiom, the author is suggesting that trouble is not due to nature; instead it is a result of human activity.

> 5:7 To be human is to be born to trouble as surely as sparks fly upward.

This verse has a far deeper meaning than might be seen at first glance. The vicissitudes of the human situation are linked to *bnai reshef* (sparks). Rashi contends that it is impossible for a human being to refrain from sinning and therefore be punished. He explains that *bnai reshef* are angels. Because of their supernal status they are untouched by the blandishments of Satan and the Evil Inclination. So they are able to fly on high.

> 5:8 If it were me, I would seek God. I would place my plea before God.

While the literal translation of this verse could yield "However, I would seek God," we are following Rashi's explanation of "Were these chastisements to have come upon me, 'I would seek God.'" After all, this is a theological text whose ultimate goal is to urge the individual to develop a closer relationship with God. This would be the author's suggestion even had Eliphaz not explained the cause of Job's problems as Job's own fault. It is what we would suggest, as well, although the context in which it is made—the game being played with Job by God and Satan—continually threatens to undermine the suggestion.

> 5:9 God does great things beyond understanding, wonders beyond counting.

While this reads as a general description of God, it continues the message of the previous verse. It is as if to say, "Place your faith in God even if you have concerns about what took place between God and Satan that impacted on Job." If what happened to Job reflects an act of the divine will which we cannot question or an act of divine wisdom which is beyond understanding, we end up with a faith which ultimately will allow everything for God and for us.

> 5:10 God gives rain to the earth and sends water to the fields.

Again these are general statements about the role of God in the universe. But it is also an explanation as if to say, "Irrespective of what God allowed Satan to do to Job, 'remember that God gives rain to the earth and sends water to the fields.' Thus, you should seek out God [as per 5:8]."

> 5:11 God brings up those who are low and brings to safety those who are in distress.

These descriptions of God may remind the reader of some of the descriptors used in the second paragraph of the Amidah prayer, the central prayer of Jewish liturgy, repeated three times daily.

> 5:12 God foils the plans of the cunning so that their hands can achieve no success.

If the book of Job is an example of the Bible's wisdom literature (defined as those books that emerge from the experience of humans rather than through divine revelation), this statement seems to run counter to such a notion.

> 5:13 God traps the cunning by their guile and the advice of the clever is made precipitous.

This reads more like the author's wish than a statement of fact. The Targum relates this verse to what happened to Pharaoh in Egypt—just as it had done in the previous verse: "By their own wisdom, God captured the wise men of Pharaoh and God directed against them the advice of the insidious astrologers." The reader should be reminded of Pharaoh's words referring to the Israelites who had grown numerous in ancient Egypt: "Come let us deal wisely with them" (Exodus 1:10).

Rashi offers folk wisdom in the context of this verse. It emerges from his understanding of the last word of the verse *nimharah* (literally, speedily—which we have rendered as "made precipitous"): any advice given in haste is ultimately folly.

> 5:14 They will encounter darkness during the day. They will fumble about at noon as if it were night.

This is further explication of the previous verse. Darkness and night, for Rashi, are simply synonyms for the failure of the "guile" and the "advice" of those in the previous verse to achieve their goals.

> 5:15 God saves the poor from a sword in their mouth and from the hand of the powerful.

While is not clear whose "mouths" create such mortal danger—it could be the mouths of the people or their enemies—the Targum attempts to clarify the verse by suggesting this translation: "God saves God's people from being killed by their mouths and God's unfortunate people from the hand of the powerful Sovereign Ruler." For Ibn Ezra, the "mouth" is mentioned because the destruction of the people comes through famine. He further argues that if God wants to do so, God can chastise humans with drought—which leads to famine. However, if they repent and return to God, then God will answer their prayers with rain.

> 5:16 So that the poor may hope and injustice shut its mouth.

If God saves the poor, as is suggested in 5:15, and this is witnessed or known by others, then it gives hope to the poor—that they, the poor, too may be saved from their unfortunate circumstances.

> 5:17 Happy, then, is the person whom God chastens. Don't reject the instruction of the Almighty.

This verse serves as a conclusion to the previous verses. Since the statements made in these verses seem obvious, then the chastening of the individual—the chastening of Job—is for one's own good, and will bring the individual happiness in the end. So don't reject what God tells you to do. For Rashi, the chastening is really *yissurim* (suffering). But just as God has healed such pain in the past, God will do so in the future. That is why Job should not reject such chastisement. Rather, he should accept it.

> 5:18 God hurts and binds up. God smashes and then God's hands let loose.

Reminiscent of the kinds of things we read in the book of Lamentations, the statement that the author of Job puts into the mouth of Eliphaz is the notion that God is the source of all that befalls us: pain and the removal of pain, illness and the recovery from illness are all due to God.

> 5:19 God shall deliver you from six troubles. Nothing bad shall happen to you from seven [troubles].

The use of paired numbers (e.g., "six" and "seven") as a rhetorical form is found elsewhere in the Bible.

> 5:20 God will save you from death in the midst of a famine. God will save you from the sword in the midst of war.

This verse identified the specific kind of saving that God will undertake that is enumerated in the previous verse. The Targum wants to identify the salvation even more specifically as similar to the one endured by the Israelites in Egypt and the war that was fought against Amalek. By looking at what God has done, the reader is assured of God's power and what can happen in the future—both to the people and to the individual.

> 5:21 You will be concealed from the scourge of the tongue. You will not fear from destruction were it to come.

This continues the theme of the previous verse. Although the precise reference or action described as the "scourge of the tongue" is not clear, nor is the source of "destruction" (unless it is an acknowledgement once again of God as the source), Rashi suggests that Satan's tongue and the "scourge" are two of the calamities alluded to in 5:19. For Ibn Ezra, the "scourge" is a reference to *lashon hara* (evil speech, gossip) which Gersonides claims is the cause of all kinds of terrible arguments among people.

> 5:22 You will laugh at destruction and famine. You won't fear the wild animals of the earth.

Through Eliphaz, the author is presenting the notion that faith in God and following God's way will protect the believer from natural calamities.

> 5:23 For even the stones of the field will be on your side and you will be at peace with the wild animals of the field.

This is the author's description of real tranquility. We have idiomatically rendered *breetecha* (literally, your covenant) as "on your side." The Targum explains "the stones of the field" and the "wild animals of the field" in a telling manner: "For the tablets of stone which were given publicly in the field will be your covenant and the Canaanites who are compared to the wild animals of the field will make peace with you."

> 5:24 You will know that your tent is at peace. You will miss nothing when you visit your home.

A home is supposed to be the source of tranquility and peace for the individual. The Targum takes the first clause to refer to "your house of study" and the second clause to mean "when you arrange the dwelling for your rest, you will not be injured." Rashi's sense of the verse is far more wide-reaching. He understands the verse to mean that wherever you will be, you will know that your habitation is secure.

> 5:25 You shall know that you will have many children and your descendants will be as the grass of the field.

This verse has some resonance with the promise to Abraham in the book of Genesis (15:4–5): "Behold, the word of God came unto him [Abraham], saying: 'This person will not be your heir; but the one who comes out of your own body will be your heir.' So God took him forth outside and said: 'Look up to the heavens, and count the stars, if you can count them'; and then God said to him: 'So shall your offspring be.'"

> 5:26 You will come to the grave in ripe old age, like sheaf gathered at its [proper] time [of harvest].

While this verse speaks of death, it is the kind of death that reflects a life well-lived. The individual dies only after making a contribution, applying God-given gifts to life. The verse contains the word *celach*, which appears nowhere else in the Bible. It is usually defined as "ripeness" or "ripe age," which we have rendered as "ripe old age."

> 5:27 Look, we have examined it. That is how it is. Listen to it and you will know something.

Since we are at the conclusion of the chapter, Gersonides seizes the opportunity for Eliphaz to offer a lesson in philosophy to Job and through Job to the reader. His lesson contains two elements: the improvement of society and the improvement of the individual. Society is improved—even maintained—by the belief that sin is punished and virtue is rewarded. The individual is improved by receiving philosophical insights.

GOOD INCLINATION AND EVIL INCLINATION

The Rabbis identified two complementary sets of drives that coexist in each person. One set of drives, which may be classified as libidinal drives or urges—including sex, hunger and the like—are grouped under the term *yetzer hara* (the inclination to do evil). While these drives are not evil in and of themselves, left unchecked, they may lead the individual to evil. For example, while the sexual drive may lead an individual to procreate, it can also lead to lust and illicit sexual behavior. Similarly, the hunger drive can lead an individual to nourishing his or her body with food, but it can also lead to obesity. The *yetzer hara* is kept in balance by the *yetzer tov* (the inclination to do good). But this inclination also needs to be kept in balance. Both the *yetzer hara* and the *yetzer tov* serve a purpose. For example, an individual who gives *tzedakah* (charitable giving)—driven by an inclination to do good—runs the risk of placing himself or his family in jeopardy should he or she give all his or her money to charitable causes.[1]

LASHON HARA (DECEITFUL SPEECH)

The Rabbis were so concerned with the potential harm inherent in speech that, employing a word game, they suggested that harmful speech is equivalent to what the Bible calls *m'tzora* (a kind of serious skin affliction, like leprosy). They used the root of the word (*m-tz-r*) as an acronym for *motzei shem ra* (the emergence of an evil reputation) and argued that gossip and slander were equivalent to murder. They then classified gossip as a kind of deceitful speech. Even when the details of the conversation were truthful, they were not to be spoken. Because the Rabbis felt that mostly women engaged in such gossip, they were particularly restrictive about communications between men and women. However, they did not understand what has been argued by modern social scientists, that women often communicate with one another and establish relationships by sharing intimate details about themselves and others without any intent for harm.[2]

AMIDAH

The core prayer of Jewish worship said while standing. Originally containing eighteen blessings, it now contains nineteen. The first three and last three blessings are constant, while the middle section changes depending on the holiday and sacred time during which it is recited.

---

1. Kravitz and Olitzky, *Kohelet*, 41.
2. Adapted from Kravitz and Olitzky, *Mishlei*, 106.

Chapter 6

> 6:1 Then Job answered:

THIS VERSE INTRODUCES A series of connected verses in which the meaning of each one is dependent on the understanding of the one that follows. The formula "answered and said" (without the latter word in the translation for the sake of English) often presents a formal declaration. (See Genesis 31:43.)

> 6:2 Would that my grief might be weighed out and my suffering placed together on a scale.

As part of Job's response to Eliphaz, he tries to communicate the depth of his suffering. However one understands his statement, it is clear that he is trying to demonstrate the unbearable extent of his pain.

> 6:3 Surely it would weigh more than all the sand of the sea! That's why my words make no sense.

Any words would be inadequate to express Job's pain. And he finds any measurement unsatisfactory. Rashi notes that it is common for a drunkard to mumble his words. Although he is not suggesting that Job is drunk, Rashi does seem to indicate that what Job is trying to express is as hard to understand as the "mumblings" of someone in a drunken stupor.

> 6:4 The arrows of the Almighty are indeed into me. My spirit sucks up their poison. The terrors of God are set in array against me.

Job presents himself as if shot through with poison arrows. As a result, his death is both imminent and certain. In the throes of death, Job is portrayed as beset with all kinds of frightening visions.

> 6:5 Does the wild ass bray when it has grass? Does an ox bellow when it has fodder?

The author is trying to explain what is a natural reaction coming from Job. The use of the uncommon verbs *yenhak* (bray) and *yegeh* (bellow) are onomatopoeic words whose sounds indicate their meanings. Rashi explains that Job asks: "Do I cry out for no reason? If a dumb animal is silent when its needs are met, an ass does not bray when it has grass to eat nor does an ox bellow when it has mash, so would I be still were my needs to be met."

> 6:6 Can something that is tasteless be eaten without salt? Does the juice of a mallow have any flavor?

While the meaning of *chalamut* (mallow) is not clear, it complements what was said in the previous verse. The sense of both verses is simply to state the obvious.

> 6:7 I refuse to touch it. Such food makes me sick.

If the prior sentence is a metaphor for tasteless food standing for meaningless arguments, as the former provides little nourishment and the latter little sense, then in this sentence Job refuses to touch the food or respond to any kind of arguments that Eliphaz has provided.

> 6:8 Would that I would get what I ask. Would that God would give me what I hope for,

> 6:9 That God would decide to crush me, to let loose the divine hand and finish me off.

This comment comes as no surprise. Job doesn't ask that he be spared the pain and suffering that he experienced. At this point, he only wishes that God would end his life which is the substance of his request. Ironically, this is precisely what God required Satan to refrain from doing if God allowed Satan to proceed with his experiment with Job.

> 6:10 This would be my consolation. I would jump for joy even in my pain. Although God has no compassion [on me], I have not denied the word of the Holy One.

This verse presents a surprisingly profound expression of faith, especially when it is read in conjunction with the previous verse. Job is disgusted with his life. He asks God to take his life. At the same time, Job's faith in God remains steadfast.

The classic commentators struggle with Job's expression of faith in the midst of his pain and are looking for a realistic way for its expression in the text. Even as pious scholars, they find his faith unsettling and disturbing. Lashing out at God would be a natural and expected response from someone who has suffered as has Job. Had Job lashed out at God, the book would not have been published. Critical to the book of Job is the notion that Job, in some manner, has accepted what has happened to him.

> 6:11 What strength have I that I should hope? What future have I that I should hold out?

The sense of this verse is clear. Job's strength is diminished by his suffering and he lacks any sense of hope or optimism for the future. So his question is really a self-reflective thought. He thinks to himself, "Why should I bother? I have nothing left to hope for."

> 6:12 Had I the strength of stones, were my flesh bronze.

While this verse appears incomplete, it is really Job's own response to the question he posed in the previous verse. It is as if he said, "Had I the strength of stones or were my flesh bronze, then [maybe] I would be able to be hopeful or anticipate the future."

> 6:13 Is it not that I have no help and that success is driven away from me?

Job's sentiment is that because he cannot turn to God, since God has not been willing to take his life, he has nowhere else to turn for help.

> 6:14 The one who is discouraged should have steadfast love from one's friends, even if one forsakes the fear of the Almighty.

Job is telling his readers that his friends should support him even if his faith in God diminishes. Perhaps the Targum offers us the best translation even if it does so by adding words: "That person who has withheld steadfast love from his friend has forsaken the fear of the Almighty." Rashi contends that steadfast love would consume such a person.

> 6:15 As treacherous as a wadi, so have been my brethren. As the flowing together of wadis, so they move away.

To emphasize his plight, Job chooses an image from nature that would have been readily understood in ancient Uz. A wadi (*nahal*) is a riverbed that is dry throughout most of the year. It fills with water only during the winter rains. Once filled, the wadi may become a roaring torrent. As a result, the wadi is not a dependable source of water and may even become a source of danger. Just like when one wadi joins with another, the speed of the flowing waters increases, so his brethren, who individually failed to help Job at one point, now collectively speed away from him, rather than responding to his needs.

> 6:16 Darkened by ice and hidden by snow upon them.

This verse continues the image that was initiated by the author in the previous verse. In the winter, the riverbeds are even more dangerous than they are during other seasons of the year. Although they are now visible since they are filled with water, one may step into them and be carried away.

> 6:17 When they dry up, they disappear. When it gets warm, they are gone.

Wadis exist even in the absence of water. They simply have a different appearance. In the winter, there is water in the wadi. In the summer, when the waters dry up, the wadi disappears, so to speak. The dry river bed is hardly visible. Taking its cue from the great flood reported in the book of Genesis but without referencing it, the Targum reads this verse as a moral lesson: "When a generation incurs guilt, a flood is heated up to boiling into which they are cast and so are wiped from their place."

> 6:18 The caravans snake around. They go to the wasteland and perish.

Ibn Ezra contends that *orchot* does not mean "caravans." He takes it to mean "paths," because he understands *yeelphatu* to mean "to be made crooked" or "to twist." He relates this verse from Job to the previous verse that refers to wadis and explains to the reader that water normally runs downhill. However, when the water in the wadi becomes heated, it rises, evaporates, and disappears.

> 6:19 The caravans of Tema looked. The traveling companies of Sheva hoped.

This verse continues the sentiment expressed in the previous verses. *Haleechot* (traveling companies) is a synonym for *orchot* (caravans). Nevertheless, it is unclear as to what the caravans were looking for or what they hoped for. We can imagine that the caravans were looking for / hoping to find water to satiate their thirst, only to find dry riverbeds.

> 6:20 They were abashed, because they were confident. They arrived and were ashamed.

It is not made clear by the author in this verse why they were ashamed.

> 6:21 Now you have become his. You see a terror and you are frightened.

This verse contains what scholars refer to as a *k'tiv/k're* problem. This is the difference between the text that is written and how it is customarily read. The *k'tiv* has *lamed-alef* (not) and the *k're* has *lamed-vav* (his). Even were we to accept the *k're*, it is not clear to whom or to what "his" refers. If "his/His" refers to God, one might wonder why a believer in God would be so frightened and ashamed. If it refers to something else, one still might wonder what would be the relevance of the second clause in the verse.

> 6:22 Did I ever say, "Give me something" or "Use your wealth to bribe someone for me"?

All of these bribes would have been used to prevent the tragedies that befell Job.

> 6:23 "Save me from the power of an enemy" [or] "Redeem me from the grasp of the powerful"?

This is a continuation of the previous verse and the listing of favors that Job claims he has not asked of anyone. Up until this point, Job has not asked for help. However, now those who see his need pretend that they have no idea of what afflicts him.

> 6:24 Teach me and I will be quiet. If I have been wrong, enlighten me.

For Eliphaz, for whom human suffering is divine punishment for sin, what Job has endured is proof that Job is both a sinner and a hypocrite. Job's response is a way of saying, "Prove that I have sinned."

> 6:25 How painful are honest words. But who among you can [offer] rebuke?

Job verbally attacks his accusers. The Targum reads the verse in an ironic way: "How seasoned are these correct words and who among you is fit to rebuke?"

Rashi takes the first clause as Job's plea: "If my words were true, you would say that you would have accepted them?" Since Rashi understands *hokeach* to mean argue, he takes the second clause to mean "Who among you can argue [with me]?"

> 6:26 Do you think to argue about words and treat what the despairing say as wind?

Job continues his attack on his accusers. Rashi understands the first clause as "Do you think to clarify words" but understands the second clause as "words as meaningless as the wind."

Ibn Ezra offers a little more clarity to Job's intent. He takes the first clause to mean, "You argue only with words because you have no proof." He reads the second clause as "You think my words are as empty as the wind." Thus, Ibn Ezra understands the verse as Job's plaint, "You think that your words are correct and the words of someone who is in pain to be as meaningless as vapor."

> 6:27 You would bring down disaster even on an orphan and would dig a pit for your friend.

Job's words are becoming increasingly accusatory and reflecting his frustration and disappointment with his friends. Ibn Ezra interprets the verse as Job's statement, "You are so without pity that you bring down a wall, or something like it, even upon an orphan. You are so bereft of feeling that you would even gather together and rejoice at what happened." Ibn Ezra also relates the digging of the pit to trap the unfortunate and unknowing friend to the "bringing down of the wall."

> 6:28 And now please look at me. Would I lie right to your face?

In this verse, Job confronts his friends directly. He wants them to see him as he is, suffering without cause and thereby challenging their view of the world and of God.

> 6:29 Think again. Let there be no mistake. Think again. My innocence still stands.

This verse follows directly on the preceding verse. Job's sentiment is striking. He wants to make sure that his friends are clear about his situation. Job is unwavering in his claim of innocence. And he wants to make sure that his friends also understand and agree that he is innocent of any wrongdoing that would incur such punishment as he has sustained. The context of the verse suggests that Job is claiming that his friends simply do not understand his situation. Their mistakes are reminiscent of the French folk saying, "Some things are worse than sins; they are mistakes."

> 6:30 Is there malice on my tongue? Can my taste not discern threats?

It seems to us that Job is saying to his friends in this verse, "I have not lied, but I can tell that you don't believe me and want to treat me as a sinner and hence a danger in your midst."

K'TIV AND *K'RE*

These are technical terms referring to the way the text is written (*k'tiv*) and the way it is suggested to be read (*k're*). This distinction was a compromise suggested by the Masoretes for certain biblical words, so that the text could be read and interpreted correctly without changing the text itself. For this reason, certain words appear in the [Hebrew] text twice in a row, once smaller and without vowels (*k'tiv*) and once with vowels (*k're*).[1]

---

1. Kravitz and Olitzky, *Mishlei*, 13.

Chapter 7

> 7:1 Do not humans have forced labor upon the earth? Are not the days of humans like those hired out?

JOB CONTENDS THAT HUMAN existence is not free at all. Individuals are compelled—in one way or another—to act by things out of their control, like a person drafted by a king to do royal work who is not free to avoid the king's command. Such a situation is minimally worse than the "prisoners of starvation" who labor for wages so that they can eat.

In order to maintain gender neutrality, we have translated the second half of this verse in the plural rather than the singular. The word *tzvah* can have a military meaning as "troops" or a civilian meaning as "forced labor." In this context, it means the latter.

Rashi connects this verse to those that precede it. For him, Job is saying, "This is what I have been telling you. Listen to me. How can I keep quiet in the face of all that has happened to me? You know that there are set circumstances and times in which each person must live. Like a hired laborer who has a set period of work at a particular wage, so I have a set burden given to me."

> 7:2 As slaves yearn for shade and as hired servants hope for their wage,
>
> 7:3 I have indeed inherited months of disaster and they have appointed for me nights of need.

We have again translated this in the plural. These verses are connected. As a result, they must be understood and interpreted together. Rashi offers an expanded meaning: "Like a slave who labors and gasps all day, yearning for the shadow of evening, and like a hired servant who yearns for the setting of the sun, for the servant expects to be paid a wage at evening having worked all day."

The shade of evening provides both the slave and the worker with respite from the sun, but it also indicates that it is the end of the workday, as Ibn Ezra reminds us.

> 7:4 When I lie down, I ask, "When am I going to get up?" But the night stretches on and I am fed up tossing and turning until dawn.

This is an easy image to which most people can relate. Perhaps our burden has never been as great as Job's. Nevertheless, things that trouble us have prevented us from sleeping and we simply wait for the sun to rise so that we can get out of bed. At night, alone, we are particularly vulnerable to our pain when there is little to mitigate it.

> 7:5 My body is clothed with worms and clods of dirt; my skin is puckered and disgusting.

Job looks as bad as he feels. What has happened to him has affected his body and his mind. In order to emphasize both his state of mind and his physical condition, the Targum translates the second clause as "my skin trembles and wastes away."

Rashi wants his readers to fully understand Job's condition so he describes it as a specific skin disease that affects those who live in caves and is caused by the soil found in them. (However, there is no indication by the author of Job or by Job's own words that he ever lived in a cave.)

> 7:6 My days pass faster than a weaver's shuttle and they end without hope.

This reminds the reader somewhat of the contemporary expression of folk wisdom, "The years are short and the days are long." Job knows that his life is short. But he is also despondent, because he sees no potential for joy, happiness or optimism in them.

Rashi attempts to take the verse a little more positively. He understands the first phrase to mean "my fortunate days pass faster." He points out that the speed of the weaving process has made the weaver and his tools metaphors for speed as in the phrase *kepaditi c'oreg chayai*, "I have rolled up my life like a weaver" (Isaiah 38:12). Rashi then takes the last clause to mean that Job no longer has any hope for good fortune.

> 7:7 Remember that my life is but a breath. My eye will never again see good.

At first read, the two parts of this verse appear to be two unrelated statements. The only thing that ties them together is that they are both related to Job's short and painful life on earth. But perhaps since Job recognizes that his sojourn on earth is short and limited and hasn't experienced good, at least after his tragedies, there is nothing more to which he can look forward.

While there doesn't seem to be any reason to indicate this as a reference to life after death, especially since that is a rabbinic concept that was introduced after the Bible was written, Rashi nevertheless takes the last clause as proof that Job has denied the doctrine of the Resurrection of the Dead.

> 7:8 That eye that now sees me will never again see me. Your eyes are upon me and I am gone.

Although the first clause in this verse seems clear, the second phrase is not quite as clear. To whom do "your eyes" refer? If it is Job's friends to which it refers, then the last clause is parallel to the first clause: when Job dies, he will disappear from the sight and the concerns of other people. If it is God, then one might assume that even after death, Job will be seen by God.

> 7:9 A cloud vanishes and is gone just as one who goes into the grave will never come up.

This verse seems to deny the possibility of life after death. However, had such a possibility existed in the mind of the author of the book of Job, the entire problem of suffering without guilt, the burden of the book, would have been mitigated. Precisely the problem of evil, perpetrated or allowed by a loving God, assumes a this-world orientation. Conversely, one may argue that the world-to-come as the solution for the problem of evil is required to maintain the notion of a loving and caring Deity.

> 7:10 One will never return to one's house. One's place will not know oneself again.

Just like the previous verse, this one proclaims that death is the end of life. There is no life beyond this life. We die and all of our familiar places are gone to us and we are gone to them. For religions that depend on a system that affirms the principles that if one is good, one will receive good and if that good is not manifest in this life it will come in the next life, the view of Job presented here is both a challenge and a threat. It challenges the view of a beneficent Deity and it threatens the entire structure of religious belief and action.

> 7:11 Therefore, I will not be silent. I will speak in the anguish of my spirit. I will complain in the bitterness of my soul.

Having nothing to lose, Job chooses to speak out at this time. Life has brought him pain. Only death can bring an end to his pain. To emphasize the place from which he is speaking, he emphasizes the depth of his pain by offering the last two clauses of this verse, which are parallel statements.

> 7:12 Am I the sea or a sea monster that you set a watch over me?

Job presents himself as a solitary and mortal individual rather than some kind of natural or supernatural threat. Hence, he asks why is he being treated as if he were either of the two.

> 7:13 Were I to say that my bed should comfort me and my couch should ease my lament?

It is clear that the understanding of this verse is dependent on the verse that follows. Both clauses in this verse parallel one another. Rashi helps us to understand the verse by suggesting that it means, "My bed at night helps me to endure my pain so that I am able to control my complaint." In other words, if he is asleep, he is not aware of his pain and therefore does not express it.

> 7:14 But you frighten me with dreams and terrify me with visions.

This verse seems to undermine Rashi's understanding of the previous verse. Job is telling his readers that even in the midst of sleep—which should separate him from the awareness of his pain—he suffers because of what he dreams. Job's interpretation of those dreams makes him feel even worse. Job gets no relief, neither during the day nor at night.

> 7:15 I would rather be strangled and dead than have this body of mine.

This is an intentionally gruesome image. It is in his body that Job feels pain and suffers. He imagines that were he dead, he would not be experiencing pain any longer.

> 7:16 I loathe living. I would not live forever. Let me alone. My days are useless.

This verse certainly does not come as a surprise to the reader. Job hates the life he must now endure. If offered to him, he would reject the opportunity to live forever, something for which many people might yearn. He has one simple wish—to be left alone. The word *hevel*, literally "a breath, a vapor," is the only word in the verse that presents the translator with a challenge. This is the word used throughout Ecclesiastes and may be considered the notion with which Ecclesiastes is most associated. Although often translated as "vanity," as in Ecclesiastes (1:2), *hevel havalim, ha-kol hevel*, it really means "Useless, it is all useless. Everything is useless." We borrow from that translation and translate the last clause of this verse as "My days are useless."

> 7:17 What is a human that you think so much of a person? And that you pay attention to that person?

In order to achieve gender neutrality, we have translated "him" as "a person." Through the author, Job makes a basic assumption that provides a foundation for this verse. Job suffers, because God wants him to suffer. It is because God knows Job. It is because God pays attention to him. Were God unaware of Job or were God not attentive to Job, then Job would not have suffered nor have arrived to his current state. Thus, Job's suffering (and the problem of theodicy that accompanies it) is a function of God's knowledge of the individual and God's specific act of will related to that person. Were Job an inanimate object or an animal, perhaps he might have escaped God's gaze. On the other hand, were the God of the book of Job not understood from a traditional perspective, then God might not have been involved with Job at all.

Rashi sees this verse as an affirmation of the human, as well as an affirmation of the relationship between humanity and God. Thus, he translates the verse as "You have magnified humanity by paying attention to the individual and by reviewing one's deeds every morning and examining the individual every moment."

> 7:18 You review the individual every morning and test people every moment.

In order to avoid gender specificity, we have translated the second clause in the plural. Clearly, Rashi's comment on the previous verse was informed by this verse. God is aware of human actions at all times. Moreover, God puts humans into situations to see how they will respond, whether they will respond with appropriate moral intention. Humans are the only ones of divine creation who warrant God's continual care and attention. But divine attention presents problems for such creatures. Humans are only human; thus, they sin. As a result, they incur guilt and deserve to be punished. Job now complains that God knows whatever it is that he, as a fallible mortal being, has done.

> 7:19 When will You stop looking at me? Can't You leave me alone until I swallow my spit?

Job believes that God follows his every move and is attentive to him. Job expresses a desire that God pay attention to someone else and leave him alone. This second phrase is a bit peculiar. It is Job's way of saying, "Leave me alone until I die on my own."

> 7:20 O You who watch humanity, what have I done to You? Why did You set me up as an obstacle to you? Why have I become a burden to myself?

Job complains that any sin he has committed does not affect God. Nonetheless, religions that demand obedience from people to what are considered God's commands take any sin as an affront to God.

> 7:21 Why don't You pardon my transgression and forgive my iniquity? I shall soon lie down in the dust. So when You search for me, I won't be there.

This verse seems to reflect somewhat of a change in Job's argument. He finally admits that perhaps he has transgressed and therefore asks for God's mercy. Moreover, since he assumes that he will die soon and that God will not attend to him when he is dead, God might as well start being inattentive now.

Perhaps the author intentionally chose to use the uncommon verb *shachartani* (search for me) from the root *shin-chet-raysh* because of its aural resonance with the noun *shachar* (morning), so that following the phrase "I shall soon lie down . . ." implies a sense of "searching for someone in the morning."

THE DOCTRINE OF RESURRECTION OF THE DEAD

The notion of resurrection is not found in the Bible, particularly not as a reward for righteous deeds. It is introduced by the early Rabbis who lived in the first to third centuries of the Common Era and undermines biblical theology and the authority of the priests as a result. Thus, it is not found directly in the book of Job. Such theology was insinuated into Job by commentators who reflect rabbinic theology. Because this theology is part of mainstream Judaism (although it was rejected by classical Reform thinkers), it is difficult to read texts such as Job without such inferences.

The doctrine (like most Jewish beliefs) is not systematically delineated in rabbinic literature but is referred to extensively. Basically, rabbinic theology suggests that body and soul will be reunited—with the body resurrected from the grave—at the onset of the messianic era, for judgment. Those who are judged as righteous will be rewarded with a place in the world-to-come, a primary feature of this theology.

This doctrine is also reflected in Jewish liturgy, particularly in the second blessing of the core prayer called the *amidah* (literally, standing prayer) which concludes with the blessing "*mechayeh hameitim*" (Who resurrects the dead). This doctrine also led to the notion of the resurrection of Jesus in Christian theology.

WORLD-TO-COME

The eschatological concept of a world-to-come (*olam haba*) developed during the period of the Second Temple. This concept was expanded upon in subsequent rabbinic literature. While the term *olam* originally was related to space, it later took on the dimension of time. Jewish tradition suggests that a major event such as the Day of Judgment would bring this world to an end and usher in the next world, that is, the world-to-come. Heaven or paradise are terms used interchangeably to define *olam haba*. However, some make a distinction between the temporary place where souls reside prior to final judgment and the "other world" where the departed souls of "good" people permanently reside.[1]

---

1. Kravitz and Olitzky, *Kohelet*, 20.

Chapter 8

> 8:1 Then Bildad the Shuchite responded:

THIS CHAPTER BEGINS THE response of another one of Job's friends in an ostensible attempt to comfort him. According to Maimonides in his *Guide for the Perplexed* (part 3, chapter 23), each of Job's comforters present a different view of providence. Maimonides thinks that Eliphaz represents the standard rabbinic position: Job is being punished for his sins, plain and simple. Bildad, on the other hand, represents the view of the *Mu'tazila*, a group of Islamic thinkers who contended that God knows all things. All things followed divine wisdom. Any incongruities with regard to virtue and its reward, as well as vice and its punishment, would be made up in the world-to-come. (See Maimonides, *Guide*, part 3, chapter 17.)

> 8:2 How long will you say these things? Your words are like a strong wind.

Bildad is tired of Job's complaints and accusations. He says, "Your words make noise, but they don't make much sense." Rashi comes close to the contemporary American English idiom when he translates, "Your words are a lot of wind."

> 8:3 Does God pervert judgment? Does the Almighty pervert justice?

These two clauses are clearly parallel and attempt to express the same sentiment and are part of Bildad's defense of God. Bildad's position, which will be explicated in the verses that follow, reminds us that he believes that people could and should be punished for the actions of their children and other members of their family. This is part of the system that Bildad implies is just and not perverse. Bildad, like Eliphaz, must maintain Job's guilt. The repetition in the two parts of the verse emphasize the central challenge of the book of Job: If Job is not guilty, then who is indeed responsible for his suffering?

> 8:4 If your children sinned again God, then God sent them into the hand of their transgression.

This is a painful verse, to be sure, and very difficult to read, let alone defend. Is there any child who is deserving of the punishment that Job's children endured? In defense of God, Bildad's theological position is that if Job's children were punished, they must have done something—they must have sinned—in order to deserve it.

> 8:5 If you would look to God and you would plead with the Almighty,

This verse is dependent on the verse that follows for the reader to understand it. While the nature of the suggested prayer is not yet apparent, it is clear that Bildad is telling Job that he has to pray if he expects any change to occur. Rashi hints at what will be the necessary content of Job's prayers in his understanding of *teshachayr* as "you should stir up your merit." In other words, Job may be able to persuade God as a result of the merit he has accrued throughout his life.

> 8:6 If you were pure and upright, God would protect you and restore you to your proper place.

Apparently, but not surprisingly, Bildad tells Job that it is all Job's fault. Since Job was not protected, then he must have been guilty and not pure and upright. Thus, he should not expect to be restored to his former place.

The rationale behind the verse is consistent with what we have seen before in the book of Job. Suffering is punishment for sin. Repentance and remorse obviate the sin and remove the punishment. However, this is precisely what the author of Job denies. The author maintains that suffering can also affect those who have not sinned. But the author of the book of Job is unable to say that if Job and his children were punished even though they had not sinned, then a number of acts of evil have indeed been committed—and not just by Satan.

> 8:7 Although your beginning was small, your end will be very great.

It seems like this verse speaks of an increase in possessions rather than an increase in virtue. Not only does Bildad promise Job that he will be return to his previous state, he also promises Job that he will be better off economically than before. Rashi offers some perspective to this verse. While it remains hard to accept, Rashi suggests that the verse means that because Job's future end will be so great, his past beginning will seem very small.

> 8:8 Go ask the previous generation and apply what their ancestors discovered.

The context of the verse seems to suggest that Job is being asked to reflect on the past so as to derive a lesson for the present. If the "ancestors" came upon some truth, then Job is being asked to apply it in some manner.

> 8:9 For we were born yesterday and so know nothing. Our days pass by on the earth like a shadow.

Bildad's response to Job follows one attempt to deal with the problem of evil: we are simply too ignorant to understand it. This approach will be repeated later in the book in the speech from the whirlwind (chapter 38). Such an approach fails because it does not deal with what we do know. Job is presented in the book by the author as an innocent man who suffers in a multitude of ways. This suffering comes at the hands of a God thought to be good. Few people are ignorant of the conflict between the ideas of God's goodness and the existence of evil in the world. What more is there to know?

> 8:10 Behold, they will teach you. They will tell you. They will speak to you from their hearts.

This verse refers to the earlier generation mentioned in 8:8. *Halo*, the negative word *lo* (no, not) preceded by the interrogative particle *ha*, often has the meaning of "behold" as it does here.

> 8:11 Can papyrus grow tall without a marsh? Can sedge sprout without water?

Bildad argues that since nature provides examples of the relationship between cause and effect, what happened to Job must have had a cause. If one assumes that suffering is due to sin, then if suffering occurs, there must have been sin. That will be the argument of verse 13 in this chapter. However, the entire central thesis of the book of Job is that suffering may not be due to sin and that observing the supposed effect may not be instructive as to the proposed cause.

> 8:12 While it is still growing and yet uncut, it will dry out quicker than grass.

Again, a purported lesson from nature. The lack of water will affect certain plants. The reader may derive this lesson from lesser living things: all causes have their effects.

> 8:13 Such are the ways of all who forget God and so will be destroyed the hope of the godless,

While Bildad's comments are couched in universal terms, they are directed to Job. For Bildad, what Job has suffered proves that he sinned. In Modern Hebrew, the word *chanef* (godless) means "hypocrite." For Bildad, and other "comforters" of Job, Job's professions of innocence seem to be statements of a hypocrite since Job's guilt is seemingly proven by his suffering.

> 8:14 Whose confidence is put in thread and whose trust is in a spider's web.

The word *yakot* occurs only here. Its translation as "thread" is derived from the parallel "spider's web" of the last clause. The sense of both clauses is that one bereft of benefit has nothing to depend on and nothing for which to hope.

> 8:15 One may lean upon one's house, but it will not stand. One may hold it tight, but it will not last.

The subject of this verse continues from the previous verse. There is no stability in the world, nothing on which one can depend. Even if things appear to be dependable, they are not. Since the "house" mentioned in the previous verse was *bayt ackavish*, literally, "the house of the spider," it would make sense for the reader to assume that this is an idiomatic reference to "the spider's web."

> 8:16 This one is like a moist plant before the sun shines, spreading out its shoots over the garden.

In order to avoid gender specificity, we have translated "he" as "this one." It is difficult to understand the author's precise meaning here. It would seem that the plant is flourishing. If that is the case, it is puzzling how such a plant could represent the uncertain status of the sinner.

Rashi takes *ratov* to mean "moist and strong." This suggests that the fate of the sinner is strong before the time of the sinner's recompense, which is like the drying up of the plant as a result of the heat of the sun. Rashi notes that the author chooses to use such language because the author is making a comparison specifically between the sinner and a papyrus plant.

> 8:17 Its roots are wrapped around a heap of rocks and go around a pile of stones.

Rashi seems to want the reader to understand the author's image more fully. So he takes the first verb to mean "to entwine" as with branches or bushes. He then reads the second verb to mean "to plan a trap." Rashi also quotes an earlier commentator who interpreted the word to mean "to limit" or "to set up a boundary" by relating it to the phrases *mechoz cheftzam* "desired haven" (Psalm 107:30) and *mechezeh el mechezeh* "light against light" (1 Kings 7:4).

> 8:18 If it becomes uprooted from its place, then the place lies, and says, "I have not seen it."

If the plant is uprooted, it is as if it had never grown in a place, even if it has entangled its roots around the stones of the place. Rashi believes that the verse lacks some words, which he provides: "If being punished, it is swallowed up from its place." He explains that the reason that the place will say "I have not seen you" is because the destruction will be so great that the plant—a metaphor for a wicked person—will disappear and nothing of it will remain. Rashi goes on to say that the righteous may fall, but they will rise up; the wicked fall and never rise up again.

> 8:19 Behold its ways lead to despair. Yet from its dust, others may grow.

This verse appears to contain a slightly more positive outlook than do the previous verses. Although the plant ceases to exist, its remains provide nutrients for others to grow in its place.

Rashi explains the verse with the rabbinic understanding of reward and punishment as background. He argues that the wicked person may rejoice in a wicked way, but the wicked person's success will not last. On the other hand, those who have been brought low—as suggested in this verse—will grow in the end. Thus, the "other" person will be the one to rise to greatness and supplant the wicked. Rashi takes a cue from a phrase in the book of Ecclesiastes, *v'lachotay natan inyan*, read in context as ". . . To the one God does not [favor], God gives the anguish of gaining and getting—and giving away to someone else whom God does favor . . ." (2:26).

Ibn Ezra sees a simple lesson in this verse. What happens to the plant is a metaphor for what happens to those who are wicked. Because of the quality of their lives and because they take rejoicing as their highest value, they will not endure.

> 8:20 Behold God does not reject the innocent nor does God support the hand of those who do evil.

In this verse, the author places into the mouth of Bildad the standard theodicy of the time, as was hinted at in the previous verses: do good and you will get good; do evil and you will be punished. For Rashi, this verse is an encouragement for Job. God will not aid those who maltreat Job and will have mercy on him. Thus, Job will rejoice in the end—as is promised by the next verse.

> 8:21 God will yet fill your mouth with laughter and your lips with a joyous shout.

For those who have suffered tragedy, these words of Bildad sound like a well-meaning truism and are therefore difficult to accept and absorb. It is hard to imagine that life could be any different than what Job has just experienced. Simply, Bildad tells Job: things will get better. We have added the word "joyous" before "shout" in order to emphasize the intent of the verse and Bildad's offer of hope to Job.

> 8:22 Your enemies will be clothed in shame and the tent of the wicked will disappear.

This follows directly on the preceding verse. Bildad continues to reassure Job that the future will be bright. What seems to be missing from Bildad's words is the recognition that the so-called wicked worked at God's behest.

As Gersonides understands it, Bildad asks Job to repent and to implore God's mercy so that what is promised will indeed occur. Gersonides suggests that we possess an inability to understand divine wisdom, which allows bad things to happen to good people and good things to happen to bad people. While certainly apologetic, inadequate, and unacceptable from the perspective of the authors of this volume, Gersonides tells his readers that for Bildad, bad things happen to good people so that such people may gain a future reward. Even so, according to Bildad, the bad things that happen to good people are far less severe than the bad things that happen to bad people.

Chapter 9

9:1 Then Job replied,

WE HAVE TRANSLATED THE formulaic *v'yaan va'yomer* (literally, he answered and said) as "replied."

9:2 Indeed it is so! How can one be justified before God?

It appears as if Job is going to defend himself. Then he seems to agree with Bildad. But we see that this is not the case as the chapter evolves. *Yitzdak* is being used in this verse in a legal sense. In a court case, how can a human being win a case against God, no matter how strong the case? If Job's somewhat facetious argument were to be accepted, then the problem of theodicy would be easily solved. Whatever the complaint, God is always the winner. But this is inconsistent with major strands of rabbinic thinking.

9:3 If one wanted to argue with God, God could not answer the individual as one out of a thousand.

It is not clear who is the subject and who is the object of *yaanenu* (literally, he answered him) in this verse. It could either mean "the mortal could not answer God" or "the Deity would not answer the mortal." Along with the previous verse, is it that the individual could not pursue an argument against God nor defend oneself against God's arguments? Or were the individual interested in arguing with God, that person could not persuade God to respond? We believe that it is as follows: "If an individual wanted to argue with God, God could not answer the individual as one out of a thousand." In other words, God can't take the time to answer the arguments and complaints of each human being. There are just too many humans to do so.

9:4 God is wise and all powerful. Who could oppose God and be at ease?

The subject of this verse is not clear. It seems to reference the previous verse, whose subject is also not clear. We contend that the previous verse refers to the inability of the human to pursue an argument with God. Theologically, irrespective of whether one accepts Bildad's argument or Job's response, we might agree with the sentiment of the author of Job. God is wise. It is hard to simply oppose God, argue with the Deity, and be at ease in doing so.

> 9:5 God moves mountains without their knowledge and overturns them in anger.

Once again, the power of the Deity is presented by the author—and by Job. However, the book of Job is not a discussion of God's power. Rather, it is an analysis of God's sense of justice.

> 9:6 God shakes the earth out of its place so that its pillars shudder.

This verse appears to be a poetic description of an earthquake. Rashi thinks that all it takes is for God to look at the earth and it shakes.

> 9:7 God speaks to the sun and it stops shining. God blocks the light of the stars.

This verse is part of a continued description of God's power. We have translated *yachtom* (literally, He seals) as "God blocks" and added the "light of" to make clear what of the stars is being blocked.

> 9:8 God alone stretches out the heavens and treads on the waves of the sea.

More demonstration of unparalleled and unequalled divine power.

> 9:9 God is the maker of the bear, orion, the pleiades and the constellations of the southern sky.

This is a statement about God's power and oversight in the universe.

> 9:10 God does great things beyond limit and marvels without number.

This verse attempts to describe God by identifying an attribute. God does great things in the world that surpass our understanding. So numerous are these wonderful things that we are unable to count them.

> 9:11 Were God to pass me, I would not see God. Were God to go by me, I would not know it.

This is an attempt by the author to explain the unknowable quality of the Deity.

> 9:12 Were God to snatch [someone] away, who could stop God?
> Who can say to God, "What are you doing?"

Just another example of the power of God. However, subtly implied in this verse by the use of the specific example of the author is the question of theodicy. This is not just about the power of God. Rather, it is also about the justice of God.

> 9:13 God does not restrain divine anger. Even those who came
> to help Rahab cowered before God.

This verse suggests something of the mythological background of ancient Israel and this book. Biblical authors were aware of the popular myths held by inhabitants of the region. Rather than try to disabuse people of these myths, they incorporated them into the folk literature of ancient Israel, adapting the theology as necessary. Rahab was one of the mythical sea monsters in medieval Jewish folk literature. It is possible, however, that Rahab was being used as the "symbolic designation of Egypt." Nevertheless, this verse makes it clear that God can express divine anger in such a way that no one is safe when God is angry. And there is no way to get out of God's way.

> 9:14 How can I answer God? What arguments can I choose
> against God?

Finally Job returns to his own situation. It isn't that Job has no argument against God. Rather, Job realizes that he has no power to bring it against the *force majeure* of the Deity. We have translated *devarai* (literally, "my words") as "arguments."

> 9:15 Were I innocent, I would not answer. I would plead with
> my judge for mercy.

As we have seen in the previous verse, it is the balance of power that makes Job's innocence irrelevant.

> 9:16 Were I to cry out, would God answer me? I don't believe
> that God would hearken to my voice.

This verse reflects Job's disillusionment and despair. He is clearly speaking from his experience. If God is presented as embodying absolute power but not absolute justice, then the human response to such a God would be utter despair.

> 9:17 God would smash me with a storm. God would multiply
> my wounds for no reason.

Job's despair continues to worsen. The absolute and arbitrary power exercised by monarchs in the ancient world was carried over into the presentation of the notion of God in this section of the text and particularly in this verse. With such a God, Job can neither argue with God nor expect divine justice. Just as it was with a king of his time, to question authority was to invite disaster onto himself. So one approach to the problem of evil is to be silent and not dare to question God.

> 9:18 You don't let me catch my breath before you start filling me with bitterness.

In an effort to maintain a gender-free translation, we have translated in the second person rather than the third person as the Hebrew has it. It is still being addressed to the Divine. God is unrelenting. Job has no break from his suffering. As soon as one source of pain leaves him, a second one arrives to take its place.

> 9:19 If it is a matter of power, God is [admittedly] strong. But if it is a matter of justice, who will testify on my behalf?

A God who possesses absolute power can summon anyone. However, it will be difficult to find someone to testify on Job's behalf against such a Deity.

> 9:20 If I were innocent, my mouth would declare me guilty. If I were upright, it would call me crooked.

In this verse, it is clear that Job is presenting the reality of power even in the purported realm of justice. Unfortunately, it seems that power often trumps virtue.

> 9:21 Although I am upright, I don't know who I am. How I despise my life!

Power can overwhelm the individual. Even if the truth can vindicate the person, that person is still unable to defend himself or herself. The notion of being upright is an interesting one. Perhaps Job is referring to his still being alive. It is similar to the contemporary idiom, "I am still standing." With all that he has been through, Job is somehow still standing. But that is all he is able to do.

> 9:22 It is all the same. That is why I said, "God destroys both the upright and the wicked."

More charges against the Deity. Destruction comes to both the innocent and the guilty without differentiation. For Job, there is no divine justice at all. Rashi colors Job's statement by adding the word *b'olam* (in this world).

Thus, Rashi implies that while there may be no justice in this world, there will be justice in the world-to-come.

> 9:23 Were some scourge to bring sudden death, God would mock the despair of the innocent.

Job has moved beyond his initial accusations against God. Not only is God unjust, Job now charges God with being unfeeling and vicious.

> 9:24 The earth is handed over to the wicked. God conceals this from the eyes of the judges. If it is not God, then who is it?

This verse presents the problem of evil in its fullness. If God is conceived as omnipresent, omniscient, and omnipotent, then how can God allow such evil to exist? If evil exists, and God is as Job conceives God to be, then God is involved by being in the presence of evil. God knows about it and does nothing to prevent it from taking action on the innocent. Thus, God becomes tainted by evil.

> 9:25 My days pass faster than any runner. They run away without seeing any good.

This is both Job's perspective on the value of his life and his sense of imminent death.

> 9:26 They speed by like papyrus boats, like an eagle swooping down on its prey.

The context of this verse suggests forward movement, rather than standing in one place.

> 9:27 Were I to say, "I will forget my complaint, I will forgo my anger, and I will be cheerful,"

> 9:28 I fear all that I would suffer, for I know that you will not acquit me.

Is Job prepared to make a compromise? It is clear that the author has Job putting on a "happy face" in order to cover up his pain. It seems like Job is about to offer God a deal of some sort.

> 9:29 If I am already guilty, why should I struggle in vain?

Why should Job bother to present his case if God—and the divine court—have decided that Job is guilty? It seems like a fruitless endeavor.

> 9:30 Were I to wash myself with snow and cleanse my hands with soap

> 9:31 then you would dunk me into slime so that even my own clothes would loathe me.

There is nothing that Job can do to convince God that he is innocent. In a bitterly ironic fashion, reflecting the world in which he lives, a world in which power rather than right rules, the author of the book of Job suggests that nothing can help Job's case. Even if somehow Job could get hold of snow, in order to melt it for washing, and soap to clean his hands, equally difficult to attain, he would still be considered a dirty sinner.

Job's plaint is that were he to have cleansed himself in every possible manner, it would not have availed him. Something would have happened to make him appear as if he were a dirty sinner—or be treated as such.

> 9:32 God is not a human like me that we could come together into court.

Job understands that the issue is not the justice of Job's cause. Rather, it is the power of God that is at the heart of the matter. How can a mortal face such power? Even if the mortal in on the side of truth and justice, can that mortal win against God? Clearly, Job contends that the mortal can never win against God.

> 9:33 There is none who could reprove us both or lay a hand on the two of us.

Job's complaint is that there is no neutral judge. Neither Job nor God could be neutral in Job's own assessment. Moreover, there is no one who could restrain God's power, however virtuous Job might be.

> 9:34 Would that he take away his staff that fear of him would not terrify me.

While we usually translate terms to make them gender free, we left the pronouns in this verse in the masculine form, because the antecedent is unclear. So "he" could refer to the person or official who would be in a position to reprove God and who in the context of the verse seems to be nonexistent. Or it could refer to God who has the capacity to make the case against Job seem more fair. As it stands, Job suffers real pain. "His staff" terrifies Job, as do his fears.

> 9:35 I would speak were I not frightened, but that is not how I am with myself.

While the words in the last clause of the verse are clear, its sense is not. Literally, the clause reads, "for not so am I with myself." It seems to suggest that Job is aware that this is not typical of his own behavior.

Chapter 10

> 10:1 I am disgusted with my life. I will let my complaint spew out. I will speak out of the bitterness of my soul.

BY THIS POINT, JOB feels like he has nothing more to lose. Since he feels that he stands condemned irrespective of what he does or says, he might as well say what is on his mind. The Targum adds to Job's level of despair by translating *nakta* (am disgusted) by *itgezart naphshi* (my soul / my desire is cut off). Rashi translates the same verb as *mikottet* (vexed) and thus explains the first clause to mean "My soul is vexed and I am still alive." He sees a connection to the use of the verb in the phrase *unekotetem befneechem*, "you will loathe yourselves in your own sight" (Exodus 20:43). He is clearly referencing the content of the verse as well.

For Ibn Ezra, Job's disgust comes from his ambivalence about speaking out or refraining from doing so. Regardless of which choice he makes, Job feels that he will lose.

> 10:2 I would say to God, "Don't convict me. Tell me: What you are charging me with?"

Job imagines himself in a legal proceeding. Before he is convicted, he would like to know for what crime is he being charged.

> 10:3 Do you enjoy oppressing and rejecting the work of your hands and smiling upon the plans of the wicked?

Continuing his imagined confrontation with God, Job is asking the basic questions asked by all who suffer: "Why?" Why is Job suffering? Why do we suffer? Why has Job been punished for something that he knows that he has not done? Why do we suffer when we feel that we too are innocent? Does God enjoy malicious delight in Job's suffering? This is the quandary of the ancient philosophers, which echoes throughout the entire book of Job: in the presence of evil, God is either powerless to remove it or vicious in allowing it to remain. For Gersonides the question is even more pointed.

Since he takes the last word *hofata* to mean assurance or brilliant light, it means that God does more than just allow the evil to transpire. God actually provides evildoers with the assurance that they can act without fear of punishment or provides the light in which they can see their actions more clearly. By providing such divine light, God is providing evildoers with the same assurances that they can carry out their plans.

> 10:4 Do you have eyes of flesh? Do you see what a human sees?

These questions may be understood in two different ways—either as a description of what is or as a challenge of what ought to be. Does God see, like a human might, what is merely apparent and not see what is ultimately true, or should not God see what humans cannot see?

> 10:5 Are your days like the days of a mortal? Are your years like those of a human

The implicit challenge here is that of any anthropomorphic understanding of the Deity. How alike can God be to humans without denying that difference which makes God, God? And how unlike humans can God be without losing a connection to humans?

> 10:6 that you should inquire about my guilt and investigate my sin

This is a continuation of the previous verse. The question is repeated: Why bother? If Job has already been convicted, what is the point of further investigation?

> 10:7 knowing that I would not have been found guilty, no one could save me from your hand?

If God is all-knowing, then God should know that Job is innocent. If God is all-powerful, then God can do whatever God wishes to do to Job, irrespective of whether Job is found to be innocent or guilty. In either case, what Job suffers challenges the notion of a beneficent Deity. If Job is innocent and suffers nonetheless, then the all-knowing God is either unable to prevent that suffering—and hence weak and not worthy of being God—or God is cruel and can prevent the suffering that God allows and also not worthy of being God. If God's relation to Job is that of arbitrary power, of a master to a slave, then Job's innocence or guilt is irrelevant. God's concern for virtue would likewise be rendered moot.

> 10:8 Your hands formed and made me all at once. Will You now change and destroy me?

Job acknowledges God's role as Creator, as well as God's power in the world. The verse is somewhat resonant of the dialogue between Jonah and God when God created shade for Jonah and then quickly provided a means for the shade to be removed. (See Jonah 4:5–8.)

> 10:9 Please remember that You have made me as clay. Would You return me to dust?

This is a reference to the end of God's creative process, as Rashi suggests in his commentary. God undertakes the effort to create Job. And now Job asks why God would want to immediately return him to the dust from which he was formed.

> 10:10 Didn't you pour me out like milk and curdle me like cheese?

While this may not seem like a positive image, it is indeed. Milk and cheese can support the lives of shepherds without any need of slaughtering the sheep and goats from which the milk comes.

> 10:11 You clothed me with skin and flesh. You assembled me with bones and sinews.

Because Gersonides wants readers to understand the specific anatomy that Job is describing, he takes *tseechayni* (you assembled me) from the root *caf-samech-hay* (cover, conceal) rather than from *sin-chaf-chaf* (to block) or from the root *samech-chaf-chaf* (knit together, assemble). He notes that the bones and the sinews are inside the body and conceal the more important inner organs. The bones and the sinews also make movement possible. Thus, the design of the body gives it more permanence.

> 10:12 You have given me life and shown me love. Your care has kept my spirit.

Job now pleads his case in a different way. God has taken care of him. So Job now asks God to continue to do so. It makes sense that the author would have Job change his way of pleading given the world in which the author lived and the concept of God he held. If such power is absolute, whether it is possessed by a sovereign ruler or by God, then the one making the plea to either a sovereign ruler or God must be careful. The one who pleads to a sovereign ruler or God may be guilty of *lese majeste* (offending the dignity of the ruler) and incur a far worse punishment than the one being threatened.

> 10:13 Yet, there were things You kept concealed. I know that this was in your mind.

Having stated in the previous verse that God has formed him and watched over him, Job now states that God has a purpose for him: Job, as is suggested by the verses that follow, is to live free from sin. We have understood *belvavecha* (literally, in Your heart) as "Your mind." To make this translation more idiomatic, we have moved the translation of this word to the second clause of the verse.

> 10:14 Were I to sin, You would catch me. You would not clear me of my sin.

The notions that God knows and God cares apply here. For the author and for the generations who read the book and follow classic rabbinic theology, the theological formula is simple: if humans sin, they will be punished.

> 10:15 Were I guilty, woe is me. Were I innocent, I could still not lift up my head, being filled with shame and satiated with misery.

Even innocence won't allay Job's pain.

> 10:16 Were I to hold my head high, you would hunt me like a lion and would again work wonders against me.

There are two levels of meaning to this verse and what the author is trying to describe. Were Job to act haughty, that is, hold his head high, then God would punish him for being arrogant. Were Job to hold his head high so that it could be seen—similar to the literal meaning of the idiom "to stick his neck out"—then God would be able to see him and hunt him down, much like a hunter does when seeing an animal's head above the brush. So although Job acknowledges his innocence, he contends that humility—subservience—in the face of power is the best course of action to take.

> 10:17 Because of your anger, You bring new witnesses against me, an army of successive waves against me.

Job feels that he cannot win, no matter what he does or how innocent he may be. Were he to be acquitted of the undetermined charges against him, God would bring new witnesses like an attacking army, one group after another, to accuse him of wrongdoing.

For Rashi, the "witnesses" attest to the succession of illnesses and pain that afflict Job, proving that he is indeed guilty of transgression. Why else would he undergo such suffering were he not guilty? The *chalifot v'tzavah* are the changes of times and seasons. This gives the sense of continuous progression that the author is trying to intimate in the verse.

> 10:18 Why did you take me out of the womb? I should have died before any eye had seen me.

> 10:19 Would that I had never been or had been brought from the womb to the tomb.

This is a feeling that readers have probably heard expressed by people who have suffered misfortune, usually rendered as "I wish that I had never been born." Job repeats a notion that he has stated previously. The author of Job includes it for emphasis.

> 10:20 Are my days few? Leave me alone. Let me have a little rest

If Job's death is imminent, he wants God to just leave him alone, if only for the short time he has left on earth. Job has had enough and cannot bear any more suffering.

> 10:21 before I must go to a land of darkness and deep gloom and not return from it.

In the previous verse, Job asked to be left alone. In this verse, he offers an explanation. Job believes that he will soon die. Thus, there is no point for him to suffer further.

There is a popular etymology for the word *tzalmavet* (usually as the "shadow of death" as in Psalm 23:4), as if the word were an unintended compounding of *tzyl* (shadow) and *mavet* (death). However, it is more likely that the word (both here and in Psalm 23) is simply the plural form of *tzyl* and therefore means shadows. Thus, it is the valley of shadows or "deep gloom."

> 10:22 A dark land, like darkness itself, of deep gloom and disorder, where even light is like darkness.

In a poetic manner, the author presents his belief that death is darkness, oblivion, and the absence of any meaning. Had the author believed that somehow we transcended the death of our bodies, then there might have been a way out of the problem of evil he presents in the book of Job. One of the Kalam groups, the Mu'tazila, according to Maimonides (*Guide* 3:17), believed that all wrongs would be righted in the world-to-come. (See comment to Job 8:1.) In this verse we learn that if the end of life is the end, then there is no recompense, no notion of reward and punishment. There is simply nothing.

MU'TAZILA, ASHARIYA AND KALAM

These three Islamic schools of thought which focused on reason and rationality date to the eighth and ninth centuries in what is now Iraq. Because of the relative freedom enjoyed by Jews in countries subject to Islamic rule during that time (the so-called Golden Age), Jewish philosophers such as Maimonides were heavily influenced by such an approach to religious scholarship. Kalam comes from the word which literally means "speech" or "word." It came to be used as a theological response to philosophy, particularly Aristotle's philosophy and his denial of creation. Kalam also arose as a theological justification of Islamic law, since there were elements in Islamic tradition (and in other traditions) that held that Fate, or the will of God, determined all things. However, without free will, one cannot justify law. Hence Kalam always had two elements: Unity and Justice. The unity of God is proven by creation; a creator God can work miracles, reveal a law and back that law with sanctions. Thus, God is free to create and command. It therefore follows that God is just, because humans have free will. If one sins, the individual meant to do so and therefore the punishment that individual receives is just. So God is free to command and humans are free to obey.

The Mu'tazila (literally, separatists) stressed God's wisdom and the Ashariya stressed God's will. The former would have a problem justifying God's acting while denying the reality of divine attributes; the latter tended to back to more traditional beliefs and held that within all divine attributes there was a real substratum of meaning. The founder of the former was Wasil b. Ata who died in the year ca. 748. The other sect arose in 912 when Abu-al Hasan Ashari argued with his teacher over the problem of God's concern for human welfare and what is best for humans. As a result, it can be considered a more traditional view.

DIVINE ATTRIBUTES

There are two ways of discovering what are the attributes of God. The first way emerges directly from the list of attributes in the Torah (Exodus 34:6–8) that find their way in the liturgy during the High Holidays and prior to the reading of the Torah on holidays that occur on weekdays. The second is taken from the list compiled by others such as Moses Maimonides or as found in liturgical expression, translated into the hymn *Yigdal*, sung at the conclusion of many worship services, particularly on Shabbat.

Chapter 11

11:1 Then Zophar the Naamatite began to speak.

THE AUTHOR NOW INTRODUCES another friend of Job to "comfort" him.

11:2 Are all these words not to be answered? Does having a big mouth make someone right?

Zophar steps forward to answer Job. He intimates that no one else is willing to do so.

11:3 Will your prattle silence people? Will you mock and no one put you to shame?

This is an admittedly odd form of speech for someone who both wants to answer Job's questions and comfort him as a friend. It is clear that the author is using this friend to present another view to the reader. The reader must remember that if Job is innocent then it is God who is guilty. This is what is at stake for the comforting friends of Job.

11:4 You say [to God], "my teaching is pure and I am innocent in your eyes."

Zophar is already implying that Job is not as innocent as Job claims.

11:5 O that God would speak and open divine lips against you

This is what is anticipated in the previous verse. For Zophar, Job's claim of innocence is false and a sign of Job's hypocrisy. If one believes that suffering evil is a sign of doing evil, then anything that the sufferer might say would be taken as hypocrisy.

11:6 And tell you the secrets of wisdom. Wondrous is prudence.
Know that God has forgotten part of your sin.

Implied in this part of Zophar's statement against Job is the notion that God's punishments are always moderated, namely, "God has forgotten part of your sin." Otherwise, all humans would be constantly and severely punished and Job's punishment would have been far worse than what he experienced.

> 11:7 Can you find the ultimate meaning of God? Can you seek out the purpose of the Almighty?

This question certainly transcends the specific book of Job, as well as the answers that the book intends to address. But it is important for the author to place these questions in the midst of such a discussion since they go right to the heart of the matter. The notion of the unknowable quality of God, as well as its contrast with the limits of human knowledge, is often found in theological discussions. However, as Hume points out (in his *Dialogues on Natural Religion*, part 4), how do the theists who proclaim the utter incomprehensibility of the Deity really differ from the "skeptics or atheists, who assert that the first cause of all is unknown and unintelligible?" Rashi understands the implications of Zophar's challenge to Job. He reads it as an air of presumptuousness on the part of Job: "Do you think that you have mastered everything?"

> 11:8 They are higher than the highest heavens. What can you do? They are deeper than the underworld. What can you know?

It is unclear whether *sheol* (translated as "the underworld") was understood by the writer as a specific place with a specific name or a general term. We take the word to have a generalized meaning: "the underworld."

> 11:9 Their measure is longer than the earth and wider than the sea.

Even as a metaphor, this is quite a substantial measurement.

> 11:10 Were God to pass by and arrest you and assemble a court, who could argue against God?

What seems to be suggested by the author is a kind of divine indifference: God acts without much intention. God could even apply a judicial process against Job—in terms that moderns who have lived in totalitarian states could well understand. On a whim, God could arrest Job, bring him up on charges in a court that God could control without anyone being able to appeal against such a false judgment. This verse seems to present Zophar's argument that God can do whatever God wants to do, without being questioned, and without any means for appeal.

> 11:11 For God knows worthless individuals. When God sees sin, shall God not pay attention?

The implicit meaning of Zophar's statement is that Job is a sinner, one of the "worthless individuals" to which the verse refers. What Job suffers, he deserves to suffer. While this may be an explanation as to why Job suffered, it certainly provides no comfort.

> 11:12 An empty-headed person can no more be made smart than can a wild ass be born as a human.

This verse seems to be a proverb of some sort. The word *navuv* (literally, empty or hollow) appears elsewhere in the Bible in the description of a chest made of boards (Exodus 27:8 and 38:7).

> 11:13 Yet were you to prepare your heart and stretch out your hands to God,

This verse is an introduction to the verses that follow. Here Zophar is offering hope to Job. Zophar takes Job to be a sinner. Thus, he is offering Job the opportunity to repent and receive surcease from his pain. Just to make sure that the reader understands the purpose of the action with one's hands, the Targum adds "in prayer to God."

Not to be outdone, Rashi takes the first clause to mean "if after [your] suffering, you would concentrate your mind" and the second clause to mean "and stretch out your hands to God—with a plea of mercy."

> 11:14 if you will cast off the sin that is in your hand and not allow malice to dwell in your tent,

For Zophar, Job's punishment is proof of Job's guilt. Thus, it is up to Job to change his situation. Were Job to remove the evil that is the cause of his punishment, then he would be free of his suffering.

The Targum translates *aver* (sin) as *shekar* (falsehood). Job complains that he suffers for no reason. For the Targum, this complaint is a lie.

> 11:15 then without blemish you could lift up your face. You could stand firm and not fear.

To Zophar, suffering implies guilt. There is no way to interpret suffering otherwise. Job's tormented face reflects the evil that he has wrought. If Job would only admit to the sin for which he is being punished and repent, then he would have a chance to have a future without blame and without pain.

The Hebrew word *mutzak* (stand firm), from the root *yod-tzadee-kuf*, can also mean "emptied out." The Targum understands it in the latter meaning as *tehay senin maychabilah* (emptied out of sin).

Rashi understands the first clause to mean "Then you will be certain that you can lift up your face from under the blemish which you, yourself, have caused." Rashi takes the last clause dealing with *mutzak* to mean "stand firm" as in the phrase *metzukay aretz*—"the pillars of the earth" (2 Samuel 2:8).

> 11:16 You will forget your troubles. You will recall them like water that has already flowed away.

This verse presents the reader with a powerful notion. Suffering pain is terrible, but the memory of the cause of that pain is overwhelming. Each time one remembers the source of the suffering, the pain is renewed. Job is now promised relief from his pain—and the ability to forget the pain, as well. The image of "water" flowing suggests the American English idiom "water under the bridge."

> 11:17 Your life will be brighter than noonday. [Even] darkness will be like morning.

This verse is a response specifically to the darkness Job described in the previous chapter. The entrance of light into a person's life implies the cessation of suffering and freedom from pain. The uncommon word *cheled* can be translated as "world." Thus, the first clause might read, "Your world will be brighter than noonday." Because the Targum takes *cheled* to mean *gushmah* (body), it surprisingly translates the first clause as "Your body will be brighter than noonday." Then the Targum adds an explicit theological twist to the second clause by translating it as "Though one may walk through the deepest darkness, before God, it will be like morning."

Rashi sees the verse in a different manner entirely. Relating *cheled* to the phrase *cheled c'ayin negdecha*—"My age is nothing before You" (Psalm 39:6)—he explains the words as "time" or "luck." Thus, he interprets the first clause as "Your luck will be brighter than the light of the moon." But he is not satisfied with his own explanation and offers an alternative. By relating *cheled* to *chaledah* (rust), Rashi suggests that the phrase means "Your darkened place will be brighter than the light of the noon."

While offering several interpretations of specific words in the verse, Ibn Ezra's main concern is that the verse is a metaphor. Job is being told that if he repents, his life will be brighter than noon and his weariness (that is, his old age) will be like morning. In other words, his youth will return and he will be restored.

> 11:18 Because there is hope, you will feel secure. You can search, lie down, and still be safe.

While this verse is a little difficult to understand, it reflects Zophar's main message. If Job repents, everything will change. Job may even venture into dangerous places without fear. The root *chet-pay-raysh* means "to dig, to track, or to search." The sense here is to dig around, to search for things that might be covered over and might present a danger to the finder were they revealed.

As was the case with the previous verse, Ibn Ezra reads this verse as a metaphor as well. Since he takes *chafarta* as "you will dig," he suggests that Job "could dig around the walls of the city."

> 11:19 You can lie down and no one will make you afraid. [As a matter of fact], many will flatter you.

Not only will Job be safe and people will leave him alone, the changes he makes in his life will induce flattery. He will become someone important. People will seek his presence.

> 11:20 The eyes of the wicked will wear out, [seeking] their lost escape route. Their hope [thus] will turn to disappointment.

Our translation attempts to join together the various clauses in this verse. In a pious manner, the author has Zophar summarize the notion that Job has suffered because he has sinned. If he wishes to be free of pain, he must repent. If he does not repent, he will continue to suffer.

Rashi understands that this verse is being directed to Job. "The eyes... [that] will wear out" are those of Job's enemies. Although they turn to gaze at Job's wickedness, they will not be able to see it. Rashi thinks that every use of the phrase "of eyes wearing out" in Hebrew refers to one who wishes to see something but is unable to do so. He offers the reader the example of the phrase *v'aynecha r'ot v'chalot*—"Your eyes shall look and fail with longing" (Deuteronomy 28:32). He takes *manos* (escape route) as *miftach* (secure place) and thus understands the last clause to mean that the wicked will be disappointed when they don't receive those things for which they hope.

SHEOL

Sheol was another name for Gehinnom, outside the western wall in Jerusalem. This is mentioned in the Bible in various places (including Joshua 15:8) as a valley that formed the boundary between the tribes of Benjamin and Judah. This valley served as a dump where the city's refuse was placed and the carcasses of animals and executed criminals were thrown. Jeremiah prophesied that the area would become a "valley of slaughter" and a burial place (Jer 7:32). Thus, in post-biblical literature, it took on the identity of hell where the wicked are punished. However, no allusion to this really exists in the Bible. In Genesis, Sheol is simply the abode of the dead (Gen 37:25). The rabbis located Gehinnom in the bowels of the earth (*Eruvin* 19a) and in the heavens or beyond the mountain of darkness (*Tamid* 32b). For the Talmud, the form of punishment for the wicked is not clearly articulated but it is associated with some form of fire.[1]

---

1. Kravitz and Olitzky, *Mishlei*, 55.

Chapter 12

> 12:1 Job answered, saying:

THIS IS THE INTRODUCTION to Job's response to Zophar.

> 12:2 Truly, you are [everyman,] one of the people and wisdom will die with you.

Job's facetious statement reflects his bitter feeling. He is like everyone else. No one special. A prime example of the human species and the human predicament. Rashi understands the last clause of Job's statement as "Do you think that all wisdom will die when you die?"

> 12:3 Just like you, I, too, have a mind. I am not your inferior who does not know these things.

Job has been preached to long enough. He is no fool. He now responds. Rashi reads Job's response as "You think that I don't know God who reigns supreme can impose the divine will and prolong the ease of the wicked. You are only mocking me." Ibn Ezra is the source of our translation of the last clause as "Who does not know these things?"

> 12:4 I have become a laughingstock to my friends. I was the one who called on God and God answered me. While I am totally innocent, I remain a laughingstock.

Job feels that he has been answered by God. Thus, he feels justified. Nevertheless, he has not been accepted by his friends. They continue to mock him. Rashi sees this clearly. He argues that this verse is Job's complaint—motivated by the provocation of his friends. Job cried out to God. God answered him. Job is condemned by Zophar, in particular, even as he proclaims his innocence. We agree with Ibn Ezra who finds it surprising that one who cries out to God might still be subject to the belittling of friends.

> 12:5 In the opinion of those at ease, disaster is worthy of contempt. It is what happens to those who are tottering on their feet.

Those untouched by tragedy think that tragedy is the fault of the one who suffers. It is the sufferer's recompense. This is the view of the so-called comforters of Job: Job got what he deserved. He suffered, because he deserved to be punished.

> 12:6 The tents of the violent are at ease. Even those who provoke God are secure in all that God has brought into their hand.

While not using the same words, Job repeats the well-known sentiment: *tzadik v'ra lo v'rasha v'tov lo*, the innocent suffer evil while the guilty enjoy good. Even those whose sins are manifest still prosper. What they have done has not cost them anything.

> 12:7 But go and ask the animals and they will teach you or the birds in the sky and they will tell you.

What is it that animals know? As the verses that follow will indicate, they know the power of God, a power that is not always applied in what humans might call an ethical manner. As history has taught us, those without power are often those who plead for justice. Those with power need not look for justice or be concerned with it.

> 12:8 Or speak to the earth and it will teach you or the fish of the sea will tell you.

The animals will provide insight, as will the birds and the fish. Even inanimate earth can provide us with insight.

> 12:9 Who among all of them does not know that the hand of Adonai has done this?

The notion of an all-powerful Deity carries with it the problem of evil. If God controls all things, God is therefore responsible for all things, good and evil. Thus, the question is presented by Job: is God all powerful, is God all good?

> 12:10 In the divine hand is the soul of everything that lives and the spirit of all human flesh.

God is involved in everything. There is nothing of the living world that is not under the influence of the Divine.

> 12:11 Does not the ear test words and the palate taste food?

This verse is self-explanatory in its rhetoric. Rashi understands the verse to be Job's question, "Why don't those who hear of God's work not know it; it is as obvious as the taste of food is to the palate."

> 12:12 Wisdom is with old people and understanding with those who have lived long.

Like the previous verse, this is a rather commonplace notion—placed by the author into the mouth of Job. Rashi twists the phrase somewhat to read that those who are old know that God has wisdom which is different than our understanding of wisdom as the accumulated experience of living. Wisdom is not revelation nor does it come from revelation.

> 12:13 With God is wisdom and power. God has counsel and understanding.

This is a description of some of God's attributes and abilities.

> 12:14 What God destroys cannot be rebuilt. What God locks up, no one can free.

This verse speaks to God's ultimate and complete power. The Targum suggests that the final clause is a reference to the finality and completeness of the grave. Gersonides simply suggests that it is "the prison in which a person will be placed and never opened."

> 12:15 When God holds back water, everything is dried up. When God sends them forth, the earth can be overturned.

More descriptions of God's powerful abilities and attributes. Events in nature are understood as a result of the power of God. Rashi refers the last clause to what happened to the generation of Enosh (considered by Rashi to be the first idol worshippers) when water covered a third of the world.

> 12:16 God has both strength and sound wisdom. The one who goes astray and the one who leads others astray belong to God.

God is the source of all—physical and spiritual. The relation of the last clause to the first clause is to claim that the fool and the one who takes advantage of the fool are given over to divine power—at which point the problem of evil becomes manifest. Why should such a situation emerge?

That is why Rashi identifies the human as "the one who goes astray" and Satan as "the one who leads others astray." For Ibn Ezra, God knows when a person commits an unintentional sin and God knows when someone leads another person to sin.

> 12:17 God leads away counselors totally bereft and makes judges foolish.

Even humans who are among the wisest and have the reputation of being the smartest are uninformed when it comes to knowledge about the Divine.

> 12:18 God opens the bonds of sovereign rulers and ties a belt around their hips.

While the words of this verse are quite clear, what the author is attempting to say with them is not quite so obvious. Two different actions are described. First, God opens something which binds or obligates sovereign rulers, namely kings. Second, God closes something around those rulers. The first action implies an act of freeing. The second action suggests imprisonment of some sort.

For Rashi, it is a statement about how God removes kings from their reign and thereby takes away their oppressive power over people. He reads the second statement as a reference to the time when those kings were first in God's favor and, as a result, God granted them power.

> 12:19 God leads away priests totally bereft of sense and ruins those of great lineage.

This reflects the sentiments of the previous two verses. Those who appear to be close to God and therefore have greater understanding of divine ways know very little.

> 12:20 God removes speech from those [whom God] trusted and takes away discernment from the elders.

As a result, there is no one left to offer advice. Those whom one might depend on are rendered mute. Those who can speak are bereft of understanding. The Targum adds *keshot* (the truth of) before "speech" to clarify the first clause. Rashi adds to our understanding of the verse by suggesting that even those who are "trusted" can slip up on occasion in their statements. For Gersonides, those who "are trusted" are those who speak too quickly or those too certain of their own wisdom. He goes on to explain that the elders are a reference for the wise.

> 12:21 God pours out contempt upon princes and loosens the girdle of the strong.

This verse continues the string of actions associated with God from the preceding verses. Thus, this action by God is not limited to those in absolute power. It extends to the various leaders down the line, as well.

> 12:22 God reveals out of the darkness what is hidden. God
> brings into the light what is completely dark.

This verse moves into an area of more positive descriptions of the actions of God, while nevertheless acknowledging the extent of divine power. We have already noted (see Job 10:21) that the translation of *tzalmavet* as "shadow of death" is a popular, if incorrect, etymology. Rather, it should be translated, particularly in this context, as "completely dark" or "gloomy."

> 12:23 God makes nations great and then destroys them. God
> spreads out nations and then leaves them alone.

More descriptions of the extent of the power of God. In this case, however, divine power extends beyond the individual or even the group, to entire nations.

To help the reader understand the extent of God's actions, the Targum translates the second clause in the verse as "God destroys the spread of strongholds of the nations and drives them out." Rashi notes that there is a view that this verse refers to the scene at the Red Sea when the Egyptians overtook the Israelites (Exodus 14). Pharaoh thought that God had agreed to drown the Israelites in the Sea as he had the firstborn of the Israelites drowned in the Nile. God had allowed the Egyptians to apparently succeed so as to wreak vengeance on the deities of the Egyptians and to drown the Egyptians in the Red Sea. This is a view that Rashi rejects.

> 12:24 God makes the leaders of the people of the land mindless
> and so makes them wander in trackless wilderness.

In these verses, the author of Job presents a variant form of the folk saying, "Man proposes and God disposes." In its otherwise literal translation of the verse, the Targum adds *chochmat* (wisdom of) before *libah*, its translation of "heart, mind" to make clear to the reader what has been affected. Rashi takes the last three words *b'toho lo darech* to mean "in a wilderness where there is no way." Ibn Ezra reads the words a little differently. He takes *toho* to mean madness, that is, the leaders have misled the people with mad counsel. No matter the specific translation, the meaning of the verse is clear. God is intentionally fouling up the leaders so that they will mislead the people and get them lost—with no opportunity to discover their way once again.

> 12:25 They fumble about in darkness without light. God makes
> them stagger like a drunkard.

This verse concludes the various statements that precede it. God totally disorients the people. Their leaders are of absolutely no help. The people are lost and there is no one to help them find their way.

RED SEA

This body of water is at the south of Israel through which the Israelites crossed into the land of Israel. Due to a mistranslation, it has come to be known as the Red Sea, but it should be called the Reed Sea or Sea of Reeds. Technically, it is an inlet of the Indian Ocean between the continents of Africa and Asia. It connects in the south to the Indian Ocean at Bab el Mandeb and the Gulf of Aden. In the north is the Sinai Desert, the Gulf of Aqaba and the Gulf of Suez (which leads to the Suez Canal).

WISDOM AND THE OLD

The ideal in Judaism—unlike in contemporary American culture—is usually personified in old age. The experience of living far exceeds any limitations in body and physical prowess. Wisdom is associated with aging since wisdom—rather than revelation—is gained through the experience of living. Who better then to benefit from such experiences than those who have lived long? However, wisdom doesn't come from the simple accumulation of years. Rather, wisdom emerges from gaining insight from the personal experiences of the individual.

Chapter 13

13:1 Behold my eye has seen all this. My ear has heard and understood it.

THIS IS NOT HEARSAY. Job, as the speaker, has witnessed it all.

13:2 What you know, I know. I am not your inferior.

Job now takes on his accusers and so-called friends who ostensibly come to comfort him. He tells them that he knows what they know. They are not superior to him.

The Targum understands the last phrase a little differently. It translates as *anah layt paraysh ana minchon*—I have not separated from you. In other words, do not reject me. I am one of you.

13:3 Nonetheless, I would speak to the Almighty and I want to argue with God.

Job is prepared once again to take his case to God and is not interested in defending his life or his actions to his friends. The pivotal word in this verse is *hocheach* (argue), which can also mean "rebuke." It's a strong word to use about God. It is also a key word in the entire chapter, appearing in different forms in verses 3, 6, 10, and 15. It also appears in Leviticus 19:17: "You should not hate your brother in your heart. [Rather,] you should rebuke your neighbor and not bear sin because of your neighbor." Rashi reads Job as making an even more emphatic statement. He sees Job saying, "I wish only to speak to God. I want to argue with God." In other words, Job will not even take the time to speak to his friends. He has no interest in speaking to them at all.

13:4 Yet, you smear me with lies. You are all worthless as healers.

Finally, Job blurts out the words we have wanted him to say all along. His friends are not friends. His comforters offer no comfort. They came to heal and instead cause him more pain and suffering. The Targum's translation is far more graphic. The Targum expands the sense of the two words *rofay elal* by adding the words *c'masay elel umordaka d'palta sakina* (like healers [dealing with] offal and spoilt meat where the knife [used in flaying] has slipped). Rashi explains *toflay sheker* (smear me with lies) as "make up lies." He brings a rabbinic interpretation that the word *elil* (worthless) means the sinew of the throat, the cutting of which is always fatal.

> 13:5 Would that all of you would shut up. For you, that would be wisdom.

Finally, Job explodes. He tells his friends to just shut up. That would be the best thing that they could do for him.

> 13:6 Now hear my case. Listen to the arguments of my lips.

Job now changes his approach entirely and resorts to a legalistic argument.

> 13:7 Will you speak for God with malice? Will you talk for God with deceit?

Job claims that the arguments made by his comforters are statements to defend God although they may be false. For Rashi, it means that the comforters actually came to defend God armed with false statements.

> 13:8 Will you show God favor? Will you argue God's case?

This verse continues the legal theme established on God's behalf in the previous verse. Using Job's voice, the author is implying that the one who argues on God's behalf will not be fair and will, instead, show deference to God.

> 13:9 Would you turn out well were God to investigate you? Can you mock God as you might mock a human?

By placing all the blame for suffering on Job as a way of defending God, Job's comforters are lying. In doing so, they actually mock God, who is the source of truth. Rashi suggests that were God to investigate the comforters, God would find them to be liars. The same comforters would be mocking God were they to say that it was for the sake of God's reputation that they became liars.

> 13:10 If you were to show God favor in secret, God would certainly reprove you.

This statement parallels the verse in the Holiness Code, "You shall not . . . favor the person of the mighty but you should judge your fellow fairly" (Leviticus 19:15), even if the one described as "the mighty" is God.

For Rashi, this statement is designed to make it clear to the comforters that they have made false statements. Rashi wonders whether the comforters actually think that what they are doing will not become known to God.

> 13:11 Should you not be terrified by God's greatness? Should not divine dread fall upon you?

In an otherwise literal translation, the Targum adds the phrase *cursei dinah* (thrones of judgment) to emphasize the context of God's justice. Rashi understands *se'eto* (God's greatness) as "God's awesome power."

> 13:12 What you mention is comparable to ashes. Your answers are answers of clay.

The author is attempting to tell the reader that the words of the comforter have no meaning. They will have little existence. Like ashes, they can be blown away with only a little wind. Like clay, they crumble and will not endure.

> 13:13 Be quiet and I will speak, no matter what happens to me.

Job has now thrown down his challenge. Unlike his comforters, he will speak the truth irrespective of the consequences.

> 13:14 Why do I put my flesh in my teeth and put my life in my hands?

Since the author has Job speak in such a manner that one clause parallels the other, one may conclude that the phrase "my flesh in my teeth" is an idiom that means "my life is at risk."

> 13:15 Were God to kill me, for that I might hope. Yet I will argue my position in front of God.

Job is not hoping; he is challenging. Does the clause mean that in spite of everything Job still places in hope in God? Or does it suggest, as we believe it does, that an exasperated Job says that, even in the face of death, he still chooses to challenge God and God's divine justice?

Rashi translates this verse somewhat differently than what appears to be the author's intent in writing Job's words: "Behold, if God were to kill me I would not depart from God, and I would always hope in God['s deliverance]. Therefore, there is neither rebellion [from God] nor rejection [of the Divine] in my words."

> 13:16 God too will be my salvation. For before God, no hypocrite can come.

Trusting in his own innocence, Job believes that God will be on his side. In the end, Job feels that his innocence will be established, since, unlike his "comforters," he did not seek to favor God with flattery. In order to make the meaning quite clear, the Targum translates *chanef* (hypocrite) by the Latin loanword *dilator* (informer, sycophant). Rashi understands the verse to be Job's claim that if he is open with God, God will be on his side. Rashi sees this verse as an interpretation of God's words to Job's friends at the end of the book: "You have not spoken correctly to Me as did My servant Job" (Job 42:7).

13:17 Hear, O hear my words. Let your ears take in what I say.

Job continues pleading with his listeners.

13:18 I have prepared my case. I know that I will win.

Job seems to be winding down his appeal. He feels more secure now that he is before God, whom he considers to be the true judge. He believes that he will win his case. In a legal context, *etzdak* (I will be righteous) may mean "I will be acquitted" or "I will be vindicated." But in a more idiomatic manner: "I will win [it]." Rashi takes the words to mean, "I have arranged my argument. I have my points in mind to respond [to any questions]."

13:19 Who could argue with me? Were it so [that one could], I would be silent and die.

The sense of the second clause is that Job is so certain of the justice of his case that only power—divine power—could cause him to be silent and suffer the death penalty which he feels would be the result of an unfair trial.

Rashi sees the verse a little differently. He reads it as "If I could not argue [my case], I would be silent and die." And Gersonides reads it even more differently than does Rashi. He suggests that Job is telling his reader, "Telling of my pain brings me a measure of relief. Were I not able to speak of my suffering, I would die." The comments of Rashi and Gersonides reflect the stance that Job is taking throughout this chapter. He expresses the importance of speaking up—a timeless lesson, to be sure, particularly resonant in our own day.

13:20 Only don't do two things to me. Then I [on my part] will not hide myself from you.

Job is not asking God not to do something. Rather, Job is asking God to do something, anything.

Rashi takes the word "two" to suggest two places and two kinds of judgment. The first judgment occurs in the heavenly court. The second occurs in the human court. Thus, Job is making a request to be judged by one court but not by two different courts. As Rashi understands the verse, Job is saying to God, "If You enter into judgment with me then I will not hide from Your face. If I am judged by the heavenly court, I will confess my sins."

> 13:21 Keep your hand far off me and let not fear of you terrify me.

Understandably, Job continues to be afraid. These two requests seem to be what was requested by Job in the previous verse. If Job is going to plead his case before the Highest Judge, then to be fair, the Judge should not exert pressure on him.

> 13:22 Call and I will answer. Let me speak and respond to me.

Silence from God is the worst punishment imaginable to the believer. It means that either God does not want to respond or that God has severed the relationship with the individual. There is no greater feeling of isolation for the individual. So this verse should be understood as part of Job's plea to God to enter into dialogue with him, albeit in a legal manner.

> 13:23 How many things have I done wrong? Make known my sins.

This is a brash and demanding statement.

> 13:24 Why do You hide your face from me and think that I am your enemy?

There's another word echo here with verse 20. Job says he won't hide himself and now asks God not to hide the divine face. Job challenges God: am I suffering because You think that I am a sinner and therefore your foe?

> 13:25 Will You terrorize a driven leaf? Will You pursue dry chaff?

Job is helpless against divine power. Like a leaf moved by the wind, like chaff moved by the breeze, Job cannot control events in his life. He needs nothing further to make him aware of his frailty.

> 13:26 For You write down bitter things against me and make me inherit the sins of my youth.

In previous verses, it seems that Job gave up searching for a reason that could explain his suffering. But he returns to that theme again. He cannot let go of it. Beginning in this verse, Job wonders whether his suffering is punishment for the sins he committed during his youth. Even were he to discover that it is punishment for something that he did as a young person, it still seems that such punishment is unfair. In reading this verse, Rashi writes that Job is concerned because God is writing down the "bitter things," that is, those bitter words that he uttered due to his suffering, rather than recording the good deeds that Job performed. Ibn Ezra sees these "bitter things" (*merarot*) as "rebellion" (from the Hebrew word *meri*). For Gersonides, the "bitter things" are the harsh decrees and bitter experiences that Job has been forced to endure.

> 13:27 You put my feet into stocks. You control my ways. You make a mark around the soles of my feet.

In striking language, Job complains that God controls where he goes. It is as if Job's feet were shackled into stocks so that only God could decide where Job could go, as well as whether he could even move. By marking Job's feet, God would be able to know wherever Job went.

Since the Targum understands *sad* (stocks) as *sheya* (cement), the image is made even more clear and contemporary. And since the Targum sees *shorshay* (soles) as *seemyonay* (shackles), the first and last clause of the verse are read as "You set my feet into cement.... You set my feet into shackles." Whether the reader follows the Targum or Ibn Ezra's suggestion that this is simply Job's statement that God has set limits on Job's movement, the general sense is the same. In Ibn Ezra's understanding, "the soles of my feet" is simply a metaphor for the entire human being. Job is limited by God and cannot go anywhere unless God gives him permission to do so.

> 13:28 And so I am like a rotten wineskin, like a moth-eaten garment.

Job, unable to move, unable to develop, unable to live in the world as he would like, now compares himself to common objects that have decayed and have been reduced to uselessness.

HOLINESS CODE

This is a reference to Leviticus 17–26 which—according to some scholars—at one time may have been an independent collection of materials that was later incorporated into the book of Leviticus. This is particularly likely, because its style is markedly different from the remainder of the book of Leviticus. These chapters of Leviticus are designated as the Holiness Code because they contain basic behaviors that separate (make holy) the Israelites from the rest of the ancient peoples. In Leviticus 19, the people are told *kedoshim tihyu* (be holy), what Rabbi Eliot Malomet considers to be one of the three charges of being Jewish: be holy; be a blessing; choose life. Regardless of its origins, the Holiness Code is now an integral part of the book of Leviticus.

Chapter 14

> 14:1 A human born of a woman has few days and much trouble.

THIS IS A RATHER morose statement that is consistent with the themes of the entire book. It is a comment on the lowly state of humans. Using the word "Adam" here makes it a bit of wordplay, that is, Job does not see himself as Adam, created by God, but as Adam, born of woman. In the *Akeidat Yitzhak*, a fifteenth-century Spanish commentary, the author, Rabbi Isaac ben Moses Arama, suggests that someone with this outlook on life can use it as an excuse not to expect much from oneself.

> 14:2 Like a flower, one springs up and then withers. Like a shadow, one speeds away and does not remain.

This verse continues the depressing mood established by the previous verse—and the rest of the book. Once again, the fading flower and the moving shadow are used as images for the frailty of human existence. This verse echoes Psalm 90, as well as other themes we often find in Yizkor (memorial) services.

> 14:3 You have fixed your eye on this. Will you bring me into judgment with you?

Job now argues that he is too insignificant to stand with God in any Divine court. The verse might better be understood as "Despite the fragility of human life, you have your eye on us and bring people to judgment." Like the first two verses in this chapter, the author claims that his life, like any human life, is too insignificant to be of consequence to God. Nevertheless, God examines us and judges us.

> 14:4 Who can make something pure out of something that is impure? No one!

Job's plaint is an anticipatory echo of other religious doctrine—including early Jewish doctrine (see Genesis 6:5; 8:21) that human beings are corrupt by nature. Job is arguing, therefore, that if he were a sinner, it would not be his fault. He was made—by God—that way.

The Targum provides us with a more satisfying answer for Job's question: "Who can make a person pure who is made impure by sin? Only God can forgive him [or her]."

> 14:5 Human days are measured. You determine the months. You have set a boundary which humans cannot pass.

The implicit argument that Job is making with this verse is that since human life is limited, why should God bother with him? After all, he will soon die anyway. By adding a few words at the beginning of its otherwise literal translation, the Targum changes the meaning of the verse and thereby attaches hope to it. The Targum begins the verse with *een la yetoov* (if one does not repent). This suggests that a person's life can be extended through repentance.

From Rashi's commentary, we infer that Rashi also understands the bleak meaning of the verse as a reference to the one who will receive the requisite punishment for leading a wicked life. The day of death has been set for such a sinner. For such a person, life is reckoned in months rather than in years.

> 14:6 Stop looking at humans. Let them succeed. Let them be paid like day laborers.

Job is pleading that since his life is so short, he should be allowed his reward, like a day laborer who receives wages for the day. In order to avoid any gender specificity, we have translated this verse in the plural, even though it is written in the singular.

For Rashi, the verse has a specific purpose. Job now pleads that since his days are limited, God should lessen his pain so that he can enjoy his (brief) old age. He is like a day laborer looking forward to receiving his wages before he passes from this world. For Rashi, this verse reflects Job's utter isolation.

> 14:7 A tree can still have hope [even] if it is cut down. It can sprout again. Its shoots will not fail.

While this verse appears to be optimistic, it continues Job's theme of desperation. Unlike the life of a human being, a tree can survive what seems to be its death. Its roots remain and new shoots will appear. The situation of the human being is far different. The next three verses are an extended metaphor about a tree, which is then compared to a human in verse 10.

> 14:8 Were the root to grow old in the earth and its stock die in the dust,
>
> 14:9 Even if there is only the scent of water around, it will bud and produce branches as if it were newly planted.

It takes very little water to revive a seemingly dead tree. Alas, as stated in the next verse, when people die, they are dead.

> 14:10 But when humans die, they are carried off dead. People perish and where are they?

This verse is translated in the plural to avoid any gender specificity. It is quite clear. While the apparent death of trees is not final, the death of humans is final. Keeping in mind that Job loses his family, Gersonides makes a reference to Joshua who cut off Amalek in an attempt to destroy his future progeny. Unlike a tree that has seed, Job too will be totally cut off with nothing coming after him since his children are gone.

> 14:11 As the waters disappear from the sea, the river will dry up completely.

We have followed Rashi's understanding of this verse. Rashi argues that the first clause sets up the conditions for the second clause. Rashi understands "the sea" as the source of "the river." Thus, if the former dries up, then the latter will be affected and will be dry forever. We chose to translate the expression—*yecherav v'yavesh*—that includes two synonyms, into one expression, "will dry up completely."

Unlike other commentators, Ibn Ezra reads the verse as a metaphor for human beings. When people die, they disappear completely. There is no trace of them, although their Source never disappears.

> 14:12 [As with the waters,] so a person lies down and will not arise. Until the heavens vanish, humans will not awake or stir from their sleep.

The implicit argument here is that just as the heavens will never "vanish," humans cannot rise up from their death. Nature may be immortal, but human beings are indeed mortal.

> 14:13 Would that You would conceal me in the underworld, hide me until Your anger had past, and then set a time and remember me.

This is a rather anthropomorphic verse; the author has Job describing God as a tyrant who has bouts of uncontrollable anger which eventually dissipate. Job hopes that he could outlast such bouts and be remembered when God, as it were, would no longer be angry. Some translations read verses 13 to 17 as being conditional. Job wishes it would happen.

> 14:14 If a person dies, will that person live again? I anticipate that my relief will come for my days of service.

"Relief," in this verse, is being used in the military sense, as one who takes the place of another on duty. In its translation, the Targum assumes the rabbinic doctrine of *techiyat ha-maytim* (Resurrection of the Dead) as a reward for the righteous. In doing so, the Targum shifts the meaning of the verse by adding *rashiya* (wicked) after the translation of "person." Such a person will not "live again."

> 14:15 If you call, I will answer you. Do you desire the work of your hands?

This turn of phrase is clearly intentional by the author. Usually, it is God who tells the people, "Call on me and I will answer you." There might be a conscious echo on the part of the author of Psalm 91:15. In this case, it is the human who invites God to do the calling and the human who promises to answer. A more idiomatic translation of the first words of the second clause would yield a deeply puzzled Job asking, "Don't You care for me?"

> 14:16 Now you count my steps. You don't watch over my sins.

The two clauses in this verse seem to contradict one another. If God pays so much attention to Job that his very steps are noted, one would anticipate that Job's sins would be noted, as well. Rashi understands *tishmor* ("You . . . watch") as carrying the same meaning as *shamar* as in the phrase "*v'aviv shamar et ha-davar*" (Genesis 37:11) which Rashi understands as "And his father waited rather than punishing [Joseph]." Thus, for Rashi, the last clause means, "You will wait rather than punish my sins." In support of this, Rashi refers to a Talmudic passage, "Let no one say, wait (*shamar*) for me next to a place of idolatry" (Babylonian Talmud, *Sanhedrin* 63b).

For Gersonides, the "waiting" is a delay in punishing Job for his sins. He understands these sins as Job's confession of guilt which Gersonides considers Job's sins to be comparable to those of the people of Sodom. But he is making a linguistic argument since Gersonides believes that "sin" means "punishment," referring to Lamentations 4:6.

As a result of these insights, perhaps the second clause of the verse should be translated as "You don't wait [to punish] my sin," yielding the opposite of Rashi. God punishes now without waiting.

> 14:17 My offenses are sealed in a bag and You cover over my guilt.

Job's sins are apparently concealed. One may assume that they are concealed either from God or by God. Yet the previous verse suggested the opposite: God was aware of every sin that Job committed and hastened to punish him for them.

The Targum presents the reader with a different view of the verse by indicating where the "transgressions" are "sealed" and taking "cover" to mean "join against": "My offenses are sealed in the Book of Remembrances and You join with others claiming my guilt."

> 14:18 But as surely as a crumbling mountain collapses and a rock moves from its place,

This verse sets up the next verse. It describes the effect of erosion in nature and the power of water to wear away even the hardest of rocks, just as the effect of constant suffering wears away any hope a person might have of being saved from additional suffering.

> 14:19 As water wears away stones and as downpours sweep away the dust of the earth, You destroy human hope.

This is a rather strong statement. Job describes natural processes in this verse. Slowly but surely, drop by drop, water dissolves the hardest rock and can move, particle by particle, the dust of the earth. Similarly, constant suffering and chronic pain, moment by moment, eats away any good feeling that a person may have and undermines any hope that the person may have for an end to such suffering.

> 14:20 You overpower people and they go away. You change their face and send them away.

Job laments the disparity between God's power and human weakness. However, this verse can also refer to aging. As people age, their mental ability and their physical agility may diminish. Aging is also reflected in a person's face. Eventually, the end of old age is death.

To avoid any gender specificity, we have translated this verse in the plural. The midrash applies this last clause to Adam in the garden of Eden. Prior to his sin, Adam appeared one way. After disobeying and eating the fruit, his appearance changed (Genesis Rabbah 11:2).

> 14:21 If their children are honored, they do not know it. If their children suffer, they do not understand it.

If the reference in this verse is aging—with the memory loss and dementia that sometimes accompanies it—then those who suffer such things lose awareness of those people who are close to them. Thus, not only do they suffer but their children suffer as well. The verse might also refer to people who die and do not live to see their children succeed. It is perhaps the converse of Psalm 128:6 "and see your children's children."

> 14:22 Only their own flesh pains them. Their own soul mourns for them.

Following the approach we used in previous verses, we have translated this verse in the plural to avoid gender specificity. Apparently, the author wants to emphasize that for the two actions to have meaning ("pains, mourns"), then the person has to still be alive.

For the Targum, it seems that the person who is afflicted is actually dead. In its otherwise literal translation of the verse, it adds *rechasha* (worm, maggot) in the first clause to explain the "pain" and *bayt dinah* (the Court) to explain why the "soul mourns." This refers to judgment in the world-to-come.

Apparently, Rashi senses a similar notion in the verse when he quotes the rabbinic adage, "Maggots are more painful to a corpse than a needle [stick] would be to a live person" (Babylonian Talmud, *Berakhot* 18b).

GREAT DAY OF JUDGMENT

While there are a variety of interpretations regarding what will happen when the Messiah comes, at the end of days, most will agree that it will be an individual and collective Day of Judgment. Individuals will be judged for their deeds as a prerequisite for living in the world-to-come. This Day of Judgment is approximated on Yom Kippur which is also known as Yom HaDin, "the Day of Judgment."[1]

---

1. Kravitz and Olitzky, *Mishle*, 204.

Chapter 15

15:1 Then Eliphaz the Temanite replied,

THIS BEGINS THE EXPLANATION of another of Job's so-called comforters.

15:2 Would a wise person answer with windy notions or fill one's belly with the east wind?

The idiom used here is comparable to the English expression, "You are full of hot air." A wise person would not waste time by providing an answer to Job—or Job's question and suffering—with "hot air."

15:3 Would one present a useless argument? Would one use words that don't convince?

Eliphaz continues the sentiment expressed in the previous verse.

15:4 But you destroy reverence and diminish prayer before God.

Eliphaz raises the perennial question: Does questioning the ways of God diminish the believer's connection to God?

15:5 Your guilt instructs your mouth so that you choose the language of the cunning.

Eliphaz has already judged Job to be a sinner. Therefore, he will pay no attention to Job's arguments.

15:6 It is your mouth that will condemn you, not me. It is your lips that will testify against you.

As noted in the previous verse, nothing that Job said could convince Eliphaz. According to Eliphaz, Job is guilty, end of story.

15:7 Were you the first person born? Were you brought forth before the hills?

Eliphaz now challenges Job in a different way: How do you claim to be so smart? Do you have primordial wisdom? The author might intentionally be echoing Psalm 90:2 in this verse.

> 15:8 Did you hear God's secret? Have you restricted wisdom to yourself?

Eliphaz is mocking Job by asking, "Where did you get this unique knowledge of yourself?"

> 15:9 What do you know that we don't? What do you understand that is not within us?

Again, Eliphaz mocks Job, "Do you have some special information that no one else has?"

> 15:10 Those who are grey, those who are still older, and even those who are older than your parents are on our side.

As in previous verses, we have offered a gender-free translation. The argument made by Eliphaz assumes that age grants wisdom and those who have lived longer than others have amassed more experience of the world than those who have not.

> 15:11 Are the consolations of God not enough for you? Is a softly spoken word not good enough?

The author has Eliphaz challenge Job's words and deny Job's suffering. Surely, God has provided some end to whatever Job has endured. Why then does Job continue to complain?

> 15:12 Why has your mind deceived you? What are you winking at?

Although the first clause literally means, "Why has your heart taken you?" since the ancients thought that the heart was the place of thinking, we have substituted "mind." For the writer, the heart has taken Job to error, so we have translated it as "deceived you."

Since winking in many cultures is a method of indicating some secret message, the reader has to determine the message that Eliphaz thinks that Job is sending.

> 15:13 You rage against God, pouring out words from your mouth.

This translation assumes that *ruach* (wind, spirit) also means anger in accordance with Ibn Ezra's suggestion which is based on Proverbs 29:11. Hence, "to respond with anger" can idiomatically be translated as "rage."

> 15:14 What human can be in the right? How can one born of a woman be innocent?

We have an echo of an ancient view of humanity that finds its place in our world as well. Those who hold this perspective contend that to be human is to be depraved. Viewed against some divine ideal model, no person can be meritorious. While such a model may be a goad for human achievement, if being human means being necessarily corrupt, then such a goad is essentially useless. If no "human can be in the right," and no one "born of a woman can be innocent," then why bother with any kind of ethics? There are theological systems which require such a view of humankind in order to have God intervene to save God's lost creatures. However, that raises the question: if God, Master of the universe, made human creatures in such a defective manner, could one not then blame God as a bad designer?

> 15:15 God puts no trust in holy ones and even the heavens will not be cleared [or found innocent] in divine sight.

This last phrase is quoted in the High Holiday prayer *Unetaneh Tokef*.

> 15:16 How much less despicable and corrupt [are the holy ones compared to] humanity, who soaks up iniquity like water.

This verse is connected with the one before as part of an *a fortiori* argument, an argument based on a stronger reason. If the angels, heavenly beings, are still not considered pure and trustworthy, how much less can humans expect God to consider us pure? The ultimate question is the same: What kind of Creator is God if nothing on high and nothing here below can be trusted?

> 15:17 Hear me out and I will explain it to you. I will tell you what I have seen.

Eliphaz begins to argue, here and in subsequent verses, from what he thinks to be the generality of experience.

> 15:18 [Here is] what those who are wise proclaimed, holding back nothing from the tradition of their ancestors.

Rashi thinks that "those who are wise proclaimed" means that those who are wise confessed their sins, and "they did not conceal" their sins. He takes such a confession as Eliphaz's implicit argument in the verse: Judah confessed his wrongdoing with regard to Tamar and was not ashamed (see Genesis 38:15ff.); Reuben confessed his wrongdoing with regard to Bilhah (see Genesis 35:22 and Genesis 49:4). The confessions ultimately brought them reward. Therefore, Job should confess his own wrongdoings.

> 15:19 To them alone was the land given. No stranger has passed among them.

To whom was the land given? By whom and why? This verse affirms the tradition that the land of Israel was given to the Jewish people by God. The plain meaning of the verse refers to the wise ones of 15:18 who shared the traditions that they were given. The implication is that Eliphaz has a duty to speak his truth (as indicated in 15:17), because reward comes to those who share the wisdom they received from their ancestors.

> 15:20 A wicked people are tormented all their days. Even the number of a tyrant's years is reckoned against him.

In order to avoid gender specificity, we rendered this verse in the plural. However, since it's reasonable to assume that the tyrant in this time period was a man, we left the male object of the preposition as "him." Both clauses of this verse echo the hope that somehow those who are sinners will not get away with their crimes. Those who now enjoy unchecked power will receive a payback in the end for every year that they lived. Eliphaz here states with certainty that right will triumph over evil even in the face of evidence to the contrary.

> 15:21 Fear rings in their ears. Even at a time of peace, someone is coming to rob them.

This verse continues to speak about those mentioned in the previous verse. For Eliphaz, wicked people are never at ease. They hear, although no one else can, the sounds of oncoming dangers. They can't depend on peace to protect them from harm. Someone is coming to get them. The choice of the words by the author points to the paradoxical situation of financially successful people who live in fear that someone will come and rob them of what they have acquired (especially if they have acquired it through evil means or tyranny noted above).

> 15:22 They do not believe that they will come out of the darkness. They expect the sword.

Wicked people are here portrayed as fearing for their lives at all times. When night falls, they think that someone is waiting to kill them. The wicked feel that they cannot get out of darkness, *teshuvah* (repentance) is somehow not accessible to them.

> 15:23 They wander about looking for bread. Where is it? They know that the day of darkness has already been determined.

Again, wicked people are described as suffering for their sins. Not only do they fear death, as indicated in the preceding verse, they are also afflicted with hunger as they wait for the final moment.

> 15:24 Anxiety and distress terrify them. They [those who are charged with meting out punishment] overpower them [the sinners], like a sovereign ruler prepared for the onslaught.

We know that some of the most wicked people seem to have enjoyed life and continue to do so. Few persons bemoan the evil that they have done. Many bemoan the evil done to them. It is not everywhere at all times apparent that evil people feel remorse. Biblical writers hope that this is the case that evil people necessarily feel remorse, because it reflects their belief in a God of justice.

> 15:25 Because they would stretch out their hand against God and play the hero against the Almighty.

As in previous verses, the charge in this verse is directed against Job by Eliphaz. Eliphaz claims that by denying his guilt, Job is attacking God. For if Job suffers and is not guilty, then God—who is responsible for all things—is unfair.

> 15:26 With stiff necks and thick strong shields, they will charge at God.

If *b'tzavar* "with a [stiff] neck" is a metaphor for "defiance" or "arrogance," it is not the usual term for such notions in the Bible. We are more used to seeing *keshay-oref* "hard-necked." Rashi understands the word to mean "the stretching forth of the neck is a means of provoking God."

> 15:27 Although their faces are covered with their fat and their waists bulge with fat.

Although it may be misleading to compare cultural expectations, one would not expect a warrior to be overweight. One wonders if Eliphaz is suggesting that the one who rashly attempts to attack God was not physically up to the task.

> 15:28 They dwelt in deserted towns, in crumbled houses which no one else would inhabit that are destined to become heaps of rubble.

The imagery of this verse is clear. Such people who challenged God would be unable to live in a society with other human beings. They have begun the process of decay and therefore will live in places that are empty and similarly decaying.

> 15:29 They will not become rich, nor will their wealth endure.
> Nor will their property spread through the earth.

We continue to translate in the plural to avoid any gender specificity in the verse. Once again, Job is told of the punishment that will follow the person who challenges the justice of God. As if Job doesn't have it bad enough, Eliphaz is warning him of what might happen should he continue to challenge what has happened to him, as well as its cause.

> 15:30 They will not escape the darkness. A flame will scorch their shoots. They will be blown away by the breath of the divine mouth.

Whatever the specifics, people who challenge God will receive a terrible punishment, says Eliphaz. This notion is challenged by streams of Jewish thought including *chutzpah clappei malah* (chutzpah in the face of Heaven) made famous particularly by Levi Yitzchak of Berditchev.

It may be that in this verse Eliphaz threatens that even the grave ("darkness") will not provide refuge to those people who challenge God. In addition, the descendents ("shoots") of such people will not avoid punishment. They will suffer wherever they are.

> 15:31 Let no one be deceived and trust in that which is worthless, for what you get back is worthless.

As in previous verses, we have avoided a gendered translation although the Hebrew is written using singular masculine pronouns and verbs. There is a kind of inverse relation here between the verb *ya-amin* (he will believe, trust, depend) and *shav* (worthless, deceitful, nothing). The verb, whatever its precise translation, means to assume that something is real. The noun, however it is translated, means something that does not have substance; it is not real.

> 15:32 Their days will fill up before their time. Their branches will not be fresh.

One may understand this verse to mean that ill-fated individuals will die young, that is, before their time, without progeny.

> 15:33 They will be like a vine casting off its unripe grapes or like an olive tree, shedding its blossoms.

To those of us who are not involved with the growing of grapes or the harvesting of olives, the images in this verse may not be clear. What is obvious is that the metaphor presented by the author suggests the premature loss of something of great value. This verse, therefore, continues the imprecations of Eliphaz against anyone who would challenge the justice of God.

> 15:34 The company of the godless shall be desolate. And fire will consume the tents of those who take bribes.

This verse reads like a proverb that is being quoted and then applied by the author as a response by Eliphaz to Job. The phrase "consuming fire" is a term used to describe God in Deuteronomy 4:24 and 9:3, as noted by Ibn Ezra.

> 15:35 They conceive trouble and bring forth transgression and their bellies prepare guile.

The author is using the image of conceiving and birthing in this verse. Like the previous verse, this verse also seems to be an aphorism that the author wants to share in the name of Eliphaz.

KAL V'CHOMER

This is an *a fortiori* argument (defined as from more to less or major to minor). This particular principle is part of a set of principles developed by Rabbi Ishmael (second century CE) in response to Rabbi Akiva's attempt to develop a logical system of sorts to derive meaning from the Torah. Rabbi Ishmael derived thirteen principles or *middot* (which are included as a form of study in the morning service of traditional prayerbooks) for the purpose of rendering legal decisions or drawing legal conclusions. There are other methods used for biblical commentary, but the process of *kal v'chomer* is used both in the Talmud and in the Bible.

This method is used as a form of inference when there are two connected cases—one lenient and one more stringent. If the lenient case has certain restrictions, then by applying the principle of *kal v'chomer*, the more stringent case also has these restrictions. Similarly, if the stringent case has leniencies, then, through the application of *kal v'chomer*, one can apply these leniencies to the more lenient cases.

Chapter 16

> 16:1 Job then replied,

WE HAVE ONCE AGAIN rendered the Hebrew phrase, considered by many to be an Aramaic form of expression (*va'ya'an va'yomar*—literally, "he answered and said") as "then replied."

> 16:2 I have heard such things so many times. You are all tedious comforters.

Job has heard all these arguments before. They are repetitive and they don't address his situation nor do they provide him any comfort. Perhaps it is Job who is tired out from listening to his so-called friends.

> 16:3 Is there no end to your inane words? Who incited you to keep arguing?

There is an echo in this verse of the *da'at ruach* mentioned by Eliphaz in Job 15:2. The Targum renders the phrase *divrai ruach* (inane words) as *meelay d'zika* (windy words). These are words that are full of air, words without substance, an echo of Ecclesiastes' notion of "*hevel*"—a wisp of wind—usually translated as "vanity" or "nothingness."

> 16:4 I can talk just like you. If only you were in my place, then I could make speeches against you and I could wag my tongue at you.

It is not that Job does not know how to respond to the arguments of Eliphaz and his other comforters. He knows the assumptions under which they operate and the arguments that follow from those assumptions. It is the assumptions that are faulty, particularly the assumption that presents suffering as a proof of past sin. If that is false, then all of the arguments built on it are also false. Were the situation reversed, Job, knowing the assumptions and arguments of his comforters, could bring the same arguments against them.

Job is saying, "Were you to have experienced what I have experienced." The sense of the phrase might be better understood by "were you in my skin" or "were you in my shoes."

We chose to translate the last phrase idiomatically; literally, it is "I could wag my head at you."

> 16:5 However, I would support you with my mouth and the moving of my lips would bring you relief.

Rashi takes *need sefatai* (which we have translated as "moving of my lips") to mean "I move and complain now [and cry out]." He understands the remainder of the clause to mean: (In the future) I will be relieved; I will not cry out nor will I move as I do now.

Gersonides reads the words as if to provide real comfort to Job. He takes *need sefatai yachsoch* to mean "As I console you with my words, they will remove your pain."

> 16:6 If I speak, my pain is not eased. And if I don't, it does not go away.

Whether or not words are used, Job's situation will not change. Speaking or not speaking will not remove his pain.

> 16:7 Now, O God, You have exhausted me. You have made my family desolate.

Ibn Ezra claims that it was Job's pain that "exhausted" him. He contends that it is Job's mourners who have been made desolate (or, according to Rashi, been silenced).

> 16:8 You have caused me to be shriveled and this is evidence; My gauntness argues against me.

For those who believe that the marks of suffering are an indication of sin, Job's weight loss is proof that he has sinned rather than the result of what he has endured.

> 16:9 Storing up hate against me, my enemies have fixed their eyes upon me. In their fury, they have ripped me apart and ground me with their teeth.

Surprisingly, Rashi takes *tzari* (my enemy) as a reference to Satan rather than to God. While we have translated the verse in the plural to avoid any gender specificity, we too agree that Job is speaking of his enemies as God.

> 16:10 People are always joined against me. They open their mouths wide to mock me and they slap my cheeks scornfully.

In this verse, Job complains that his situation has attracted mockery and contempt rather than pity and compassion.

> 16:11 God has handed me over to evil ones and thrown me into the hands of the wicked.

Beyond the pain due to illness and the distress due to mockery, Job now has to endure the depredations of the truly vicious since he has no support from God or "good people." As Rashi understands the verse, Job complains that God has given him over to wicked people for their sport.

> 16:12 I was at ease but You crushed me. You grabbed me by the neck and smashed me. You set me up as Your target.

In order to avoid gender, we have translated the masculine third person as the second person so that Job's complaint about God is directed to God. Job graphically describes God's actions as harsh and cruel.

> 16:13 Your archers surround me. You stab me through the kidneys without mercy, pouring my gall on the ground.

Perhaps it is more threatening to be surrounded by archers rather than by an onslaught of arrows coming from every which way.

> 16:14 You attack me again and again. You charge at me like a warrior.

Although *peretz* means "breach," as in a breach in a defensive wall, and *yephretzayni* means "he makes a breach into me," we have attempted to give a sense of the verse through an idiomatic translation. *Yarutz* generally means "he will run." However, the context of the second clause suggests "charges" as the more appropriate idiomatic translation.

> 16:15 I have sewn sackcloth on my skin. I have put my glory into the dust.

Gersonides' translation would yield a verse that reads far more smoothly and is more readily understood: "I have put sackcloth on my scabs. I have put dust on my head." Both are signs of mourning, but the former suggests a profound level of suffering and Job's disfigurement as a result. Such a translation also allows for an easier transition to the following verse.

> 16:16 My face is flushed from weeping and my eyelids are darkened,

In the verse, Job explains how he looks. His suffering has affected his face and eyes.

> 16:17 Even though my hands have done no violence and my prayer is pure.

Rashi explains that Job's prayer was pure, because he never cursed anyone nor plotted evil against anyone. Rashi might also mean that Job did not wish anyone harm nor did he accuse anyone of evil.

> 16:18 O earth, do not cover my blood. Let there be no resting place for my cry.

Job wants his death to be visible if he dies. He does not want his plea as an innocent man who suffered wrongfully to accompany him to the grave. Rather, he wants his plea for justice to be heard beyond the end of his life. Job wants his example to stand. Justice is due to him. The assumption of many that suffering is a result of doing evil is unjust. In a sense, Job's wish has been fulfilled. So many generations later we are still talking about him and using him as an example of a righteous person who suffered through no fault of his own.

> 16:19 Yet even now, my witness is in the heavens. God, who would testify on my behalf, is in the heights.

While the Hebrew of the second clause merely identifies the subject as male, not necessarily God, God is clearly indicated by the context. So we have identified the subject as God (but not necessarily male). This position is supported by Rashi's comment on the verse, as well. Rashi explains that "my witness" is God, the Creator who knows the ways of Job. This verse is a statement that reflects Job's disappointment in God. Job acknowledges that God stands witness to all of his actions but he isn't able to rouse God to act justly.

> 16:20 My friends scorn me, so my eyes pour out tears to God.

Because Job finds no real friends to offer him comfort, he turns to God as the only outlet for anguish and pain.

> 16:21 Let God arbitrate between a person and God, just as an individual might do so with a friend.

To avoid gender specificity, we have translated *gever* (man) and *ben adam* (simple man, mortal) as "person" and "individual." This raises questions regarding the relationship between the two clauses. Is the arbitration of God the same as when one advocates one's position with a friend, a mere mortal? Moreover, how does this verse relate to the previous verse which suggested that because mortals mocked Job, he poured out his plea to God in tears. Just two verses back, Job seemed to proclaim his faith that God would be his witness.

Perhaps the Targum sensed the problem of internal consistency and its coherence with other verses when it began its otherwise literal translation of the verse with the word *ephshar* ("it is possible") ["as a person might argue. . . ."].

Rashi takes the two clauses as a wish for equality: If only one could argue with God in the same way that one might argue with another person!

> 16:22 In only a few years, I will go on a journey from which I will not return.

In this verse, Job expresses his ultimate despair. He will die soon and his demand for justice will not be met. For a more idiomatic translation, we have not translated *yetayu* (will pass), rendering the opening words as "in only a few years" instead of something like "a few years will pass."

Chapter 17

> 17:1 My spirit is destroyed. My days come to an end. The grave is before me.

IN UTTER DESPAIR, JOB now speaks. There is no end to his suffering and no sympathy from his friends. Rashi comments on the last two words and emphasizes: I am ready to be buried.

> 17:2 Surely my mockers accompany me. My eye rests upon their provocation.

Rashi translates the first clause as "Indeed, people have gathered around me, to mock me as they [seem to] console me." For Ibn Ezra, the first clause means "His friends are mocking him." For the last clause, we have followed Rashi's understanding of the word as *b'haknatechem* (upon their provocation).

And the last clause means, according to Ibn Ezra, in which he translates the word from a different root as embitter thereby yielding, "I cannot sleep while they embitter my life."

> 17:3 [I] set now my pledge to you. Who else will shake my hand in agreement?

Although the intention of the first clause is difficult to decipher, we think it means that since Job wants to come to an agreement with God, he asks God what it is that God has to offer as a pledge. The "shaking of the hand" is a sign here, as in many other cultures, that an agreement has been accepted.

Gersonides explains the entire verse in this way: "Pay attention to me. Respond to my words as I would argue with You. Give me a surety in which I can trust that You will respond to my words for it is my desire to contend with You and not with these people."

> 17:4 You have kept them from understanding. Therefore, do not esteem them.

In our translation, we have not translated *lebam* (their hearts), which in context means "their minds," because it is assumed in the phrase "from understanding." Rashi understands the last clause as addressed to God: "Because they have been kept from understanding, Your glory will not be exalted by them."

> 17:5 For some benefit, you might speak to friends, although the eyes of your children fail.

To avoid gender specificity, we translated this verse in the second person, rather than the third person of the Hebrew. If it is about God, then it is now directed to God.

> 17:6 You have set me up as a popular byword. I have become the one in whose face they spit.

In this verse, Job presents his situation to the reader. He is viewed with contempt by all with whom he comes into contact.

The Targum picks up on the word *tophet*, which elsewhere in the Bible refers to a locality devoted to pagan sacrifices. Because in later Hebrew, the term became a synonym for hell, the Targum translates the word as *Gehinnom*. It, therefore, translates the first clause as *v'gehinnom min l'gav ehay* "I have been as one within hell."

Rashi reads *tophet* to mean *toph* (drum) and takes the last clause to mean "I have become a drum before all the people." The drum is used because it is an object to be beaten, or it is an instrument through which merriment is expressed.

Ibn Ezra takes the first word *hetzegani* (He has set me up) as a reference to Job's pain. By seeing it as a reference to Job's pain he is saying, "My pain has set me up" or "presented me." Taken with his understanding of *limshol* Ibn Ezra seems to understand Job to be saying: "My pain has made me an example and a byword." This statement which Job makes seems to be true until this day.

> 17:7 I am so troubled. I can barely see. My guts are like a shadow.

Although a literal translation would be "Because of grief, my eye is dimmed and my inner members are like a shadow," we have attempted more of an idiomatic translation to convey the force of Job's pain. There seems to be an echo of Psalm 6:8 in this verse.

The Targum translates *yetzurim* with the Greek loan word *kelastayr* (beauty of features). Since the term also suggests "shining face," the Targum suggests that Job's face changed from being bright in appearance to a shadow.

For Rashi, the term *yetzuray* means "those body parts by which I was created." On the basis of the phrase *cee yetzer ha'adam ra me'nurav*—"the devisings of the human heart is evil from youth" (Genesis 8:21), Gersonides, on the other hand, understands *yetzuray* as "my thoughts." Once again, we see the tension between what might be considered the innate goodness of the human being struggling with the drive to do evil.

> 17:8 The upright are astounded at this. The guiltless [are] aroused against the godless.

It would seem that the author wished that Job's condition would somehow stir up sympathy for him. But as the speeches of Job's so-called "comforters" indicate, that wish was never realized.

Rashi understands the last clause to mean that when those who are free of guilt hear the meaningless flattery of the mockers, they are upset enough to contend with them.

> 17:9 Yet the righteous will hold on to this way and those with clean hands will increase their strength.

Rashi takes the first clause to mean that the righteous will withstand the assembly of flatterers.

> 17:10 Would that all of you were to return, please come. Still I could not find a wise person among you.

In this verse, Job addresses his comforters. Since they do not or cannot or will not understand his situation, whatever they say will be useless. He will not find wisdom among them.

> 17:11 My days are past. My plans are smashed. And so are the wishes of my heart.

Neither the past nor the future has any meaning for Job. He has not received what he hoped for in the past and he is sure that he will not get what he wishes for in the future.

> 17:12 They have changed night into day and yet have diminished the light before the darkness.

To an otherwise literal translation of the verse, the Targum has added *meslakin* (remove) before its translation of *choshech* (darkness). It does not identify who "remove(d)" or who or what *yeshyavun* "changed" in the beginning of the verse.

For Rashi, it is the mockery that Job endured that has changed the night into day. Because of the pain he suffers, he is unable to sleep at night.

Even the daylight seems shortened and fleeting as he remembers that mockery during the day. Rashi finds support for this notion in the word *karov* (close) which can also mean shortened or fleeting as in Genesis 19:20, Job 20:5, and Deuteronomy 32:17.

> 17:13 I might hope that the grave would be my home and that I might spread out my bed in the darkness.

This verse is connected to the verse that follows. On the basis of a previous verse (14:5) in which the word *eem* (if) precedes the verb, Rashi concludes that *eem* has no interrogative function. Rather it has a declarative function as "since" (rather than "if"). Hence, the first clause should be understood as "I would expect that the grave would be my home." And the second clause yields "and that I would spread out my bed in that grave."

> 17:14 I will call the pit my father and the worm my mother and sister.

For Rashi, Job names "the pit" as his "father" since he will rest in that place for many days, as if it were his father, since he thinks that the pit (read: grave) awaits him. These two verses, 17:13 and 17:14, contain extremely striking images. It is clear that Job is feeling like he has hit bottom or has bottomed out, to use a more contemporary expression. He can go no lower or feel any worse than he currently feels.

> 17:15 Where then is my faith? Who then will gaze on my hope?

Job recognizes that any faith in the future has totally eroded. Although the Hebrew text uses the same word *tikvatee* (my hope) twice in this verse, we have chosen to translate it in different ways for literary reasons, as does the Targum which uses the words *sevari* and *metinati*. However, it could be understood that Job repeats the words in order to emphasize how terrible he feels, how awful is his situation, and how he is losing faith.

Rashi understands the verse to mean "Who will oversee the speedy delivery of witnesses on my behalf?" Job ties his hope to the arrival of witnesses because he feels like they might be the only chance for his vindication.

> 17:16 The shoots of the netherworld will go down and together we will travel down to the dust.

It is not clear how "shoots," something growing, could be related to *Sheol*, also called *Gehinnom*, the nether-world, the place of death. However, Gersonides points out that *baday sheol* means "the poles of Sheol," that is, the extremities of Sheol. If Sheol is the center of the earth, as Gersonides claims, then in it is the ultimate dust of the grave. This would be the absolute opposite of the heavens as the highest point of the world.

Although *bad* seems to be a masculine noun, the construct *baday* appears to be treated as a feminine plural. So we get *teradna* (from the root *yod-raysh-daled*) as "go down, descend"—they [feminine] will go down.

If we read *naychat*, a verb, instead of *nachat* (a noun meaning calm, ease), then we understand the word as "travel down."

The Targum begins its translation of the verse with the word *tandu* (with a load of grief, in trouble). It then translates the first clause as *l'bayt kevurata tachtawn* (they are descending to the grave). It translates the last clause as *een c'chada al afar sharan* (indeed they rest together upon the dust).

Rashi takes *baday* to mean the parts of the body which will go down into the grave in order to finally rest in the dust.

Chapter 18

18:1 Bildad the Shuchite responded.

ANOTHER OF JOB'S COMFORTERS begins to speak.

18:2 When will you stop with these speeches? Think. And then we will talk.

Bildad is so convinced about his position that he considers everything that Job has said to be just words, words without sense.

Gersonides understands the verse to mean that Job has brought many repetitive arguments in his discussion with his comforters. For Gersonides, Bildad is saying that Job never completes his point. He goes from one point to another without making a persuasive—and progressive—argument.

18:3 Why are we thought of as cattle, dullards in your sight?

The word *neetmeenu* in this verse is either from the root *tet-mem-ulef* or *tet-mem-hay*. If it comes from the former root, it would mean "we are unclean." However, if the word comes from the latter root, then it means "we are wooden-headed." In other words, the context suggests it to mean "we are seen as stupid."

The Targum translates the word with *teemana* from the root *tet-mem-ayin* which can mean "darkened, dull" or "inaccessible to argument." We think that the word "dullards" carries both the meanings.

18:4 You tear yourself to pieces in your anger. Will the earth be deserted for your sake? Will some rock be moved from its place?

Bildad reproves Job for his anger. Because he cannot understand Job's situation, he cannot understand Job's anger. Not only does Job suffer, but he also feels betrayed. The assumption that if one did good, one would be rewarded has proven to be false. The underlying notion that the God whom Job worshipped was the guarantor of good is now in doubt. To suffer and to lose one's grounding in the universe is sufficient reason to make anyone angry.

According to Rashi, Bildad directs his speech to Job: "You are destroying yourself by your anger. Do you think that your virtue somehow changes the laws and rules that govern the earth?" We have followed Rashi in translating the verse all in the second person. Taking "Rock" to refer to God, Rashi understands Bildad's statement to mean "Do you think that God [the Creator] will change divine knowledge or divine qualities?" He uses the word Creator (*Hayotzer*) as a play on the word for rock *tzur*.

> 18:5 The light of the wicked will be put out and the spark of its [the wicked person's] fire will not shine.

This reads like a proverb that Bildad is quoting in this verse. Readers should note the onomatopoetic quality of the word *yedach* (will be put out).

> 18:6 The light in the tent of the wicked will be dark. The lamp above the wicked will go out.

Ner refers to an oil lamp. Candles were not yet invented when this verse was written. The Targum specifies that the person in the darkened tent is the wicked person mentioned in the previous verse. The metaphor of light and lamp is used in this verse. A similar image is found in Job 21:17. Both are echoes of Proverbs 6:23, "For a commandment is a lamp and instruction is light."

> 18:7 The strength of the step of the wicked is weakened. The wicked's own plan casts down the wicked.

We follow the emended reading of *yaytzaru* from root *tzadee-rayshraysh*—to be compressed, hampered, or weakened instead of reading *yaytzaru* from the root *yod-tzadee-raysh*: to form, create.

> 18:8 The wicked is caught in the net by the feet and goes back and forth in its mesh.

The author provides a striking metaphor of people who cannot escape from a situation which they have made. This verse may remind the reader of Job 13:27.

Rashi takes the verse to mean that the person described by Bildad—specifically Job—will be caught in a net from which he cannot escape.

> 18:9 A trap will catch the wicked by the heel. A sling will grab the wicked.

We translate the uncommon word *tzammim* as "a trapping device" or "sling." The Targum understands the last clause as *yitkofu aloi gavraya* (men will attack him), translating *tzammim* as men. We have attempted to avoid gender specificity, translating the male pronouns with the noun: the wicked.

Ibn Ezra thinks that *tzammim* may mean "those who thirst," that is, those who thirst will seize the wicked.

> 18:10 A snare is hidden in the ground for the wicked. A trap lies for the wicked in the path.

In the course of this verse and the previous one, the author has provided the reader with four different terms for four different kinds of traps: *pach, tzammim, chevel* and *malcodet*. Thus, the translator is obliged to find different translations for each of these terms. This is especially difficult since we are neither hunters nor trappers, nor are we experts in the hunting/trapping practices of the biblical period.

> 18:11 Appalling horrors surround the wicked, harassing their every move.

The challenge with translating this verse is found in the tension between a literal and idiomatic translation. The first clause has three words: the adverb *saviv* (around, 'round about); the verb with suffix *beatuhu* (they terrify him); and the plural noun *behalot* (terrors, horrors). The word appears five times in the book of Job and only ten times in the entire Hebrew Bible.

One could translate: "terrors terrify him around [him]." While that would be a literal translation of the Hebrew text, it would lose its aural quality. The second clause has two words: *v'hefeetzuhu l'raglav*. We translate it from the root *pay-vav-tzadee* as "harass." *L'raglav* literally means "to his feet." While "harassing his feet" might be literal, it makes little sense in English. Thus, we translated it as "harassing every move."

For Rashi, Job's "terrors" are *sheydim* (demons). It is they who knock Job off his feet and beat him to the ground.

> 18:12 Trouble hungers for the wicked. Disaster is ready for its fall.

The Targum provides two interpretations for this verse that are not direct translations. They might be described as midrashic interpretations in which the author takes a great deal of license to expand on the text, much like the Rabbis do in their sometimes fanciful interpretations of biblical text in the rabbinic midrash. The first interpretation of this verse by the Targum is: "May famine be his first born and trouble destined to be his wife." This interpretation is based on the fact that *ono* can mean "his trouble" or it can be associated with "first born" as in the phrase "*Reuven b'chori . . . reyshit oni*—Reuben, you are my first born . . . the first fruits of my strength"

(Genesis 49:3). *Tzlao* (his fall) can also be understood as "his rib" like the rib taken of Adam to become Eve: "*Va-yekach Adonai Elohim et ha-tzelah asher lakach min ha-adam l'ishah*—and the rib which Adonai, God, had taken from the man, God made into a woman" (Genesis 2:22). From this, the Targum interprets "his rib" as "his wife."

The second interpretation, "May sorrow hunger for him and trouble be at his side," depends on an understanding of *on* as "sorrow," as in Rachel's dying words naming Benjamin as "*ben-oni*—son of my sorrow" (Genesis 35:18). *Tzalao* (his fall, his rib) can also mean "his side" as discerned in the phrase "*l'tzela ha-mishkan*—the side of the Tabernacle" (Exodus 26:20).

> 18:13 Devouring bits of the wicked one's skin, death's first born devours parts of the wicked.

The parallelism of Job rarely uses the same word in both verses. Our translation is an attempt to reflect this. We understand the subject of the second clause to be the subject of the first clause as well. Evil was personified and given quasi divine status as Satan earlier in the book of Job. In this verse, we have the remnant of the belief that death was part of life and even had an existence of its own, complete with a child. Such a personification and deification of death was found in many places in the ancient world and in ancient Near Eastern cultures with an iconography of death like some wild beast, slowly devouring a living person, savoring each piece while life still clung to it. This is the stuff of nightmares. While Judaism did not deify death or develop graphic iconography, the literary figure of the angel of death, a supernatural being, has remained in Jewish literature. Here the author of Job sees Death as a person, having its own first born child.

> 18:14 The wicked will be snatched from the security of one's home and brought before the sovereign of terrors.

This verse includes an ancient image of horror which has had a modern revival. Someone is arrested, on what charge is not clear, and taken before some authority figure who can do whatever he or she wants to the person.

Ibn Ezra takes *tzadayhu* "[he] was brought" to refer to that person's views and hopes. Like Gersonides, he thinks that "king of terrors" is a metaphor that refers to the greatest terror a person can imagine: death seizing a person, particularly a child, unexpectedly, as a burglar might enter someone's home and kidnap a member of the family. Loss is the greatest terror.

> 18:15 Nothing of the wicked one remains in the home. Brimstone is sprinkled over the dwelling.

Utter devastation will occur. Nothing of the person who was evil will remain. Moreover, the person's house will be uninhabitable in the future. Thus, any trace of the individual will be removed.

The Targum and Rashi read "the home" as the wife of the wicked person. The Targum reads the first clause and suggests that the wicked one's wife will remain in the home. But Rashi says that the wicked one's wife will remain as a widow in his home, having nothing because her husband is dead. As a final indignity, brimstone will be sprinkled over that home.

Ibn Ezra thinks that since no one remains in the home, wild or strange animals will enter it. For Gersonides, nothing remains because people will have stolen everything.

> 18:16 The roots of the wicked dry up below. The branches of the wicked wither above.

In this verse, we see a shift in the metaphor that the author is using. Yet here too we see a progression from present to future. If the roots of the plant lack sufficient water, what will grow from the roots will be weakened and wither.

> 18:17 [All] mention of the wicked one disappears from the earth. The name of the wicked one is lost to the outside world.

The horror of becoming someone completely disregarded and overlooked, like human refuse on the streets of our society whose lives when gone made no impact, is something which our modern world already knows. Here that horror is seen existing in ancient times. "Disappearing" someone is a function of power. The more power exercised, the easier it is to accomplish. Removing the mention of particular individuals is something that totalitarian regimes have done repeatedly. The Holocaust is a case in point. Many were lost for whom their children or grandchildren have no knowledge of even where they are buried.

> 18:18 The wicked one will be driven from light into darkness and excluded from the world.

"Light and darkness" are metaphors for life and death. The person described in the preceding verse, who "will disappear from the earth," is functionally dead even if their heart still beats. A person who is thrown into an inescapable prison—and will never be released—is already "excluded from the world" and "lost to the outside world."

For Rashi, the person is driven from light into darkness by a heavenly command.

18:19 The wicked one will have neither child nor descendant among the people, nor anyone surviving in the place the wicked one once lived.

In this verse, Bildad sketches a truly morose situation. It is not enough that Job will suffer in his own life. But he will have no survivors to remember him.

18:20 Those who come after will be astounded by what happened as those who came before were seized with terror.

The Targum translates the word *sa'ar*, which we have translated as terror, by *alolah* (windstorm) since that is one of its meanings. Gersonides also understands the idea of a storm.

Rashi explains that the first clause suggests that those who follow Job will be astounded when they hear the report about Job's calamity.

Ibn Ezra takes *achronim* (those who come after) to mean that those who come after are persons as wicked as Job. He reads *kadmonim* (those who come before) as reference to his friends.

18:21 This is surely the dwelling of the sinner, the place of the one who does not know God.

The first clause in this verse has a plural pronoun (these) and a plural noun (dwellings) while the second clause speaks of a single "place." To bring both clauses into balance, we have translated the first clause in the singular: "this" and "dwelling." Rashi takes the verse as the final end of the wicked.

ANGEL OF DEATH

Known as the *malakh ha-mavet* in Hebrew, Death is personified as an angel, sent by God. While there is some debate as to whether the Angel of Death appears explicitly in the Bible as a being or only an abstract concept, the Angel of Death does emerge clearly in rabbinic literature and in Jewish folklore. While the Angel of Death can act only on the behest of God, folk legends have arisen filled with methods to deceive the angel and thereby thwart its plans. For example, when someone is very ill, they are often renamed Chaya or Chayim (meaning life) to confuse the Angel of Death were it to visit.

Chapter 19

19:1 Job replied:

19:2 How long will you torment me and beat me down with words?

FOR A MORE IDIOMATIC translation, we have used "me" as a translation for the word *naphshi* "my soul." Rashi derives the uncommon word *togeoon* (you torment) from the noun *toogah* (grief). This word is also found in one instance in the book of Proverbs and the book of Psalms.

19:3 You have tried to humiliate me ten times. You attack me without shame.

Although the imperfect form of the verb *tachleemayni* can mean "you constantly humiliate me" as well as indicating future action ("you will humiliate me"), the context of the verse here and elsewhere suggests that Job has not been humiliated once in ten attempts. Thus, we have added "have tried" in our translation. The sense of the Targum's translation is "Although you [have tried] to humiliate me ten times, you [still have the gall] to make yourselves known to me." Rashi explains the "ten times" as a reference to those speeches that have occurred until this point in the story. According to Rashi, Job is accusing his friends of treating him like a stranger.

19:4 If, indeed, I have made a mistake, that mistake remains with me.

Job begins to analyze the nature of his so-called "wrongdoing" in this verse. It is as if he were to say "I own my mistakes." The author uses the root *shin-gimel-hey* as a verb, meaning "to sin inadvertently" and as a noun meaning "an inadvertent sin." For a more idiomatic translation, we have rendered the verb as "made a mistake" and the noun as "mistake."

Rashi understands the last clause *iti taleen*—which we have translated as "remains with me"—as "I will be the one to suffer blows because of my mistake."

> 19:5 Indeed, if you assume superiority over me, to reproach me for my shame,
>
> 19:6 know then that God has wronged me and surrounded me with a divine net.

Because these verses represent one complete thought, we have placed them together. Ibn Ezra seems to treat it as fortress rather than net. If we relate the last clause of the second verse to the first clause in the same verse, Job says that God has made his path through life impassible and impossible.

> 19:7 Although I scream "violence," no one responds. Even though I yell, there is no justice.

While Job has sought justice from God in heaven and from his friends on earth, he has not received it. To provide readers with an idiomatic translation of the verse, we have rendered *lo e'ahneh* (I am not answered) as "no one responds."

Rashi makes it clear that Job is crying out against violence.

> 19:8 God has fenced off my path so that I cannot pass. God has set darkness upon my ways.
>
> 19:9 God has stripped glory from me and has taken my crown from my head.

While it is not explicit that these verses are referring to God, the context of the previous verses, to which these are linked, suggests that Job continues to cry out to God and accuse God of injustice. While Gersonides clarifies "my glory" to mean "my wealth," that is the only comment that the classic commentators make on these two verses. The accusation against God is powerful enough to stand on its own.

> 19:10 Round and around God tears at me so that I am no longer there. God has uprooted my hope like a [dead] tree.

The savagery of the attack that Job describes is like being attacked by a wild animal who tears off a piece of flesh and then comes around from a different direction and tears off another piece of flesh and then another, and then another so that that the one being attacked dies, in a slow and horrid manner, literally piecemeal.

> 19:11 God's anger is kindled against me. God considers me an enemy.

To explain his plight, Job assumes that God is angry with him. Somehow, he has become one of God's enemies. A common response to suffering is for the sufferer to believe God is angry with him/her; God is punishing the individual. Although Job protests his innocence, he still believes that God is causing his suffering, and believes it comes from God's anger.

> 19:12 God's troops mass against me. They have besieged me. They surround my tent.

As presented, the three clauses suggest three stages of military action: first, the advance of massed forces; then, the siege of the fortified locality; and finally, surrounding the target in preparation for attack. Job personalizes all of this—the troops are amassed against him, the siege is upon him, and it is his own tent that is surrounded.

> 19:13 God kept my brethren far from me. Those who knew me have become strangers to me.

Job's suffering has not brought his family and friends closer, as is often the case when someone suffers misfortune and loss. Rather, Job's situation has driven his family and friends away from him. That distance is due to their assumption that virtue brings reward and vice brings punishment. They think that since Job suffers, he must be being punished for his sins. Those who were once near Job now keep their distance because they do not want to be associated with a sinner nor negatively impacted upon by his sins.

> 19:14 My relatives fail to appear and my friends have forgotten me.

> 19:15 Those who live in my house, even the maidservants, consider me a stranger. In their eyes, I am now a foreigner.

Job complains that he has lost status in family, community, and his own home to such an extent that even his household pays him no regard. No one recognizes him anymore. He has become a nonperson.

There's a repetition in this verse with the word *zar* used in both 19:13 and 15. The image of estrangement, becoming strange to those around him, is in this verse, and them being strangers to him is in 19:13. In the middle, 19:14, he speaks of how they have ceased to appear and forgotten him. This sense of isolation seems to be the heart of these verses.

> 19:16 If I call my servant, the servant does not answer. I have to beg the servant with my own mouth.

No one pays attention to Job, even his own servant.

> 19:17 It is abhorrent to my wife that I breathe. I am loathsome to my closest kin.

There is an echo in this verse from 19:13 and 15. The context suggests that Job's marital problem is that he is alive. His wife hates the fact that he is still breathing. To use an American idiom, "she hates his guts."

> 19:18 Even little children despise me. They talk about me when I stand up.

The sense of the verse is that Job's appearance or his suffering causes many to turn from him. Since they believe that suffering is divine punishment for sin, they turn away from him because they view him as a sinner. It is true, however, that we turn away from suffering even when we don't believe that the person who is suffering is being divinely punished. For Rashi, Job is saying, "If I am despised by children, then how much the more so am I despised by princes."

> 19:19 Those closest to me abhor me. Those whom I loved have turned against me.

Job's distress cries out to the reader in each word. It is hard to accept when those closest to us reject us.

> 19:20 The skin of my body sticks to my bones. I escaped by the skin of my teeth.

Rashi explains the first clause as a result of Job becoming thin. He explains the last clause by suggesting that Job suffered an infestation of boils and worms over all of his body except for his palate and tongue. Rashi thus explained "the skin of [one's] teeth" as the soft tissues in the mouth. Gersonides takes the "skin of the teeth" to refer to the flesh at the base of the teeth, that is, the gums. As he understands the clause, the gums were the only unaffected part of Job's body.

> 19:21 You are my friends. Have pity on me. Even though the hand of God has struck me, have pity on me.

Job pleads that by virtue of friendship itself he should warrant his friend's pity. For him, if the connections of marriage, the relationship of brothers, and the requirements of status have not brought him a modicum of compassion, he can expect even less from his friends.

> 19:22 Why do you chase after me like God? Haven't you had enough of my flesh?

Job feels like a hunted animal. Even worse, he feels like an animal which is being eaten alive. Those whom he trusted have belied his trust. It is bad enough that they have no sympathy for him. They also seem to enjoy seeing his downfall. Ibn Ezra comments as a reminder to readers on the words "like God," and "he is holy," suggesting that Job's friends are arrogating to themselves the role of the Divine.

> 19:23 Would that my words might be written down and inscribed in a book!

Job now hopes that although he may be at the point of death, were his words preserved in written form, his complaint might transcend his death. Like most of us, Job desired that his suffering or the message of our lives live beyond us.

> 19:24 With an iron pen on lead, engraved on a rock forever.

Job now asks that the record of his case be put on something more lasting than papyrus or parchment.

> 19:25 For I know that my redeemer is alive and in the end, that redeemer will stand upon the dust.

Perhaps the meaning of this verse is that Job hopes that God, unlike a mortal redeemer, will, without a doubt, mark out Job's grave and finally avenge his death.

> 19:26 Although my skin be peeled off, in my flesh I shall see God.

This verse is usually quoted out of context—the second clause quoted without the first clause, outside the context of Job's misery. It seems that here Job refers to one of the most horrendous acts of ancient torture: the flaying of a live person. Even if such a torture would be applied to him, Job hopes that he would still see God as his redeemer.

> 19:27 I myself shall see the redeemer, with my own eyes and no one else's. How I yearn for this.

While Job does not specifically make reference to the Redeemer, we have translated it as a reference to its antecedent in 19:25 in order to avoid gender specificity.

In our rendering of the last clause, we have attempted to present an idiomatic translation of its three Hebrew words. The literal translation of *calu cilyotai b'chsaykee* would be "My kidneys are consumed in my breast." As is apparent, that is neither proper anatomy nor English usage. *Kelayot* (kidneys) were believed to be the seat of feeling. Hence, "consumed" could mean "used up" or "exhausted." *Chayk* means "chest cavity" or "bosom, breast." One might translate the verse as "My deepest feelings are exhausted within me." However, we think that our rendering best fits the sense of the text and its context.

> 19:28 If you say, "Don't chase after him, for the root of the matter is found within him."

Job's enemies believe that they need not pursue him to attack him thereby causing him additional suffering since Job's very nature is the cause of his suffering.

> 19:29 Do not be afraid of the sword yourselves, for wrath will bring the punishments of the sword, that you may know that there is judgment.

Job's statement to his "comforters" who bring him only grief is that they should look within instead of looking at him. If they think that he is evil by nature, then they too are intrinsically evil. Instead of looking gleefully to his punishment, let them fear their own. Their smug and pious anger against him will lead to divine anger against them.

There is a *k'tiv* (written) and *k're* (read) reading of the last word of the verse. The written form is *shaddeen* and it is to be read as *shaddon*. Both readings can be understood, and we have translated, as "there is judgment."

In its translation, the Targum amplifies the text: "Fear the sword because God will be furious at those transgressions worthy of death by sword. For you should know that the True Judge is the Master of Judgment." Rashi understands the "wrath" as due to those who increase the number of sins punishable by the sword. "What you may know" means that you will know the secret of the punishments which come upon the wicked. He alludes to a tradition that is found in the midrash that *shadeen* is to be understood as *yesh din ba'olam*—there is judgment in the world.

GOEL

The *goel* or "redeemer" is the one charged with the responsibility of restoring the rights of another and avenging the wrongs done to that person. The redeemer was the nearest male blood relative, often referred to simply as a "kinsman." If someone was unable to redeem their inheritance as a result of personal poverty, it was the duty of the kinsman to redeem it. During the biblical period, this kinsman redeemer avenged deaths, claimed inheritances for poor family members, and married the widow of a dead male relative.

Chapter 20

20:1 Then Zophar, the Na'amatite replied.

20:2 My thoughts cause me to respond, also because I have been silent.

THE AUTHOR OFFERS THE reader a motivation for Zophar responding at this point in the dialogue with Job.

20:3 I hear the censure which is an insult to me. But my deepest understanding will answer on my behalf.

Rashi contends that the first clause means "I hear the pain of my shame with which you berate me. Therefore, the spirit of my understanding moves me to answer you."

Ibn Ezra reads the first clause as "I have reproaches from you" and the second clause to mean "the spirit of my understanding will answer me."

20:4 Surely you knew this from of old, from the time that Adam was placed on the earth.

This verse introduces the verse that follows and can be understood only in the context of it. The Targum understands *adam* as *bar nash* (man) rather than Adam, the first human. Rashi understands this verse as a question: Don't you know the manner by which life proceeds from the beginning of time?

20:5 That the rejoicing of the wicked is soon over and the joy of the godless lasts only a moment.

In its otherwise literal translation, the Targum renders *chanef* (godless) by the Latin loanword *delator* (informer). This is an unusual choice of words for this commentary/translation. Rashi reads the first clause as "it comes quickly and goes quickly" and the second clause as "it cannot be lost." Rashi's concern is that the text spells out that it is short and goes away.

> 20:6 Even if their arrogance reaches the heavens and their heads touch the clouds.

This verse may remind the reader of Isaiah 14:13–15. Those who think that they can reach the heights are essentially arrogating themselves to the role of God. This verse has been rendered in the plural, referring to "the wicked" in the previous verse, in order to prevent any gender specificity.

> 20:7 Like their own dung, they will be lost forever. Those who once saw them will say, "Where are they?"

Zophar thinks that however pretentious are the wicked, in the end they will disappear. His is the standard assumption of the time that virtue is rewarded and vice is eventually punished.

> 20:8 Like a dream, they will fly away and no one will find them. They will be cast away like a vision of the night.

Rashi tells readers that those who previously knew the wicked person will be unable to find that person.

> 20:9 The eye that caught sight of them will see them no more. Nor will their place look upon them.

It seems that the author has put into the mouth of Zophar the notion that the wicked will be seen only for a moment and only in an unusual manner.

> 20:10 Their children will make amends to the poor and their hands will give back their wealth.

Since Zophar believes in a God who brings justice into the world, he tells Job that the wicked will not "get away" with their wrongdoing. Oppressing the poor is a common trait of the wicked. If the wicked live long enough, they will be forced to return what they have stolen to the poor in one way or another. If they do not do so, their descendents will have to return the "ill-gotten gains."

> 20:11 Although their bones are filled with youthful strength, it will lie with them in the dust.

The sense of this verse is that however we are filled with youthful vitality, that vitality eventually vanishes and we will die. Rashi believes that the wicked will die suddenly, while still full of strength.

> 20:12 Although evil is sweet in their mouths, they will still hide it under their tongues.

Evil is something that is savored, but it is concealed. This reflects the human condition. Rashi explains this verse as a metaphor. It is the way of the wicked that if something is pleasing to them ("sweet in their mouths") and it is not yet time to act on it, it will be hidden ("hide it under their tongues") until the time is ripe for successful action.

> 20:13 They will spare it but not let go. They will keep it within their mouths.

The metaphor of evil as something in the mouth returns. In this verse, it is something that is held in one's mouth. It is not swallowed or spit out. As the generations of humanity can attest, evil is so attractive that although we should get rid of the plans to do wrong, we do not do so. We may hold off from swallowing (that is, acting on those plans) but we keep the plans. At a certain time, our defenses against evil may weaken and we may act on those plans.

> 20:14 Their food within their bowels will turn into snake poison within them.

This is powerful language—a serious stomach ache. Rashi tells the reader that the digestive upset including the transformation of food into snake poison, fated for the wicked, will occur on a particular fateful day, that is, perhaps the day of judgment.

> 20:15 They will vomit all the wealth that they swallowed. God will purge them out of their belly.

The author continues the hope that the wicked will not get away with their crimes, what they amassed unjustly will be taken from them. This is an understandable hope but not a common reality. The supposed strength that people think they have, the inability to digest or absorb the ill-gotten gains, reflects the frailty of the human body as compared to God's power. This is a harsh critique of evildoers that calls attention to the need for humility, of admission of our frailty as humans, of realizing that we cannot swallow or absorb the material things we try so hard to attain.

> 20:16 They will lap up snake venom and the viper's tongue will kill them.

Starting with 20:12, the author has suggested that wickedness is related to the mouth—where it occurs—and is punished through the mouth and what is connected to it: the digestive tract.

> 20:17 They will never see the rivers, streaming with honey and cream.

It seems that absolute luxury in the biblical world is expressed in terms of "honey and cream." One is provided by the farmer; the other is provided by the shepherd. See Psalm 81:17 for another notion of what cream might be (cream of wheat) with honey. Deuteronomy 32:13 also has the notion of nursing honey from the rock, in contrast to what the author of Job previously said above of nursing from snake venom. Were the verse to be taken literally, one might wonder where such "rivers" might exist. Thus, it seems clear that the verse is indeed a metaphor. Rashi explains that the marvelous river will be in *gan eden*, in Paradise.

> 20:18 What they struggled to get, they will have to give back. They will not consume it. They will not enjoy the profit from their trade.

This verse suggests that the wicked person will fail in business. There is an echo in the Hebrew of 20:15.

> 20:19 For they oppressed and abandoned the poor. They seized houses which they had not built.

It may be that we are reading elements of the present into the past, but this verse suggests the same immoral method we see today of creating schemes by which the poor lose their homes.

> 20:20 Since their desire has never let them know any serenity whatever treasure they have provides no escape.

The "treasure" is not satisfying, because the more you eat, the more you want. Thus, the same amount of meat seems to be progressively less.

Gersonides understands the last clause to mean that all the desired wealth which the wicked person amassed will be lost to them. Nothing will remain. We can understand this as another way of saying, "You can't take it with you," or as an expression of the fact that the wicked will be punished. Either way, stealing and coveting do not avail.

> 20:21 Nothing remains for them to consume. Therefore, their good fortune will not last.

This verse is linked to the imagery above by following up on the word *chayil* with *yachi*. The author once again expresses the sentiment that the wicked will suffer in the end, yet the experience of Job seems to undermine even this hopeful statement.

> 20:22 Although they may have much, they will have pain. The
> hand of every laborer will come against them.

Rashi understands the first clause to mean that although the wicked will be able to fulfill their own desires, pain will yet come to them. He explains the second clause as "everyone's hand will have power over them and the hand of the poor will cause [them] pain." Ibn Ezra contends that the workers will rise up against the wicked.

> 20:23 When they fill their bellies, God will kindle a burning
> anger against them and will rain it upon their flesh.

Zophar, as the author presents him to the reader, continues with the notion established by previous verses that those who have amassed unjust wealth and power will not be able to enjoy their ill-gotten gains; they will not even be able to enjoy a good meal. They may be able to eat, but they will suffer. There is a constant underlying hope that justice will triumph.

> 20:24 Although they may flee from a spearhead of iron, they will
> be pierced through by a bronze arrowhead.

It seems clear that although the Hebrew text has *keshet nechoshet* (literally, a bow of bronze), it is not the bow which does the piercing. Rather, it is the arrow which is shot from the bow. Moreover, bows were made of various kinds of wood and horn. Metal bows would have to wait until the invention of the cross bow and the cranking mechanism required to pull back the bowstring of such a bow. What is suggested here is the difference between a spear that has a wooden shaft and iron spearhead and an arrow that is made with a wooden shaft and a bronze arrowhead. One can run away from the pursuit of an individual armed with a spear. But one cannot easily run away from an arrow shot from a bow.

> 20:25 They pull it back. The point glistens with gall. They are
> gripped by terror.

In our translation of the first clause, we have taken the two verbs together as pull back (also translating in the plural to avoid any gender specificity). Thus, we understand that the wicked have received mortal wounds. The bronze arrow has passed through the liver into the gall bladder and they will bleed to death. Awareness of their impending death brings "terror" to them.

> 20:26 All that they treasure will be hidden in total darkness.
> They will be consumed by an unfanned fire. What remains of
> their tent will be ruined.

Speaking through Zophar, the author once again expresses the sentiment that the wicked will not get away with their acts of wickedness. The Targum specifies that the fire that consumes them will be the fire of Gehinnom, that is, the fires of hell.

Rashi explains to the reader that it will be treasures which were stored away that will be hidden from the wicked. Thus, the wicked will not be able to find them. It seems that Rashi is working in contrast to a verse about the righteous: Psalm 31:20.

> 20:27 The heavens will reveal their transgression and the earth will rise up against them.

There will be no place to hide. Nature itself will call out their guilt.

> 20:28 A flood will sweep away their homes—a cloud burst in the time of God's anger.

The verse suggests that the wicked will be punished by the forces of nature on the earth and from the skies, both as a result of divine direction.

> 20:29 This is the destiny that God has set for the wicked; this is the appointed heritage from God.

Gersonides uses this last verse as an opportunity to summarize his views on the chapter. Zophar, the Naamite, says, "In truth, my thoughts force me to respond to you [Job]. From the time that the world came into being and from the time that the human was created, it is manifest that the triumphs and the ease of the wicked do not last, nor does the joy of the unbeliever endure for more than a moment. However high the wicked may rise, even as high as a cloud in the heavens, they will fall. Whatever success they may have will soon disappear. They too soon will no longer be seen."

Chapter 21

21:1 Then Job responded:

21:2 Listen carefully to what I say. This will be your (last) consolation to me.

As Rashi understands this verse, were "his comforters" silent and listening to what he is about to say, that would help to console Job. The reason Rashi comments as he does is because the literal meaning of the verse is not "your consolation to me" but "your consolation." While the verse could be read that Job is consoling his comforters, it is unlikely that is the intent of the author.

21:3 Bear with me and I will speak. You can mock me after I have spoken.

Job understands his position. He knows that what he will say will not win acquiescence from his friends. Rather, it will invite further mockery.

21:4 Is my complaint to a human? Why should I not be impatient?

There is an implicit argument in Job's statement. His demand for justice is not directed to humanity. Rather, it is directed to God. One does not expect justice from humanity. But one does expect justice from God.

21:5 Look at me and be shocked. Put your hand over your mouth.

Job hurts so much that he does not want any comment. His physical appearance attests to his suffering. Rashi explains that the reason that Job has told his comforters to put their hands over their mouths is because they don't know how to respond to what he has said and will yet say.

21:6 When I think of it, I am terrified. Shuddering takes over my body.

Job tells his comforters that bringing up his past experiences, even now in the present, brings on the same symptoms of uncontrollable terror. What we have translated as "when I think of it" can also be translated as "when I remember." Rashi does not think he is remembering past experiences but rather thinking of what he is about to say in the next verse.

> 21:7 Why do the wicked survive, grow old, and increase their power?

Job asks the nagging question once again: Why do the righteous suffer evil and the wicked enjoy life?

> 21:8 Their children live securely in their presence and they see their descendants.

Job has discovered that even the ancient belief that children suffer for the sins of their wicked parents is not true. Both the wicked and their children seem to thrive.

> 21:9 Their homes are secure, free of fear. The rod of God does not smite them.

Although the text of the last clause simply has, "The rod of God is not upon them," to make sense of the phrase, we have added the assumed verb "smite them."

> 21:10 Their bulls breed without fail. Their cows deliver and never miscarry.

Even the animals of the wicked do not suffer from the sins of their owners. Moreover, they increase the wealth of their owners by producing offspring.

> 21:11 They send forth their little ones like a flock and their children dance.

The wicked are blessed with children and these children rush into life joyfully. Rashi refers the verse to the moment of birth. The babies come forth and they move around as if they were dancing. Were they to be attacked by some demon, they would fight against it. Seeing the sprightly child, the new mother can say to it, "bring me scissors and I will cut its hair."

> 21:12 They sing to [the music of] the drum and the harp. They rejoice at the sound of the flute.

Job continues to emphasize how rewarded are those who do evil. The children of the wicked are carefree, living without any burden or fear.

> 21:13 They spend their days at ease and go to their graves in peace.

We see here Job's complaint in stark relief. The wicked enjoy their lives and they do not suffer even in dying.

> 21:14 They say to God, "Don't bother us. We don't want the knowledge of your ways."

Job complains that the wicked have the effrontery to challenge God directly—in addition to their getting away with evil.

> 21:15 "Who is the Almighty whom we should serve? Of what benefit is it to us to pray to the Divine?"

What the wicked say is more than blasphemy. It is *chutzpah* (moxy). Rashi understands the wicked to be saying, "What benefit could we get by praying to God? Since 'a mist comes up from the earth' (Genesis 2:6), we don't need God at all, not even for rain."

> 21:16 Behold they don't own their own property. So I keep distant from the counsel of the wicked.

After challenging traditional belief in previous chapters, it seems that Job now affirms that very belief in the first clause of this verse. But it is a literary device that allows the author to contest that belief in the verse that follows.

Ibn Ezra understands this verse as connected to the preceding verses: all the good things that come to the wicked are not in their own hands, that is, they did not make them happen. Everything comes from God. He reads the entire verse as a strong attack on traditional belief: "In spite of all their evil, the wicked are not punished. Rather, God is the source of their prosperity. Even so, Job rejects their views." Ibn Ezra reads the first clause here as a statement: their wealth is not from their own hands; it is from God.

> 21:17 When is the lamp of the wicked ever quenched? When does their calamity ever come upon them? When does God, in anger, give them their share of destruction?

Job's challenge of the traditional belief—that virtue brings with it reward and vice brings punishment—is evident in this verse. He simply points to the life of the wicked. They live in light, not darkness. They experience neither specific suffering nor the pains that ordinary people endure.

> 21:18 Are they [the wicked] like straw before the wind? Are they like chaff that is snatched by a storm?

The author places common experience in the mouth of Job. The wicked "get away with it." They don't disappear. In fact, they have a certain permanence. Were they like chaff in the wind, then they would be impermanent.

> 21:19 Does God lay away the punishment of the wicked for their children? Let God give it to them [while they are alive] so that they may know it.

We have translated this verse in the plural to avoid any gender specificity. Job refers to another common explanation of how it is that the wicked prosper and are not punished. If they are not punished, their children are punished.

This belief, and a condemnation of it, are attested to in the book of the prophet Ezekiel (18:2). He begins by quoting a proverb: "The parents eat sour grapes and the children's teeth are set on edge." This essentially unfair belief is rejected by the prophet. Speaking for God, Ezekiel says, ". . . You will no longer quote this proverb in Israel. . . . The soul that sins is the one that will die. . . . The child will not share the guilt of the parent nor will the parent share the guilt of the child" (Ezekiel 18:3, 4, 20). Other biblical texts attest to the notion that children are punished for the sins of their parents. Ibn Ezra here references one: "Visiting the sins of the parents upon children and children's children, upon the third and fourth generations" (Exodus 34:7).

> 21:20 Let their own eyes see their destruction. Let them drink the wrath of the Almighty.

This is a straightforward verse that reflects Job's basic wish: let the evildoers be punished and let them be aware of their punishment—as a result of their wrongdoing.

> 21:21 When the number of their months come to an end, why would they care about their family, after they are gone?

We have reversed the order of the clauses to indicate more clearly the force of Job's statement. The wicked who do not care about other people in their lifetime will hardly care about members of their family after they, the wicked, are dead. This may be a further justification of why the wicked and not their children should be punished, because after they are dead they won't care about what happens to their family.

> 21:22 Can anyone teach knowledge to God, the one who judges those on high?

A person cannot teach God knowledge, but a person can confront God nonetheless. Is Job also saying that God's knowledge is so profound and so different that we earthbound mortals do not understand it? In either case, we are unable to wonder about the justice of God, so says Job. It is important to compare this verse to Psalm 94:10 which describes God as the one who instructs humans with knowledge. The context of the verse from Psalms is also about reward and punishment.

> 21:23 One person dies at full strength, totally secure and at ease.

If such a person were at "full strength," one might think that person too healthy to die. Rashi explains the verse as referring to a wicked—healthy—person who will die suddenly as a result of sin. Rashi suggests that the person looks and seems to be whole but actually is not.

> 21:24 The person's thighs are filled with fat. The person's bones are replete with marrow.

Our translation of the first clause is not as it is presented in the text. We did so in order to make better sense of the first clause and relate it directly to the second clause in the verse. Without doing so, the two clauses would seem to have no relationship to each other.

> 21:25 Yet another person dies with bitterness in the soul, never having tasted good.

This verse is related to 21:23 above. Both verses make the observation that while the wicked prosper, the innocent suffer. The verse contrasts the death of two people: one satisfied and one unsatisfied, who both die and both have the same end.

> 21:26 The two together lie in the dust and worms cover them both.

Death comes to the innocent and guilty alike. Whatever they were in life, they are the same in the grave. Rashi notes that after their death, when they lie in the grave, no one will know which one was good and which one was wicked.

> 21:27 I know what you are thinking and how you plan to wrong me.

Since his comforters operate from the notion that if one does good, one receives good and if one does evil, then one is punished, Job thinks that seeing his suffering, Job's comforters believe that Job is a sinner. Thus, they would plan to punish him further for both his thoughts and his words.

> 21:28 Yet you say, "Where is the house of the great person?
> Where is the tent where the wicked dwelled?"

Job thinks that the comforters challenge Job to show where one can see the wicked in their habitations. For them, Job will be able to provide much information about the success and the status of the wicked. Job says his comforters think you can look at someone's home and tell whether they are a good or bad person. He casts aspersions on their way of understanding material success.

> 21:29 Have you never asked the passersby? Have you never examined their reports?

This verse is related to both the previous verse and the next verse. Rashi takes the first clause to mean "You are making up stories about me." He takes the second clause (with *t'nackru*) to mean "You disregard their reports."

> 21:30 That the evil person is reserved for the day of calamity;
> that they [the wicked] will be led out for the day of wrath.

Job presents another attempt to deal with the problem of the suffering of the innocent by putting off the fitting punishment for the wicked to some time in the future.

> 21:31 Who will tell them to their face about their behavior?
> Who will make them repay for what they have done?

Once again, Job tells his comforters that the wicked get away with their crimes. We have made the subject of this verse plural in order to avoid gender specificity. We have also reversed the order of the last clause to make it read better.

> 21:32 For they are brought to their grave and a watch is kept
> over their tomb.

Even in death, the wicked are not punished. Their funerals are conducted in the same manner as are the funerals of the righteous. Ecclesiastes made the same observation: "This too did I see: the wicked brought to burial and they came and would go from the holy place and they would be forgotten in the city where thus they had acted—but this too is useless" (Ecclesiastes 8:10).

> 21:33 The clods of earth of the grave are sweet to them. Everyone follows after them and numberless are those who go before them.

It seems that those who "follow" and those "who go before" refer to those who participate in the funeral going before and after the bier.

> 21:34 How can you comfort me with prattle? Whatever is still in your responses is wrong.

Job has spoken of the truth that he sees: in life and in death, the wicked "get away with it." All the usual answers about human suffering and God's justice are not true, according to Job.

CHUTZPAH CLAPPEI MALAH

Chutzpah in the face of heaven. While not a strictly modern concept, this is a posture of standing up to and questioning God, made famous particularly by Levi Yitzchak of Berditchev (1740–1810). Levi Yitzchak, known as the Berdichever Rebbe, was a Hasidic rabbi and disciple of the Maggid of Mezritch. Because of the stance he toook in front of God—and because he was believed to be able to intercede on behalf of people—he was sometimes called the "defense attorney" for the Jewish people. This stance is a way of challenging God. Ironically, this position—and its struggle—affirm our faith in God, because it holds God responsible for what the world is and how it operates.

EZEKIEL

Sixth-century prophet who prophesied in a community of exiles in Babylon, thus one of the so-called exilic prophets. He was a member of the priestly class. A book of his prophesies is contained in the canon. He is best known for his "chariot vision" (Ezekiel 1—3:27) and "dry bones" (Ezekiel 37).

Chapter 22

22:1 Then Eliphaz, the Temanite replied,

22:2 Can a person be of use to God? Can even a wise person be of use to the Divine?

THE TARGUM INSERTS THE word *ephshar* (is it possible) at the beginning of the verse and then specifies what kind of "use" might be understood. Such a specification makes sense of the *maskil* (wise person) who might be expected to teach, if not God, then at least human beings.

22:3 Is it the desire of the Almighty that you are righteous? Is there a benefit for God if you perfect your ways?

The book of Job presents us with another theological dilemma in the words of Eliphaz. If God is perfect—and he would argue that God is indeed perfect—then why does God need us? The atheist might ask: if there is a God, what does God do for us? The theist would ask: what do we do for God? Moreover, if God doesn't care, then why should God know? This is part of the tension of Eliphaz's argument.

Rashi refers us to Job 21:21 and the phrase "why should he care about his family" (which we rendered in the plural as "Why would they care about their family?"). Rashi is saying, "Does God take pleasure or worry if your deeds are good or not? If you come to argue before God, should God come and dispute your words? Just as the wicked do not care about their families after they are dead (see Job 21:21), so God does not need to care whether we follow God's ways and are righteous."

22:4 Is it because of God's fear of you that God contends with you and comes with you to court?

Elpihaz extends the various theological notions he is pondering. This verse is about God's relationship to humans. Individual humans may fear God, but God is not afraid of humans. How then can a person challenge the Almighty?

22:5 Is not your evil enormous? Is there no end to your transgressions?

Eliphaz responds to Job's claim of innocent suffering by arguing that Job deserves whatever Job is suffering. Rashi takes Eliphaz's statement even further. He claims that God knows the extent of Job's evil ways. Thus, it is for that reason that Job suffers.

22:6 You took pledges from your own brethren for no reason and stripped them naked of their clothing.

This is a serious charge, the first of a number of charges Eliphaz will level against Job. Here he charges Job with a misuse of economic power. This is a sin that is widely reported throughout history and throughout the world. In Deuteronomy 24:10, we are instructed to return a pledged garment to a poor person in the daytime because that may be the only garment in which the individual has to sleep.

22:7 You gave no water to the weary and you held back bread from the hungry.

Eliphaz adds more accusations. Since Eliphaz charges Job with being a heartless exploiter, using his economic strength in an unjust manner, one might be led to believe that *lechem* is being used in its literal meaning of "bread" rather than its expanded meaning as "food." According to the charge levied against Job, not even bread and water, the barest means of sustenance, did Job provide to the poor with whom he came into contact Although the reader may surmise that Job will be found innocent of such an economic crime, the fact that the charge is being made reveals to us the issues that are important to the writer.

22:8 A person of power possessing land and well-respected living on it.

Eliphaz continues to press the attack. Job was a man of means and a person of status. Yet, as the next verse will charge, he did not live up to his power.

22:9 You sent widows away empty-handed and the arms of orphans were crushed.

This description is not the Job that we have come to know in previous chapters. Eliphaz describes him as heartless and ruthless. Eliphaz is suggesting that Job is guilty of neglecting the poor—something many wealthy people may be guilty of—directed at those who have no one to defend them.

> 22:10 That is why snares encircle you and sudden fear terrifies you.

Eliphaz assumes that the sins described above are the reason that Job now suffers and have caused him to fear disaster and the potential for destruction coming from every side.

> 22:11 Or is there darkness so that you cannot see and a stream of water that sweeps over you.

Eliphaz continues his suggestion that Job's sins have impaired his sight and caused him to feel as if he were drowning, submerged in water. See Psalm 32:6 and Jonah 2:4 for similar notions.

> 22:12 Is God not in the highest heavens? And look how far up are the highest stars?

Eliphaz uses the majesty of nature to challenge Job. The God who has the capacity to create the heavens and earth surely knows the true nature of Job's situation. Job, therefore, suffers because he has sinned; he cannot possibly be innocent.

As Rashi understands it, although God is enthroned on high, God does not have to descend in order to discern Job's situation. Rashi is echoing (and reversing) a Psalm here: Psalm 113:6.

> 22:13 Yet you say, "What does God know? Can God judge through thick darkness?"

Once again, Eliphaz challenges Job. A God who knows enough to create the entire world surely knows the situation of any part of it. According to Eliphaz, God knows Job and God knows that Job deserves to suffer. This verse and the following verse are both playing off imagery of God dwelling in a cloud and judging from there, such as appears in Psalm 97:2–3, 2 Chronicles 6:1, and the parallel in 2 Kings 8:12.

> 22:14 Thick clouds cover the Divine, so that God does not see, as God goes about circling the heavens.

In his own mind, Eliphaz assumes the thought of Job. Even so, there is logic to Eliphaz's position. For him, God can do no wrong. If Job suffers, it is because Job is a sinner. According to Eliphaz, God is in charge and aware. Does Job think that the cloud and fog surrounding God mean that God is unable to be cognizant? Those who read Eliphaz's words and their intrinsic logic can wonder if God were ignorant of what goes on in the world and what happens to those who inhabit it, then the problem of the suffering of the righteous would be solved.

> 22:15 Will you keep to the way of the world upon which evildoers have walked?

There's a balance here with the prior verse. In 22:14, God walks a circuit of the heavens. In this verse, a way or path has been walked by evil individuals.

> 22:16 They were snatched before their time, their foundations swept away by a flood.

While there is an echo here of the covering waters in 22:11, this verse refers back to 22:15. Eliphaz claims that those who are evil die young.

> 22:17 They said to God, "Get away from us! What could the almighty do to us?"

This argument by Eliphaz asserts that the wicked reject God with no fear of Divine retribution.

> 22:18 Yet God filled their houses with all manner of good. So I reject the counsel of the wicked.

Although the wicked reject God, God has not rejected them. The fact that God does good even to the undeserving proves to Eliphaz that God is still involved with the lives of human beings.

> 22:19 The righteous will see and rejoice. The innocent will mock them.

This verse assumes the next verse. To make the matter clearer, we have added a connecting word "saying" into the translation at the beginning of the next verse.

> 22:20 [Saying] surely their riches are destroyed and fire will consume what remains.

Rashi brings a midrash as commentary to the verse which says that when the flood came, some of the wicked were so tall that their heads were above the water. God then shortened their heights so that they would drown. Regarding the second clause, he explains that God caused fire to come down from heaven, so those who did not drown were scalded to death.

> 22:21 Be reconciled to God and be at peace. In such a manner, good will come to you.

As presented above, Eliphaz still thinks that Job is at fault. However, he gives Job what he thinks is good advice.

> 22:22 Take instruction from God's mouth and put the divine teaching in your heart.

The notion of Torah study and of Torah as a particular entity is a development of the late Second Temple period, reflected only in the latest parts of the Bible, such as Psalm 119. Since we cannot be sure when Job was composed, we have rendered "torah" as instruction, similar to its meaning in Proverbs 1:8 and elsewhere.

> 22:23 If you return to the Almighty and you keep transgression far from your tent, you shall be restored.

Gersonides explains the verse this way: "You will return to be rebuilt after you have been ruined by all these terrible things that have happened to you." He adds that it could also mean, "you will have children."

> 22:24 And if you will set your gold nuggets on the dust and the gold of Ophir among the rocks of the brook.

This verse seems to continue the thoughts of the previous verse. According to Eliphaz, this is what Job must do. He has to give up his possessions in order to return to God's favor. "Ophir" is a place name, the location of a legendary source of gold. Mention of the name suggests the gold to be found in it.

> 22:25 Then the Almighty will be like gold nuggets and be like refined silver to you.

While there is some debate among the various translations of this text (Septuagint, Vulgate, and Peshitta) as to whether the last clause suggests that silver will be heaped up or refined or in vast quantities, the message is clear. If Job follows Eliphaz's advice, he will reap a reward.

> 22:26 For then you will delight in the Almighty and lift your face to God.

This verse appears simple to understand. There might be an echo here of Isaiah 58:14. However, from the context of the previous verses, one might expect that Eliphaz would tell Job that God will delight in him and have regard for him. We delight in God only when things go well for us. Rashi suggests that the verse means that Job only has to lift up his face to ask for his needs.

> 22:27 When you pray to God, God will listen to you. And you will pay your vows.

This expression appears in Psalm 116 twice—verses 14 and 18—in the context of rejoicing, praise celebration and happiness. Everyone seeks such a situation. When we pray to God, we want to know that God hears our prayers and will respond to them.

> 22:28 Whatever you decide on will happen and light will shine on all your ways.

This verse continues Eliphaz's assumption that Job's suffering—which he still considers as punishment for Job's sins—would end were he only to repent. While this is meant to be a message of consolation, so to speak, the first part of the verse is rather shocking. Eliphaz seems to believe that when one is close to God or repents suddenly everything goes the way the person wants. This is a surprising theology in light of what we know about the world and about suffering.

> 22:29 God brings down the height of arrogance while delivering those with downcast eyes.

The Targum translates the verse as "The arrogance of the generations of which you speak will be subjugated, while those sunk in disgrace shall be delivered."

Rashi explains the first clause in this way, "If you see your generation brought low, say with assurance that it will be brought up, and it will [indeed] be brought up." He takes the "downcast eyes" of the second clause as a reference to the pain suffered as a result of sin. Nevertheless, as Rashi understands the clause, those sinners will be delivered by God through Job's prayer.

> 22:30 God will rescue the one who is not innocent, who will be rescued because of the cleanliness of your hands.

Ibn Ezra thinks that the verse means that God will rescue the person "of downcast eyes" [cf. preceding verse].

By assuming some words in the Hebrew text, the Targum's translation makes sense of the verse as "Through your merit, God will deliver a person who is not innocent and so through the cleanliness of your hands, that person will be delivered."

SEPTUAGINT

The ancient Greek version of the Bible, translated in stages between the third and first centuries BCE in Alexandria. It is the oldest translation of the Bible into Greek. The name derives from a tradition that suggests that seventy (*septuaginta* in Latin) Jewish scholars translated the Torah into Greek by a copying process that prevented any errors. The translation was made by and for the Greek-speaking Jewish community in Alexandria.

PESHITTA

An independent Aramaic translation of the Bible that is based largely on a Proto-Masoretic text. It shows some similarities to early Aramaic translations (known as the Targums). It is clear that the Septuagint was used by the translators for some of the passages. It was probably written in the second century CE.

THE VULGATE

The Vulgate is a Latin translation (early fifth century CE) of the Hebrew Bible. Along with the Peshitta and the Septuagint, they became official translations of the church. Scholars often consult these early translations for a better understanding of the meaning of specific Hebrew words.

Chapter 23

23:1 Job then responded,

23:2 Even today, my complaint is bitter. My suffering is greater than my groaning.

THE TARGUM AND ALL three of our commentators take *yadee* (literally, "my hand") to mean "my plague." Following Rashi, who adds *negay* (my wounds) to make the phrase "the plague of my wounds," we have interpreted the word to mean "my suffering." Rashi reads the first clause as "Even after all of your words of consolation, 'my complaint [remains] . . . bitter.'" He explains the second clause to mean, "My suffering is greater than my groaning—I am not crying out at the level of my pain."

For Ibn Ezra, the first clause conveys the message, "My complaint is more instructive than any other." Gersonides, on the other hand, suggests that the first clause reflects Job's desire to react to Eliphaz, "I am so bitter and so angry that I would storm against your words."

23:3 Would that I knew where to find God, I would go to the divine dwelling place.

Undeterred by the words of his so-called consolers, Job remains unwilling to accept his suffering as punishment for sins that he may have committed. Job still wants to find God so that he can be judged. Although Rashi and Ibn Ezra are unclear about the meaning of this last word in the verse, it seems clear that Job is trying to find God wherever God dwells so that he might confront the Divine.

23:4 I would lay my case before God, I would fill my mouth with arguments.

This is Job's plan of action. Once he finds God, he is prepared to present his case without delay. The Hebrew *tochechot* has been a key-word throughout. Job returns here to the metaphor of a court and of proving his case.

> 23:5 I would know the words with which God would answer me.
> And I would understand what God would say.

Job is convinced that were God to try his case, he would be found innocent of any wrongdoing. As Rashi understands this verse, Job thinks that even if God were to prevent him from speaking, he would know how God would respond to him. Job seems to be asserting knowledge and understanding of God's message. His statement would seem to raise the issue of whether people can know or understand God's ways. He is not arguing that God is inscrutable.

> 23:6 Would God contend with me with divine power? No. God would provide me with power.

In such a situation, Job believes that God would not assert divine power against him. Instead, God would empower Job.

> 23:7 It is there that the upright person might win one's case before God. So I would stand forever acquitted by my judge.

Job argues that if only he could present his case before the Eternal Judge, he might win his case. It is his only chance to clear his name. For Rashi, "there" is the place where Job and God would meet. For him, the "upright" is the one whose deeds are proper. He takes *nochach* (present one's case) as a noun: "one whose case is proven." Since Job would be free of transgression, he would "stand forever acquitted."

> 23:8 Behold, if I go east, God is not there. If I go west, I do not understand God.

Job understands the daunting nature of the task that he has set for himself. He recognizes that while God is everywhere, God is also nowhere to be found specifically, geographically. He also understands that even if he were able to find God, it doesn't mean that he would be able to communicate with the Divine.

We follow the Targum in translating *kedem* (literally, "previous" or "ahead") as east and *achor* (literally, "behind") as west. Gersonides explains that since the sun rises in the east, where it arose became east. And since the setting of the sun comes last (*achor*), *achor* came to mean west.

> 23:9 When God is at work in the north, I catch no sight of the Divine. When God swings to the south, I can't see God.

No matter where Job goes, he is unable to find God. Following the directions of the previous verse, and the interpretations of Rashi and

Chapter 23   143

Gersonides, we have translated *smol* (left) as north and *yamin* (right) as south. Ibn Ezra suggests that Job argues that if he cannot see God in whatever direction he might look, why should he attempt to deliver himself from a judge he cannot see?

> 23:10 For God knows the path that I take. God has tested me. I came out like gold.

It is not only that Job is unable to find God, God may be avoiding Job. After all, if God knows all, then God knows that path that Job takes to seek out the Divine—just as God saw Job's entire life and the actions he undertook. For Rashi, this is another statement in which Job claims his innocence. Job is confident that knowing his path, God would enter into an argument with Job and Job would emerge pure, like gold. Ibn Ezra thinks that this statement suggests that Job remains on God's path or God has been with Job on his path—this is a reflection of Job's righteousness and the life that he has led.

> 23:11 My feet have closely followed God's steps. I have kept to God's path and not turned away.

This verse reflects what Ibn Ezra contended was implied by the previous verse. Job has followed God throughout his life and does not intend to turn from that path at this point, even after all of his suffering.

> 23:12 I have not departed from the commandment of God's lips. I have treasured the words of the divine mouth more than my daily bread.

Additional contentions by Job that he has not strayed from the path that God set for him in his life. According to Ibn Ezra, this verse means that Job has stored all of the words and commandments of God in his heart (mind). Rashi contends that this verse alludes to Proverbs 30:8 in which the author writes, "feed me my allotted [daily] bread." Such bread, Rashi contends, one would be eager to store away.

> 23:13 But God stands alone and none can move the Divine. Whatever God desires, God can do.

Even amidst the suffering that he endures, Job continues to believe in God and the power of the Divine. Job believes, however, that whether or not he has been righteous, whether or not he has followed the divine commandments, irrespective of whatever action he takes, God can still disregard it all and act at will.

Rashi adds that God is unique, because God knows what people want to express to the Divine. Before people say anything, God has already prepared a response in advance.

> 23:14 God will carry out what is allotted to me. God has many such plans in store [for others too].

The Targum reads this verse as related to everything that has preceded it: "God will carry out the previous decree against me." Rashi sees this verse as a continuation of the actions, "God will not remove a hand from me until completing the punishments allotted to me that have been decreed." For him, the second statement should be read as "God has already done similar things" to me.

> 23:15 Therefore, I am terrified of God. All I have to do is think of God and I am afraid.

Job is afraid of God—whom he perceives as the all-powerful Deity. He admits his fear in God's presence.

> 23:16 God has made my heart faint. The Almighty has terrified me.

This verse repeats the sentiment of the previous verse in order to emphasize the depth of Job's fear and his despair. It simply changes the subject. In either case, Job is afraid. He is terrified.

> 23:17 I did not disappear into the darkness nor did thick darkness cover my face.

We have chosen to understand *lo* (not) to apply to both clauses. Carrying over a negation from one clause to another is not unusual in biblical literature. Rashi applies the negation to both clauses as well. He takes the verse to be Job's statement of terror. He has not been totally cut off in order to enter the eternity of the grave. So he must now endure the darkness that covers him.

Ibn Ezra reads the statement as it if it were an echo of Ecclesiastes (7:1) "the day of death is better than the day of birth." Ibn Ezra senses that Job would prefer to be cut off from life and enter the darkness from which he emerged at birth.

For Gersonides "darkness" is Job's metaphor for all of the terrible things that have happened to him. And "thick darkness" is Job's metaphor for wishing that he could not see his troubles.

Chapter 24

> 24:1 Why are times not set aside by the Almighty? Why do those who know God not see those days?

THE VERSE DOES NOT make it clear to which "times" and "days" it is referring. However, in reading the verses that follow, the reader might conclude that both terms refer to times of judgment when the divine court might be in session.

> 24:2 They keep moving boundary markers in order to pasture the flocks they steal.

The writer describes a clever way to take advantage of others. The moving of markers affects the use of the land and the animals on it. In this way, one can steal by indirection rather than by force.

> 24:3 They lead away the orphan's donkey. They take the widow's ox on pledge.

This verse identifies those who are considered to be at the bottom rung of the socioeconomic ladder in society—widows and orphans. Under the guise of legality, the wicked take advantage of those too weak to defend themselves.

> 24:4 They turn the poor from the path so that the wretched of the earth must hide together.

The author describes a phenomenon well-known to modern readers. The poor are removed from the sight of those who are better off so that it would seem that they hide themselves from view. What the author of Job complains about in biblical Israel still exists in many large cities in North America and elsewhere.

> 24:5 Like wild asses in the wilderness, they [the poor] go out laboriously looking for food. The desert provides bread for their children.

Driven from the settled land where they might have had a chance to gain sustenance, the poor have to look for food wherever they may find it. What little they may find requires traversing, like "wild asses," vast expanses in the wilderness to look for edible plants.

> 24:6 They harvest mixed fodder in the field and they glean in the vineyards of the wicked.

Rashi takes the first word of the verse, *basadeh* (in the field), to indicate "the field of others." And he reads *b'leelo* as *yevulo* (his produce). He understands *yektzoru* (they harvest) to mean that they do so in order to steal. And he thinks that the last clause means that the wicked go to vineyards that belong to others in order to pick their fruit.

> 24:7 Lacking clothing, they spend the night naked. They have no covering in the cold.

This is a terrible picture of the reality of poverty. The poor suffer when they could rest. This verse seems to be a reference to a violation of the commandment in Exodus 22:25–26 that requires the return of garments to the poor to sleep.

> 24:8 They are soaked by water streaming off the mountains. Lacking shelter, they hide among the rocks.

The word *zerem* is not common in the Hebew Bible. It only appears nine times, seven of which are in the book of Isaiah. This is the only time it is used in the book of Job. It seems to be a reference to the flash-flooding process in the Judean hills where streams come quickly through the mountains to previously dry areas and people who are caught are forced to seek high ground, clinging to rocks. The description of the poor forced to live under terrible conditions is clear. Unfortunately, what the author of Job describes has not changed much since writing the book of Job. Rashi makes the situation clear, linking this verse to the previous one. Lacking clothing to protect them, the poor are "soaked" by the water coming down the mountain. Without any other shelter, they try to find cover among the rocks and in the clefts of the boulders.

> 24:9 They [the wicked] snatch the orphan babe from the breast. They would take the poor in pledge.

Job's plaint here reminds the reader of the story of the poor widow who could not pay back her creditors. Therefore, she was threatened with losing her two sons as collateral (2 Kings 4:1). It was unethical to treat children as chattel.

> 24:10 Lacking clothing, they go about naked. Though starving,
> they carry sheaves.

The poor are being treated like animals. They lack clothing, like animals. And like beasts of burden, they may not eat what they are forced to carry.

> 24:11 Between two rows [of watchers], they press oil. They tread
> the wine presses and yet suffer from thirst.

The poor are forced to work between two rows of men watching that they do not take even a drop of the oil that they are producing. In like manner, although the poor crush grapes, they will have no grape juice—and certainly no wine—to drink.

> 24:12 The dying groan in the city. The souls of the wounded
> scream. Yet God ascribes no fault.

Job's plaint is that what has happened is so far out of God's purview that it is not even worth a prayer. Neither the deaths nor the suffering nor the screams make any sense. Job argues that they are meaningless to God; otherwise, God would be responsive to them.

> 24:13 There are those who rebel against the light. They do not
> know the ways of the Divine nor abide in divine paths.

We have translated the verse to avoid gender specificity by using the word "divine" instead of "his." As we understand the verse, the reason that "those who rebel" do so is because they do not know God's paths nor do they "abide" in them.

> 24:14 At morning light, the murderer arises to kill the poor and
> the needy. By night, this same person becomes a thief.

Since theft is a lesser crime than murder, it seems odd that the "murderer" would engage in a nefarious profession in daylight, during which time others would observe this person's actions.

> 24:15 The eye of the adulterer waits for twilight. Saying "no eye
> will see me," he masks his face.

We presume that the adulterer in the case of this verse is indeed a male and thus translate the gender specificity accordingly. We have moved from the previous verse's murder and theft to adultery. To carry out any or all of the three sins/crimes, concealment of one kind or another is necessary. The murderer looks for an isolated place or a time when others are not around to see him do his dirty work. The thief waits for darkness to hide his act of breaking into a house to steal. The adulterer thinks that no one will see him or recognize him in the half-light of dusk. In any case, he covers his face so that even if he is seen, he will not be recognized. While readers might think that an all-seeing God would know what the wicked do, the author of Job (24:12) suggests that God does not seem to see or if God does see these actions, God does not seem to care.

> 24:16 In the dark, they break into houses. In the day, they shut themselves in. They never know the light.

As in the previous verses, the malefactors think that darkness conceals their crimes—from mortals and from God. Digging through the wall of a house was the means by which a thief would gain entry. This is assumed in the verse *eem b'machteret yematzay ha-ganav* / if a thief is found breaking in (Exodus 22:1).

> 24:17 For all of them, their morning is as deep darkness. They are acquainted with the terrors of the shadow of death.

Rashi makes an interesting comment about the verse. Since these sinners are sealed away by day and go about at night to break into houses, it would seem that they have no fear of demons. Moreover, it is said of them that they are "acquainted with terrors." This proves that they are familiar with demons and, as a result, are not afraid of them. Rashi identifies the modus operandi of the thieves according to the Rabbis of the Talmud (Sanhedrin 109a). The thieves would put markers on the cellars of the houses of the wealthy to indicate where the inhabitants hid their valuables. They would then place fragrant balsam on those valuables. Remembering where in the cellar the wealthy had placed their valuables, being able to smell their exact location, the thieves would then dig down and steal them.

> 24:18 He is swift upon the surface of the water, yet their portion is cursed upon the earth. He does not turn in the way of the vineyards.

The three clauses in this verse do not seem to be related one to another. It is unclear who "is swift upon . . . the water" or who are they whose "portion is accursed upon the earth" or who it is who "does not turn in the way of the vineyards." (We have left the verse gender specific in order to emphasize the unrelated nature of the verses.) Moreover, it is not clear as to the mutual and reciprocal relations of "water" to "earth" and "vineyards." Generally speaking, this verse is about those who are wicked (and therefore cursed) who never turn to good.

> 24:19 As drought and heat suck up the water of melted snow, so Sheol will suck up the sinner.

Just as snow melts and the resultant water suddenly disappears in the face of heat, so are the wicked, upon their death, suddenly brought to Sheol.

> 24:20 The womb forgets the wicked. The worms feast sweetly on them. They are no more remembered and malice is smashed like wood.

Although the wicked may escape justice in this life, they cannot escape death. Death, as the writer of Job said at the beginning of the book, is the great equalizer. ["The wicked cease their agitation there . . . great and small [alike]" (Job 3:16, 18)]. We have translated the pronouns in this verse in plural form to avoid gender specificity.

> 24:21 They devour the barren who cannot bear and show no kindness to the widow.

This verse suggests that wicked men take sexual advantage of women known to be barren since they realize that sexual intercourse will not lead to a pregnancy. Since the widow has no one to protect her—in the social strata of ancient society—the wicked man has no reason to extend any kindness toward her.

> 24:22 God draws away the mighty with divine power. Although they may rise up, they cannot be sure of their lives.

While it is the context of the verse, rather than its specific content, that suggests the subject of the verse as God and the objects as the wicked, it is not entirely clear. All of the verbs are singular.

We follow Rashi in our understanding of the verse. "God draws away the mighty" either for punishment or for sustenance by extending time for them. He reads this as a continuation of the context of the generation of the flood; no one could be "sure of their lives" because of the great inundation of water.

> 24:23 God may allow them to rest in security. Yet God's eyes are upon their ways.

We are assuming that the subject is God once again and the object is the wicked.

> 24:24 They are exalted for a moment and then they are gone. They are brought low and snatched away. They wither like kernels of grain.

Shebolet usually means corn. In British English, "corn" is a generic word for grain. In American English, "corn" suggests maize. To avoid any confusion, we have translated *shebolet* as "grain."

The Targum makes it clear as to whom the first clause refers: *reshayah* (the wicked). For Rashi, the first clause means that the wicked will disappear from the world in a brief moment.

> 24:25 And now, if this be not so, who can prove me wrong and so make nothing of my words?

Having pointed out the evil that exists in the world in the face of the notion of a God of goodness, Job now asks his so-called comforters to prove him wrong.

Chapter 25

25:1 Then Bildad the Shuchite responded:

THIS IS THE SHORTEST chapter in the book of Job, containing only six verses.

25:2 Dominion and fear are God's. God establishes peace in the high places.

Note the liturgical use of the last clause, *oseh shalom bimromav*, in the paragraph following the Amidah (the core prayer of Jewish worship, said while standing). It was also added to the last sections of the Full Kaddish prayer and the Mourner's Kaddish prayer.

Rashi reads this verse as a response by Bildad to Job's prior statement (23:4): "I would lay my case before God, I would fill my mouth with arguments." For Rashi, God has two eloquent spokespeople to present the Divine case: "dominion" stands for the angel Michael and "fear" stands for the angel Gabriel. Thus Bildad asks Job, "Do you think that you could stand up to either of them?"

Rashi explains the "peace in the high places" as the time when the constellations appear. Since each does not see the one before it, it thinks that it was the first and is hence not jealous of the others. He also suggests that it could mean that God is able to mix fire and water together "in the high places" without the water extinguishing the fire.

Ibn Ezra explains that "dominion" and "fear" are the means by which "God establishes peace in the high places." No war exists on high. Only good is found there. Evil is found below on earth. For Gersonides, "dominion" is a matter of control and "fear" is a matter of awe. God uses them to set the arrays of heaven so that they move continually. By their movements, God is able to affect the world.

25:3 Can God's legions be counted? Upon whom does the divine light not shine?

G'dud is the singular form of *g'dudav* (literally, "His legions"). In Modern Hebrew, it means "battalion." We have rendered the whole verse without gendered possessives. Since the sun is always shining somewhere, it seems that Bildad also believes that God's light shines on everyone.

> 25:4 How can a person be justified before God? How can one born of woman be innocent?

The surprisingly implicit message in this verse is that human beings are evil by nature. Such a view of humans can be used as a means of justifying God's actions and as an attempt to solve the problem of evil. That problem asks how can a good God permit evil and why do the innocent suffer. If no one is innocent, then what is seen as evil, even suffering, can be seen as an appropriate punishment.

Rashi reads this verse as Bildad's response to Job's earlier statement (23:10), "For God knows the path that I take. God has tested me. I came out like gold."

> 25:5 If the moon is not bright, nor the stars clear in God's sight.

To make sense of this verse, it has to be connected to the verse that follows. Together, they both continue the notion that God is somehow praised if the human being is demeaned. The Targum expands the meaning of the verse in its translation: "Until the waning of the moon in the east, the sun does not shine, and the stars are not clear before God." In this verse, there is a strain resonant of the *Unetaneh Tokef* prayer said on the High Holidays—even the angels or heavenly beings are not pure in God's sight. All creation, including the moon and stars, pale before God's perfection.

> 25:6 How much less a human who is but a maggot and the child of humankind who is but a worm.

This is a very negative statement about the imperfection of creation, whether it is the heavenly orbs or earthly humans. Such statements imply a question infrequently asked: If God is such a bad creator, and God's handiwork is so rotten, then why should God be praised and revered?

The Targum adds *d'b'chayo* (in his life) after *enosh* (human) and also adds *d'bmototoye* (in his death) after *bar enosh* (literally, "son of man," which we have translated gender-free as "child of humankind"). This is reminiscent of a prayer said during the High Holidays. It is found at the end of the personal Amidah in the Yom Kippur Maariv (evening) service: My God, before I was formed I was unworthy and now that I have been formed, it is as if I had not been formed. I am dust in my life and will surely be so in my death. Behold—before You I am like a vessel filled with shame and humiliation. May it be Your will Adonai, my God and God of my ancestors, that I not sin anymore. And what I have sinned before You, may You cleanse with Your abundant mercy, but not through suffering or serious illness.

FULL KADDISH

One of numerous recitations of the Kaddish prayer, this formulaic affirmation of God is used to mark the separation of major sections of liturgy during a worship service.

MOURNER'S KADDISH

This version of Kaddish is recited by those in mourning or observing the anniversary of the death of a loved one (called a *yahrzeit* by Ashkenazi Jews), as well as the during the *Yizkor* memorial service (which is part of holiday liturgy).

MICHAEL

An archangel, he is seen as the field commander of God's army.

GABRIEL

Angel who serves as messenger for God.

Chapter 26

26:1 Job then replied,

26:2 How you have helped that one who is powerless. How you have saved the one who is weak.

THE BITTER SARCASM OF this verse is manifest. Instead of defending Job who is weak, Bildad chose to defend God who is all-powerful.

26:3 How you have advised the one without wisdom. How you have taught prudence to the many.

While the Targum translates the first clause literally, it adds *v'damai lach* (do you imagine) before translating the second clause. It translates *tushiya* as *chuchmata* (wisdom) and *lawrov* as *l'sugaa* (much, frequently).

For Gersonides, *tushiya* is a philosophical term that refers to "the divine order and pattern of those things that exist." He believes Job is criticizing his friends for not teaching this.

26:4 Who told you these words? Whose breath came out of you?

The word *neshamah* (usually translated as "soul" or "spirit") can also mean "breath." Job is alluding to the fact that God created humans by breathing into them. Therefore, our life breath (soul) comes from God.

For Gersonides, the use of the word *neshamah* suggests a different question, "Whose soul came out of you?" The question arises for him because he contends that new ideas give a person a new soul. Thus, the person who teaches new ideas gives the receiver of those new ideas a new soul since the soul is changed by the study of ideas and, as a result, the soul and the newly apprehended ideas become a new entity.

26:5 The spirits of the dead whirl around, those beneath the waters and those who dwell therein.

The Targum understands *refa'im* as those (dead) men whose bodies have become *mizmazmin* (softened through the process of decay). However, they will be healed (at the time of resurrection) as will those beneath water and those who inhabit the depths.

Since Rashi derives the word *refa'im* from the root *raysh-pay-hay* (to weaken, soften), he suggests that Gehinnom (hell) softens people. Thus, he takes *y'cholalu* as a reference to the seven circles of hell. For him, the last clause refers to the utter depths of the water.

> 26:6 Sheol lies naked before God. Destruction is bereft of cover.

In striking terms, Job says that nothing is hidden from God. Moreover, nothing is hidden from humankind. Whether Sheol is understood as death or the grave or the underworld, it is the ultimate reality for the human even as humans avoid thinking about it. All that lives ultimately dies. One might want to avert one's eyes, just as one might avert one's eyes in order to avoid gazing at a naked person. But whether we look or not, it makes no difference in the end. We die.

For Rashi, Sheol is naked so that God may see and know all that is in it.

For Gersonides, Sheol is the lowest place on earth. It is described as "naked" as a metaphorical way of saying that God's power reaches even there. The deepest depths cannot prevent the heavenly bodies from having their effect. The place is also called "destruction" since it lacks perfection, a result of being so far from the heavenly bodies. Death and destruction correspond to the lack of a form and perfection.

> 26:7 God stretches the north over the void. God suspends the earth over nothingness.

This verse intentionally alludes to the notion of *tohu v'vohu* (without form and void) from Genesis 1:2. As a parallel to "nothingness," we have rendered *tohu* as "void."

> 26:8 God ties up the waters in God's thick clouds and yet the clouds are not split between them.

The author presents the reader with a poetic image of God making a bag of the clouds, pouring the water which will become rain into them. Yet, even so, the evanescent clouds are able to hold water.

> 26:9 God covers the face of the full moon, spreading the clouds over it.

The Targum translates the word *ceeseh* as *ametitah* (thick darkness). But it also relates it to "throne" as it renders the first clause: "God joins together in thick darkness which comes from God's throne." The Targum reads the second clause as "So that the angels may not see how God spreads out the divine canopy over the clouds of divine glory."

> 26:10 God set the horizon on the face of the waters at the point where the light meets the darkness.

The author paints a striking image and assigns it to God as the Creator. The image in our verse is clear: at sea, one can look in every direction toward the horizon. For the ancients, this marked as far as the light could be seen.

> 26:11 The pillars of heaven tremble, shocked by God's rebuke.

Clearly, God is in control of the universe. It responds to God's actions, just as it did at creation. Rashi reads this verse as referring to an early stage of creation when the heavens were inchoate and only became firm and permanent when God rebuked them.

> 26:12 With divine power, God stirs up the sea. Through divine understanding, God smashes Rahab.

With the author's mention of Rahab, the dragon or serpent god of the sea, the author hints at the mythology that preceded the formation of the Hebrew Scriptures. The mention of such a myth clearly provokes the various commentators. The Targum avoids the challenge of acknowledging other gods by translating *rahav* as *gebrayah* (the giants), however undefined they may be.

Rashi connects *raga* (which we have translated "stirs up") to the phrase *oree raga* (literally, "my skin closed up")—which we have translated in this volume as "my skin puckered" (7:5)—to suggest a motion in which God gathered the waters to one place.

Gersonides understands *raga* to mean "rest," that is, God calmed the sea. He thinks that Rahab means that part of the sea that might overflow upon the dry land.

> 26:13 The heavens became bare with God's winds. God's hand pierced the fleeing serpent.

This verse probably continues God's attack on Rahab initiated in the previous verse.

> 26:14 These are only the outer limits of God's ways. We hear only a faint whisper of God. Who can understand God's thunderous power?

This verse is an affirmation of God's power, far beyond human capability and perhaps even comprehension.

Chapter 27

27:1 Job continued his argument:

WE HAVE NOT TRANSLATED the phrase *se'et meshalo* (took up his theme) literally. A literal translation would suggest that Job is telling a story. Since the context suggests that Job is making some kind of formal plea, we have rendered the phrase as "continued his argument."

Rashi reads this verse to mean that the so-called comforters of Job had stopped responding to his challenges and had become silent. He finds support for such a notion in chapter 32 where Elihu rebukes them for not answering Job.

> 27:2 As God lives, who has snatched away justice due me. The Almighty who has embittered my life,

This introductory phrase "as God lives" can be understood to be an oath that Job takes, affirming his position that he has been cheated out of the justice that is due him. Rashi quotes a teaching by Rabbi Joshua (found in *Yalkut Shimoni*, part 2, section 914:27, a collection of rabbinic narrative interpretations), who states that Job served God out of love, since only a person who loved a sovereign ruler would swear by that ruler's life.

> 27:3 As long as I have breath within me, as long as God's spirit rests in my nostrils,

> 27:4 My lips will not speak malice nor will my tongue utter deceit.

Job continues the oath he initiated in 27:2.

> 27:5 I will never declare you to be in the right. Even if I die, I won't give up my own innocence.

It should be noted that *atzdeek etchem* is a legal term ("to acquit you" or "declare you to be in the right") as in *lo aseer tumati mimeni* (I won't give up my own innocence). Although the last clause is rendered in negative terms, its meaning is clear. Job affirms his innocence. There's word play in this verse with the word *aseer* back to 27:2. Job swears by God who took or removed justice from him that he will never let go of his own innocence. Even if God gave up on Job, Job refuses to give up on himself.

> 27:6 I will hold fast to my own righteousness and will not let go.
> As long as I live, my heart will not reproach me.

Job is convinced that he is right. He rejects any argument that would undermine his innocence. For Rashi, the second phrase is an indication that Job has examined his entire life in order to be certain of his own virtue.

> 27:7 May my enemy be as one [judged] guilty and the one who would rise against me be as a transgressor.

Job's statement reads like a legal brief so we translated *c'rasha* as "one [judged] guilty," adding "judged" for clarity.

> 27:8 What hope does the godless [person] have [that] one will profit when God takes away one's life?

Translating *chanef* (godless) by the Latin loanword *delator* (informer), the Targum offers the entire verse as "What hope does an informer have that he will amass money on the basis of falsehood when God will cast off his soul?" For Rashi, the verse embodies Job's question to his "comforters": Why should I become wicked and a thief, knowing the end of anyone who steals money?

> 27:9 Will God hear [that] one's cry, when trouble comes upon [that] one?

"[That] one" refers to the godless person of the previous verse. We have translated it this way to avoid any gender specificity. Nevertheless, this identification poses a logical problem in the verse. We would expect Job's "comforters" to believe that God does not answer sinners. But if Job believes such, then how does he deal with God not answering him?

By adding the word *ephshar* (is it possible) at the beginning of verse, the Targum stresses the theological problem: "Is it possible that God will receive his [the godless person's] complaint when trouble comes to him [the godless]?"

> 27:10 Will that one delight in the Almighty? Will God call upon that one at all times?

Rashi sees this verse as a kind of emphasis by repetition, the repetition of questions about the godless person. God will no more answer the cry of the godless than the godless will delight in God.

> 27:11 I will teach you with God's help. I will not hide what is with the Almighty.

It is unclear whether Job will teach by divine help or whether Job will teach his understanding of God. The Targum's translation suggests the former. Rashi assumes the latter.

> 27:12 You have all seen this; why then do you murmur meaninglessly?

The challenge of translating this verse is to convey in English the intended various meanings of the noun *hevel*: "vapor, breath," that is, something evanescent. That sense of something transitory and meaningless is suggested by the beginning words of the book of Ecclesiastes (1:2b): *hevel havalim*, often translated as "vanity of vanities" which we render as "It's all useless. Everything is useless."

> 27:13 This is the portion that the wicked will receive from God. This is the inheritance which the violent will receive from the Almighty.

This verse introduces the punishments awaiting the wicked which will then be described in the remainder of the chapter. The use of the word *chelek* (portion) with the word *eem* (with) in the first clause suggests a financial arrangement: the "portion" is on deposit with God. As sure as God is, the wicked will get it back—and with interest. The second clause parallels the first. Without doubt, "the violent will receive their inheritance."

> 27:14 Were the children of the wicked to be many, their fate would be the sword. [Were they to survive the sword,] the offspring of the wicked would never have enough food.

We have added a parenthetical statement to the second clause to clarify the intention of the author. We have also translated the pronoun "his" as "the wicked" in order to avoid any gender specificity.

It should be noted that the punishment fated for the wicked occurs in this world and in this life. War and famine will destroy any hope that the children of the wicked will survive their wicked parent. For Rashi, the first clause of this verse explains the last clause of the next verse. The children of the wicked will have such terrible suffering and illnesses that their surviving spouses will be happy when they die and will not weep.

> 27:15 Those who escape will be buried by the plague. Their surviving spouses will not weep for them.

The word *bamavet* is difficult to translate in this verse. Literally, it means "by death." Were that the specific meaning here, the phrase in which it appears would suggest something so obvious that it need not be said. If someone is dead, that person needs to be buried. Since *mavet* (death) can also mean "an epidemic" or "plague" that leads to death, we have translated it by the latter word.

> 27:16 Although the wicked may heap up silver like dust and prepare one's clothing like clay,
>
> 27:17 The wicked may prepare it, but the righteous will wear it. As for the silver of the wicked, the innocent will divide it.

These verses have to be read together. Whatever the wicked amass will be taken. One may assume that the comparison to clay is to suggest that the wicked person has so many suits of clothing that it is as if such clothing were as easy to acquire as clay.

For Rashi, the subject of the verb "divide" is God. So he understands the last clause to mean that "God will allot the silver of the wicked to the innocent." In the last clause, Gersonides sees the innocent person taking control of the wealth of the wicked and spending it as the innocent person sees fit.

> 27:18 The wicked has built a house like that of a moth and like a booth that a guard might make.

The structure that the author of Job describes is temporary. It lacks permanence. As a result, it will soon be destroyed. According to the primitive entomology of the Rabbis and the writer of the Targum, the "moth" was thought to build its nest in decayed matter. The process of development of egg to cocoon to moth was not fully understood. Even if incomplete or unsophisticated in their understanding, the ancients perceived some connection of moths to decayed matter.

> 27:19 One may lie down rich but it [the wealth of the person] will not be available. One opens one's eyes and it disappears.

The literal meaning of the first two words of the first clause, *asheer yishcav*, is "a rich man may lie down." The literal meaning of the last two words of the first clause, *v'lo ye'aseph*, is "and will not be gathered." It is our assumption that it is the wealth of the rich person that will not be gathered.

The three words of the second clause *aynav pakach v'aynenu* can be literally translated as "his eyes he opens and is not." It is not clear whose eyes are opened and does not exist. It is our supposition that it is the eyes of the rich person which have been opened and it is that person's wealth that has disappeared.

> 27:20 Terrors sweep over the individual like a flood. A storm snatches the person away at night.

Again, the wicked are warned of future punishments. The previous verse warned of a loss of money. This verse warns of a loss of mental health.

> 27:21 The east wind carries one off and that person is gone. It sweeps one away from one's place.

Now the wicked person faces a physical attack. The very air that the wicked breathes can turn into a wind—a wind that can carry the wicked to death.

> 27:22 Merciless, it hurls itself upon the wicked. From its power, the wicked would escape.

As with some of the previous verses, it is easier to translate the individual words in the verse than the entire verse. The first word in the Hebrew text, *v'yashlaych*, is from the root *shin-lamed-caph* (to cast). This form usually has an object. None is given in this verse. We have assumed "itself" as the object. The preposition *alav* (literally, upon him) is given. To make it gender neutral, we have translated *v'lo yachmol* (literally, "he/it will have no pity") as "merciless" and we have placed it at the beginning of the first clause.

The three words of the second clause *me-yado*, *ba-ruach*, and *yevrach* are easy to translate individually but they are difficult to put together in a meaningful way. The last is the most clear. It means "he will escape, he will flee." The first word, *me-yado* (literally, "from his hand"), can also mean "from his/its power." One might think that the cantillation mark, that acts as a grammatical indicator of a clause, may be in the wrong place. Instead of ending the first clause at *yachmol*, it should have ended at *me-yado*. This would make the last phrase, "it has no mercy from its power." If one wants to retain the present word order, then *yevrach . . . me-yado* could mean "it will escape from its power." The problem then becomes how to translate *ba-ruach* (literally, "with the wind" or "by the wind").

Ruach, however, can mean numerous other things: "wind, breeze, breath, spirit, sense, mind, or intellectual frame of mind." Our rendering,

"Foolishly, the wicked would escape" is our attempt to deal with the three words.

> 27:23 People [mockingly] clap their hands and hiss at the evil person wherever is that person.

It is clear that mockery is being described here. However, what might constitute such an act then is most probably different from what might constitute an act of mockery today. In this verse, the author indicates that hands are clapped as an act of derision, rather than as an act of approbation as would be the case today. To clarify, we have added the word "mockingly."

The root *shin-raysh-kof* can mean either "to whistle" or "to hiss." Although today whistling might be considered the same as applauding, this most probably was not the case in the ancient world. Thus, we have taken it to mean "hiss."

Moreover, while both verbs are rendered in this verse in the singular imperfect form, the sense of the verse suggests an anonymous subject. We have, therefore, added "people" as the subject of the verbs.

According to Rashi, those who clap their hands in mockery are those who knew the wicked person when that person enjoyed good fortune and now see that same person disgraced.

Chapter 28

> 28:1 There is a mine for silver and a place where gold is refined.

OUR AUTHOR HAS JOB present a picture of the prized elements of the natural world so that he may compare them to what is the most precious of all: wisdom.

The Targum reads *motza* (which we translate "mine") as "exit, spring," that is, endpoint or exit point. Rashi explains Job's words this way: Why should I be wicked? If for the sake of silver and gold, these have an end. Wisdom has no end and is therefore more precious than anything else. Rashi reasons that one's wealth diminishes eventually. But wisdom never runs out.

> 28:2 Iron is taken from the dust and copper smelted from rocks.

This appears to be a lesson in earth science. But as the metaphor develops in the coming verses, it is clear the author is talking about wisdom and the propensity of the individual to do evil.

> 28:3 Going beyond the dark, past any limit, one seeks ore in completely dark places.

We continue to have a description of mining—an activity that is far from the sun and fraught with danger.

> 28:4 Far from any habitation, in a place forgotten by the passerby, the miner opens a shaft and there, far from other people, [the miner] dangles, swinging to and fro.

While this is a verse about the miner, it is really a verse about an evildoer. But the point of the verse is to demonstrate the danger in both mining and the propagation of evil. It is also possible that verses one through eleven in this chapter set up an extended metaphor which comes to a climax in verse 12. People work hard to access natural resources through mining. Thus, mining is a task that people set themselves to singlehandedly, with great effort and willing to endure great hardship. Job asks the question: are we willing to work as hard to seek wisdom? Can precious ores and gems be easier to come by than what is of greater value, that is, understanding?

> 28:5 Earth, from which food comes, is changed in its depths as if by fire.

Mining has revealed to us another mystery of nature. What seems to be normal on the surface is different at the subterranean depths. The Targum sees something more than a change in nature in the depths of the earth. According to the Targum, *Gehinnom* is where the cold of snow is changed to the heat of fire.

> 28:6 Its stones contain sapphires and gold dust is found there.

It is not clear whether the author meant to say that sapphires and gold were to be found in the same place or that they could be found in the various places where mining takes place. But the intent is the same. If you mine the earth, you can find sapphires and gold.

> 28:7 No bird of prey knows its path. No raptor's eye has glimpsed it.

The treasures revealed by mining cannot be seen from above—from the heavens. We only learn about them when workers go down into the depths of earth and bring them up.

> 28:8 No proud beasts tread upon it. No lion roams there.

The author has moved on from discussing birds in the sky and is now talking about land animals. According to the author of Job, neither birds nor animals have the ability to see into the treasures of the earth. Insights are a human quality.

> 28:9 Humans attack the flinty rock. They uproot mountains.

In this verse, we hear of the power and wonder of mining once again. Even in the ancient world, miners were able to manipulate nature. In order to be gender neutral, we have translated this verse in the plural.

Ibn Ezra argues that the verse refers to God, not humans. It is only God who can uproot mountains and split rivers with stones and flint.

> 28:10 They cut galleries in the mines and their eyes see anything of value.

Although *ye'orim* could be translated as "channels" and *batzurot* as "rocks," we adapt the translation of *batzurot ye'orim bekaya* as "They cut galleries in the mines." Such a gender-neutral translation seems to us to better reflect the so-called "wonders of mining."

> 28:11 They plug up the trickles of water, so they can bring into light whatever is hidden.

The author returns to another aspect of mining. In this verse, the author deals with the flow of groundwater, which might impede further exploration. Again, we have translated this verse in the plural to avoid any gender specificity.

> 28:12 But wisdom, where is it to be found? And where is the place of understanding?

The author has regaled the reader with visions of treasures hidden out of sight, deep in dark and dangerous mines. Yet, they can be brought to the surface to be enjoyed. The author now directs the attention of the reader to the most precious of all commodities: wisdom. But wisdom is not only hidden from the eyes of mortals, it is also hidden from their minds. This is an important verse for the entire book since it serves the author as a rhetorical shift in which the author focuses on his/her main topic. This chapter is also one which has been used by some scholars to define Job as part of what is called Wisdom Literature, that is, the experience of the human rather than revelation from a divine source as the Torah is considered.

> 28:13 Mortals do not know its value nor is it found in the land of the living.

To provide readers with a gender-free translation we have rendered *enosh* (man, human) as "mortal" which also fits the context of the verse better.

> 28:14 The deep says, "It is not in me." The sea says, "It is not with me."

While one might assume that wisdom can be found somewhere—perhaps in the depths of the sea—it is not someplace that can be located. According to Rashi, were you to go ask divers who go down to the depths to bring up pearls and sunken silver and gold, they would answer that wisdom is not to be found in the deep. For him, the second clause suggests that were you to ask merchants who sail the seas on business, they would answer that wisdom—unlike merchandise—cannot be purchased.

> 28:15 It cannot be gotten for gold nor can [enough] silver be weighed out for its price.

Wisdom cannot be purchased. No amount of money or jewels is adequate to buy it. The implication is that the gold described in this verse is of exceptional value.

> 28:16 It cannot be acquired by the gold of Ophir nor by expensive onyx or sapphires.

While the intent of this verse is the same as the one that precedes it, the author uses a different word for gold in this verse: *cetem*. The author also references a legendary place for gold: Ophir. It seems that Ophir was like El Dorado, the legendary place of gold in the Americas.

> 28:17 Neither gold nor glass compare to it. Nor can vessels of gold be exchanged for it.

Glass is common and generally inexpensive today. In ancient times, glass was uncommon and rather precious. Hence, the author could use "gold" or "glass" together as things which could not be compared to wisdom.

By translating *zechuchit* (glass) as *espacklariah* (window glass), the Targum actually increases the value of the "glass" in this verse. It is not a mere ornament. Rather, it is something larger and more expensive.

> 28:18 Corals and black crystal need not be mentioned, for the price of wisdom is beyond pearls.

The intent of the author to continue the comparison between precious jewels and wisdom is clear.

> 28:19 The topaz of Ethiopia cannot equal it. It cannot be acquired with pure gold.

More jewels are brought forward by the author to compare to wisdom.

> 28:20 Where does wisdom come from? Where is the place of understanding?

This perennial question is placed by the author into Job's mouth: Does our ability to reason and understand come from nature or from another source? Is it something that is intrinsic to our being human or is it something that we have received as a gift? In the comment on subsequent verses, we will see that rabbinic Judaism understood "wisdom" as "Torah."

> 28:21 It is hidden from the eyes of all that lives. It is concealed even from the birds of the sky.

Reflecting the poetic structure of this chapter with repetitions and echoes, this verse seems to be an echo of 28:7. This verse is not an answer to the questions asked in the previous verse, but it is does offer some insight.

> 28:22 Destruction and death say, "We have only heard a rumor of it with our ears."

The eternality of wisdom might be used to mitigate the limitations and senselessness of destruction and death. In this verse that personifies destruction and death, these forces have heard clearly of wisdom. Unfortunately, the bloody corridors of human history silently attest that humankind has barely heard of wisdom.

> 28:23 Only God understands its way and only God knows its place.

It is clear that the author is referring to wisdom in this verse.

> 28:24 For God gazes to the ends of the earth and sees all that is beneath the heavens.

This is a statement about God's omniscience. It is in contrast to 28:7, 21. Only God sees all.

> 28:25 God weighed out the wind and set a measure for the water.

In poetic terms, this verse describes creation. There is something astounding in the imagery—weighing the wind! Setting a measure for the waters which seem infinite when we look at the sea: this is a strong image of God's power.

> 28:26 God set a limit for the rain and a path for the thunderstorm.

This verse once again presents readers with the notion that all nature is controlled by God.

> 28:27 Then God saw it [wisdom] and proclaimed it. God established it and searched it out.

> 28:28 God said to humanity: "Behold, the fear of God is wisdom and to turn from evil is understanding."

This verse may be the shortest and most profound statement of the true meaning of religion. "Fear" may be too strong of a word. Jewish tradition tends to understand *yeerah* more as "awe" than "fear." The term *yeerat shamayim* (literally, "fear of Heaven") came to mean the measure of the *mitzvah* (sacred instruction) performance. In other words, fear of heaven is demonstrated through the observance of ritual and ethical commandments. However, fear of God in the Bible means basic morality. Rashi notes that there can be no true wisdom without fear of God.

Chapter 29

29:1 Job now continued his speech:

29:2 Would that I could be again as in the months gone by, in the days when God watched over me.

Were we to read this verse in light of Gersonides' philosophical approach to the text, we might read these words as the statement of one who once believed in a simpler approach to life and God. But, as it stands, this verse is a simple statement that reflects Job's hope for restored faith in God. Rashi suggests that it is merely Job's wish for his past well-being.

29:3 When God's lamp shone over my head and I walked through the darkness by divine light.

The author has provided readers with a striking image of Job's current darkness and despair. God's light had previously illumined Job's path in life. Job's life was filled with divine light.

29:4 As I was in the days of my youth, when God's protection was over my tent.

This verse continues Job's wistfulness, as expressed in the previous verses.

29:5 When the Almighty was still with me and my children were around me.

When Job was surrounded by his children and felt that he could feel God's presence, he felt comfortable and secure. This was a time before the horrible events befell Job.

29:6 When my steps were washed with cream and the rock poured out streams of oil for me.

To the modern reader, "steps washed with cream" would put the walker in jeopardy of slipping and falling. It would hardly be something fondly remembered in the past or hoped for in the future. Yet, for the writer—and the presumed reader—such a slippery situation was clearly a positive notion. Perhaps the notion of steps covered in rose petals or glittering with gold can provide a more modern image. It may be that in the ancient past, "streams of oil" provided some protection from the sun on long journeys. And we know from other contexts that oil is a sign of wealth, comfort, and protection. Oil was made by pressing olives between rocks. This image may be connected to Psalm 81:17. We might say "the streets were paved with gold" and the connotation is that one doesn't have to work for what one gets. Similarly here, butter at your feet or oil from a rock means one doesn't have to press the olives or milk the goats to be fed.

> 29:7 When I went to the gate of the city, when I prepared my place in the plaza.

By *shaar* (gate), the writer and the intended reader would understand "the place of judgment" as the place where people conducted the city's business. By *rechov*, which comes from the root meaning enlarge or widen, the writer and the reader would understand a parallel to "gate," a place where people conducted business and the authorities leveled judgments. Some might translate *rechov* in this context as an "open plaza," a nuance we tried to capture with simply "the plaza."

> 29:8 Young people saw me and got out of the way. Old people rose up and stood [in my presence].

Nechba'u literally means "hid themselves." Why would young people, particularly men as the text specifies, hide? Perhaps they were afraid of him. If the first clause is the parallel of the second, then the young men had previously shown some kind of deference to Job. And the older people, who are deserving of respect, gave their respect to Job instead.

> 29:9 Princes stopped speaking and covered their mouths with their hands.

In the context of the time in which the author lives, Job is reflecting on the respect he previously commanded. No one, not even those in power, spoke in his presence.

> 29:10 The voices of nobles were silenced. Their tongues stuck to the roof of their mouths.

This verse uses the same verb *nechba'u* as used in 29:8. In this case, we have provided a different idiomatic translation (silenced) since the referent (voices of nobles) is different.

> 29:11 Those who heard of me declared me fortunate. Those who saw me spoke well of me.

We have translated the subject of this verse in the plural to avoid any gender specificity. And again, we have tried to replicate the sentiment of the author idiomatically since "the ear that heard declared me fortunate and the eye that saw summoned me" is harder to understand. The author is attempting to suggest that anyone who had heard of Job considered him to be fortunate (and perhaps they were envious of him) and anyone that saw him wanted to be close to him (hoping that Job could be of help or that his luck might "rub off" on them).

> 29:12 Because I rescued the poor who cried out for aid and the orphan who had no one else to be of help.

Now we better understand why people wanted to be close to Job. He had a reputation of being philanthropic, especially to the economically downtrodden. This is related to questions of Job's righteousness that have been raised before. In particular, see Job 22:6–9.

> 29:13 The person about to die would bless me and I made the widow's heart sing for joy.

This verse suggests an affluent former life in which Job promised to provide support to the families of those about to die, as well as the families of those who had already died.

> 29:14 I put on righteousness as a robe and it clothed me. Justice was my robe and my headband.

Job unabashedly sings praises of himself in the past. There's an echo here of Isaiah 61:10. Rashi takes the verse to mean that Job pursued righteousness and justice with such zeal that they became associated with him as something worn on the body, whether jewelry or an article of clothing. As Ibn Ezra suggests, perhaps these articles were chosen by the author since they are visible to onlookers, as was Job's commitment to righteousness and justice.

> 29:15 I was eyes to the blind and feet to the lame.

Job recalls his past efforts to be helpful to the weak and those who had no one else to help.

> 29:16 I was parent to the poor and I took up the cause of the stranger.

Continuing his recital of his past virtues, Job tells his comforters that he had provided for the poor and, devoted to justice, he defended people he did not know.

> 29:17 I smashed the fangs of the wicked and snatched prey from their teeth.

This is translated in the plural to avoid any gender specificity. As Gersonides suggests, this is a metaphor for Job's ability to subdue the wicked and make them return what they have stolen from the innocent.

> 29:18 I thought that I would die at home. My days will be as many as those of the phoenix.

Rashi explains that the verse should be understood as Job saying, "I said to myself, due to my proper behavior, when I die, my house and my household will be cared for." He explains the second clause as a reference to the bird that will never die because it tasted of the fruit of the Tree of Knowledge. Job thought that he would live as a regenerated young person—and not as an old man.

> 29:19 My roots will spread out to the water and dew will rest all night on my branches.

In this verse, the author changes the image of permanence from a bird—whether real or mythical—to a tree which, when well-watered, will endure.

> 29:20 My honor will be renewed for me and my bow will sprout in my hand.

The meanings of *k'vodee* (literally, "my glory") and *kashti* (my bow) are far clearer than are the metaphors they represent. The first seems to reflect the perception of Job by others. The second is probably a reference to his physical prowess. However, they might both concern Job's physical abilities. Nonetheless, Job believes that both will return to him, irrespective of the suffering that he has endured. For Rashi, this will be a continual process of renewal.

> 29:21 People would listen to me and wait silently for my advice.

People stood in awe of Job. They solicited his advice and followed it. They cared what he had to say. Rashi adds to our understanding of this verse by suggesting that people would wait for the fulfillment of Job's predictions since he was a man of wisdom.

> 29:22 After my words, no one spoke. What I said was absorbed by them.

No one rose to challenge Job's words. Nor did they challenge the advice that he gave. Instead, they listened attentively so that they could understand his words completely.

> 29:23 They waited for me like rain. They gulped down my words like spring rain.

Although the image in *u'vpheehem pa'aru* (literally, "they opened their mouths wide") is clear, it is still difficult to render the phrase in idiomatic English. We have chosen to understand it as "they gulped down." The word *malkosh* (spring rain) may be familiar to readers because of its liturgical use (in the second paragraph of the *Shema* prayer, quoting Deuteronomy 11:14). Rashi offers another understanding of *malkosh*. He suggests that "for spring rain" means "for a long time"—they began speaking for a long time because they had been silent for a long time since they were eager to hear Job's words.

> 29:24 Were I to laugh at them, they would not believe it. The light of my face would not cast them down.

Why would Job have laughed at the people before him? One might hope that "the light of . . . [Job's] face" would elevate and encourage his onlookers. What then would be the point of such a "light" not "cast[ing] them down?"

For the Targum, the entire verse can be read as "I laughed for their sake. Nevertheless, they would not believe it and did not look up at the beauty in my face."

Rashi explains what the people "would not believe." It seems that although Job was an important person, the people did not believe he was still willing to rejoice with them. As Rashi continues, nonetheless, the people were afraid to approach Job and share their concerns with him.

Ibn Ezra suggests that it is well known that a ruler's levity can remove awe from him or her. Yet, Ibn Ezra argues that even though Job joked with the people, they never lost their reverence for him.

Bearing in mind the comments of Rashi and Ibn Ezra, we suggest the translation could be "Although I might joke with them, they would not take it seriously. Respect for me never diminished."

> 29:25 I chose their way and I sat as chief. I dwelt as a ruler among troops. I was like one who comforts mourners.

In this verse, one may wonder why compassion is mentioned among the indications of power. Nonetheless, it is clear that Job previously occupied an important role in the community.

Rashi says that Job was so important that he was able to tell people what to do and where to go. For Rashi, the second clause indicated that Job was honored with the best seat at any festive gathering.

THE PHOENIX

A mythical bird that lives for a thousand years, dies, and is later resurrected from its ashes.

Chapter 30

> 30:1 Now I am mocked by people younger than me, whose parents I would not have hired to tend my herd dogs.

JOB BEMOANS HIS LOSS of status. Once he was important. People hung on his words. Now young people of the lowest social status treat him with contempt. Age has provided him no protection for his loss of status. To make for a better idiomatic translation, we have translated *ma'astee* (I rejected) as "I would not have hired" and have added "to tend" to explain the reasons why such persons might have been hired.

> 30:2 What do I need with the strength of their hands, people whose vigor has vanished?

It is unclear to whom Job is referring in this verse (and the following verses). It does not seem that Job is referring to the young people who mock him in the previous verse, since their vigor has not diminished. One may doubt that Job refers to their parents, whom Job would not have hired for the lowest kind of job. Perhaps Job is thinking of his former servants, who previously did whatever he asked of them and who are now enfeebled by age. The verse contains the word *celach*, which appears twice in Job and nowhere else in the Bible. See Job 5:26, translated there as "ripe old age" and here as "vigor."

> 30:3 Emaciated from want and famine, they gnaw the dust in the desolate waste at twilight.

Job refers to those who attempt to assuage the pangs of hunger by chewing clods of earth.

> 30:4 Among the bushes, they pluck salt-wort and the root of the broom tree was their food.

In their hunger, the people are forced to eat the least nutritious plants, plants that no one else is willing to eat.

> 30:5 Driven away from other people, they are yelled at as if they were thieves.

In terms of its context, we have taken "*gev*" (usually translated as "back" or "inner self" or even "community") to mean "other people" since it is clear that they are not treated as members of the community. Unfortunately, this is how some poor people were treated—and are still treated.

Rashi is more precise as to the lot of these unfortunate individuals: they will be driven away from the city. Ibn Ezra reads the word *gev* to mean "among," that is, "they will be driven out from among people." He understands the verse to mean that these people have deficiencies. As a result, they are driven away from the people. The others yell, "Thief!" at them.

> 30:6 They live in depressions, in dry stream beds, amid rocks, and in holes in the ground.

These unfortunate individuals, mentioned in previous verses, have no homes. Even where they take refuge, their lives are at risk. The *nachalim* (stream beds) or *wadis* can fill up at any cloudburst, driving out those who make their homes there. Even worse, they could drown.

> 30:7 They bray between the bushes. They gather among the weeds.

These folks are no longer regarded as human. They are considered animals. They bray like donkeys. They gather together like wild animals.

> 30:8 Worthless people, nobodies, they were thrown out of the land.

It has been unfortunately common in history not to see the other as a human being. These people, as referenced in previous verses, are further denigrated. They are less than human, so much so, that they are not even worthy of being given a name. While there is some underlying lack of clarity as to whom the verse is referring, it does describe them as the lowest of the low so that Job in verse 9 can share how he is more scorned and disparaged than they are.

> 30:9 Now I am their mocking song and I have become their byword.

In this verse, Job now complains that he had been somebody while others were nobodies. Now he has become a nobody and those he had held in low repute now sing songs that mock him. What a downfall! For the writer of the book of Job, this is another example of Job suffering without reason. Perhaps to the modern reader, Job's experience, as expressed in this verse, is reflective of the notion that "what goes around comes around."

> 30:10 They abhor me. They keep their distance from me. Yet, they don't hesitate to spit in my face.

The author presents the reader with a telling description of being scorned. The people whom Job disparaged have distanced themselves from him in almost every sense. The only time that they approach him is to spit on him.

> 30:11 God has let my bowstring go slack. Yet God afflicts me. They behave without restraint in my presence.

In the first clause, a taut bowstring can be used as a means of defense. However, a loose bowstring leaves the archer (i.e., Job) defenseless against enemies. As a result, Job feels that God has permitted his enemies to threaten and attack him. The second clause would literally be translated as "They cast away bridle (*resen*) from before me."

> 30:12 The rabble rise up on the right. They trapped my feet. They pile their mounds of mischief around me.

This verse presents the reader with a picture of what Job is now up against. The situation has become dire.

> 30:13 They have ripped up my path. They have succeeded in destroying me, even without any help.

Again, Job complains that those who oppose him have been able to do whatever they want to keep him from pursuing his purposes. According to Rashi, the situation is even worse, since he contends that the verse refers to otherwise good people who have no regard for Job.

> 30:14 They come on as [if they were entering] through a wide breach. They roll around beneath the ruins.

Job's enemies get to him easily. He has no defense at all. The Targum explains the meaning of the verse by rendering it as "They came with the force of boulders moved to form a lane in the sea. They rolled around with great tumult." Rashi takes *c'pheretz rachav* (through a wide breach), to suggest a fence about which Job's opponents passed through in order to shame him. He understands the last clause to mean that those opponents move against Job secretly to prevent him from escaping from them.

For Ibn Ezra, this verse indicates that all manner of troubles came upon Job in a desolate place where no one could help him. Gersonides says that Job's troubles came suddenly upon him, like a flood bursting through a gap in a fence.

> 30:15 Terror turns upon me. Like the wind, it blows away my dignity. Whatever could save me moves away like a cloud.

This verse suggests that Job has no hope of salvation.

> 30:16 Now my soul is poured out upon me. Days of suffering have taken hold of me.

This idiom appears elsewhere in the Bible: 1 Samuel 1:15, Psalm 42:5 (both of which may be familiar to readers from the High Holiday liturgy), as well as in Lamentations 2:12. The author places "soul" and "poured out" together to suggest to the reader that Job's soul, that is, his life, is like a finite amount of liquid that is gradually running out from a container which will be cast away when it is empty. Job, therefore, is aware that he is close to death.

> 30:17 My bones feel pierced at night. My sinews never sleep.

Anyone who has endured the kind of pain that Job describes knows precisely what the author intends. Two different kinds of pain are described: needle-like stabs which move about and a constant unchanging pain that doesn't abate. Both contribute to making the sufferer unable to sleep. The word *orkai* appears only here in the Bible. It is meant to parallel *atzmai* (my bones) and thus refers to some other bodily part which we have translated as sinews.

> 30:18 Because of [its] great power, my clothing can't be recognized. It holds on tight to the collar of my shirt.

This is obviously not an easily understood verse. What or who possesses "great power"? What or who "holds on tight"? Is it God? Perhaps it is Job's great suffering. The context, as indicated by the preceding verses, suggests the latter. One may wonder why, whether the cause is divine or human, there is an effect on the clothes that Job is wearing.

> 30:19 God has thrown me into mud so that I have become like dust and ashes.

The Targum provides us with two translations of this verse. While the first translation is literal, the second is an interpretation: "They have made it difficult for me, like Adam who was created from mud. I am compared to Abraham who was compared to dust and ashes." (See Genesis 18:22.)

> 30:20 I cry out to you, but you don't answer me. I stand up but you just look at me.

The context makes it clear that it is God to whom Job cries out. Job makes himself visible to God and God sees him but does not seem to care.

> 30:21 You have become cruel to me. You manifest your enmity to me with your mighty hand.

Still suffering, Job continues to complain. In this verse, Job asks the essential question of God's justice: Is God cruel? Is the person who experiences God as cruel wrong?

> 30:22 You pick me up and make me ride on the wind. You toss me about in the thunderstorm.

For Rashi, being given over to the winds has the meaning of being given over to demons. He takes the second clause to mean that Job has been progressively weakened.

> 30:23 I know that you will bring me to death, to the place appointed for all that lives.

Job understands that death awaits him just like it awaits everything that lives.

> 30:24 Surely, no one would stretch out a hand to a ruin and, to one's misfortune, provide a cry for help.

It is not clear what metaphor the author is seeking to communicate to the reader. Who or what is the ruin? To whom does misfortune belong? And who will or will not help or respond to a cry for help?

If the ruin is Job, then perhaps the meaning of the first clause is that no one will stretch out a hand to save him. Or perhaps it means that no one will attack him any further. Perhaps misfortune will then come to the one who tries to help Job? Or maybe misfortune is a reference to what has already occurred to Job. If so, then who is to provide the help or the cry for help?

Because of the lack of clarity in the verse, the Targum offers two different explanations. The first interpretation reads as follows: "Not in anger does God send divine stroke [punishment] at the time of the penitent's pain. God will receive their prayers." The Targum's second interpretation: "Not for Godself will God cover the wound. Rather, God will place a bandage on the cavity (of the wound)." In both cases, it seems that the Targum's interpretation wanders significantly from the Hebrew text.

> 30:25 Did I not weep for the unfortunate? Did not my soul grieve for the poor?

In this verse, Job states that when others suffered, he had compassion for them. Yet now, no one offers to help him. Although he cared for others, no one seems able to care for him.

> 30:26 Yet when I hoped for good, evil came. When I waited for light, darkness came.

As suggested by his statement in the previous verse, Job did all of the right things in his life. Yet, these actions did not prevent him from suffering. Thus, Job denies the notion that all suffering is a punishment for sin. Rashi goes as far as to claim that Job's complaint is that he did not receive an appropriate reward for his good works.

> 30:27 My guts ceaselessly churn. Days of suffering now confront me.

We have translated *mayai* (literally, "my bowels") with the more idiomatic "guts." The suffering that Job has endured does indeed get him in the "gut," as it would any person.

> 30:28 I go about in darkness without the sun. I stand up in the assembly and cry out.

We think that the darkness mentioned here mirrors the curse given in Deuteronomy 28:29: "You will grope at noonday as the blind [person] gropes darkness." Job complains that his suffering impedes his sight as if he were going about in darkness, that is, "without the sun."

> 30:29 I have become the brother to jackals and the companion to ostriches.

The intent of this verse is clear: Job has become like one of the solitary animals that live in the wilderness.

> 30:30 My skin has become dark and peels off me. My bones burn with heat.

Job's suffering now has a physical manifestation. His skin, darkened without the sun, peels off as if he were sunburned.

> 30:31 My harp is set to mourning and my pipe to the sound of weeping.

This chapter concludes with a rather striking image of sadness. Music, which is usually considered the means by which to lift the soul, can, for Job, only reproduce sounds of sorrow.

Chapter 31

> 31:1 I have made a covenant with my eyes not to gaze at a young woman.

ALTHOUGH THE LAST WORD in the verse is *betulah* (virgin), the biological/legal status of the woman does not seem to be intended. This verse is a statement of Job's piety. Of course, Job would not "gaze" licentiously at a married woman. Such self-control would be expected of any pious person. Job, however, exhibits even more self-control. He would not even glance at an unmarried woman. We have, therefore, rendered *betulah* as "young woman."

We have also taken *mah* (usually translated as "what") here in a negative sense, to mean "not" as in *ma ta'eeru* / do not wake (Song of Songs 8:4).

> 31:2 What portion would there be from God above? What inheritance from the Almighty on high?

Job implies that his behaviors should command a reward (and not a punishment). This verse is probably connected to the previous verse. In both cases, Job asks, what could I hope to gain were I to behave that way?

> 31:3 Does not disaster wait for the wicked and misfortune for those who do wrong?

This verse presents the entire challenge of the book of Job and, therefore, may be considered its most important verse: how is it possible that "disaster" may come upon the innocent and "misfortune" plagues those who have done nothing wrong? Job is questioning the views of his "comforters," asking, "is this not true?"

> 31:4 Does God not see my ways? Does God not count my steps?

> 31:5 Had I walked with what is worthless, and my foot sped after what is false,

These verses continue the profound questioning of the previous verse: if good is to be rewarded and evil punished, can it be God does not see Job's behavior? God was counting Job's steps and should have seen whether he walked with what is worthless or his foot sped after what is false.

> 31:6 Would that God might weigh me on an accurate scale that God might know my integrity.

No matter what Job's "comforters" have said to undermine his virtue, Job is certain of it. All Job asks for is a fair trial.

> 31:7 If I ever stepped out off the path [of righteousness], if my heart ever went [astray] after [what] my eyes [have seen], if anything at all ever stuck to my hands,

This verse is the beginning of a conditional statement that should be read with the verse that follows. Because of the nature of the idiomatic expressions in the verse, we have had to add certain words in brackets.

> 31:8 Then let me sow and somebody else eat. Let others uproot what I have planted.

Job is willing to accept punishment that is merited. He objects to receiving punishment that he feels is unwarranted.

> 31:9 If my heart has been tempted by a woman and I have skulked at my neighbor's door,

Like the previous two verses, which form one statement, this verse and the one that follows also form one conditional statement. The use of the word *ishah* (woman) in the first clause suggests a married woman and the "neighbor's door" in the second clause implies adultery with someone close by, perhaps with the wife of a friend.

> 31:10 Let my wife grind for another and let others lie upon her.

While "grind" is a literal translation of the Hebrew, its sexual meaning is resonant in colloquial English, as well. Job is proposing measure for measure. Had he committed adultery with someone else's wife, which he clearly hasn't, then he would accept someone else committing adultery with his wife. This may be offensive to modern readers but it is part of a biblical worldview in which a husband controls his wife's sexuality.

> 31:11 For that would be despicable, an iniquity to be legally punished.

Job continues the notion initiated in previous verses. He admits that such behaviors would be horrible and deserving of punishment. The implication, once again, is that he is innocent.

> 31:12 It is a fire that consumes until all is destroyed. It uproots
> all my produce.

Such acts, as described in previous verses, are destructive of all who are engaged in them. Moreover, they destroy people and things even remotely connected to them.

> 31:13 If I rejected the judgment due to my male or female servants when they had a claim against me,

Another conditional case. Having denied that he committed adultery or acted in any lewd fashion against women, Job now introduces the subject of how he treated his servants. Although he had mastery over them, he asserts that he never took advantage of that power and authority.

> 31:14 What shall I do when God stands as judge against me?
> What shall I answer when God calls me to account?

Although *yakoom* (will arise) and *yifkod* (will remember) are clearly understandable, the context in which they appear suggests specific legal meanings. Here we follow others who understand *yakoom* as "stands as judge" and *yefkod* as "calls to account."

> 31:15 Did God not make others in the belly as God made me?
> Did not the same One fashion us in the womb?

The previous verse suggested a confrontation between God and Job. This verse suggests a comparison between Job and another human being. In order to avoid gender specificity, we have translated the pronoun "him" as "others."

> 31:16 If I had prevented the poor from getting what they wanted,
> if I had caused the eyes of a widow to languish,

This verse is incomplete and should be read with the next two verses.

> 31:17 If I had eaten all of my bread and not shared any with an
> orphan,

Again we read one of Job's rhetorical questions. Job implies that he didn't do anything like this. Therefore, once again, he implies that the suffering he endured is unfair.

> 31:18 Even when I was young, I raised him as would a father.
> From the moment of my birth, I guided her.

Job is speaking in inflated terms to stress his innocence. The "him" probably refers to the orphan of the previous verse. It would seem that the "her" of *anchenah* (guided her) refers to the widow mentioned in verse 16.

> 31:19 If I ever saw someone wandering without clothing or
> some poor person without a garment,

Job continues his claims of virtue. In this verse, he is even more strident in his claims. The wanderer has no claim on him, yet Job is willing to provide such a person with clothing. Even when Job was wealthy, he was concerned with the poor.

> 31:20 If that person's [the wanderer's] body had not blessed me,
> if that person had not been warmed by the fleece from my sheep,

We have rendered *chalatzav* (his loins) as "that person's body" to avoid gender specificity. The two persons—wanderer and poor person—would certainly have blessed Job for his kindness.

> 31:21 Even seeing that I had support in the court, I have never
> raised my hand against an orphan [in a legal matter].

This claim of virtue by Job speaks to a universal situation. Even when Job had wealth and power, when he might have been able to rely on his connections to "fix" a judgment in his favor, he did not do so. Even when dealing with an orphan, who was without wealth or power, Job never acted immorally, although he could have gotten away with it. We switched the order of the verse and translated "gate" as "court" since the town gate was the site of legal judgment in biblical times.

> 31:22 Then let my shoulder fall from my neck joint and let my
> arm be broken at my humerus.

Note the self-cursing of body parts as a technique of assertion seen elsewhere in Scripture, for example, "If I forget thee, O Jerusalem, let my right hand forget its cunning. Let my tongue cleave to the roof of my mouth" (Psalm 137:5, 6).

> 31:23 Fearing God's destruction and in awe of the divine majesty, I could not [act badly].

We have attempted to join the two clauses together by assuming that the meaning of *kee pachad aylay* (literally, "I was afraid"), which we have translated as "fearing," carries over to the second clause. In this way, it relates to *umese'eato* ([and to] the Divine majesty). Since it would not be idiomatic English "to fear majesty," we have used "in awe" in its place. Finally, *lo uchal* (I could not) requires an indication of what "could not" be done. We have added: "act badly."

> 31:24 If I put my trust in gold, if I had said to fine gold, "You are my security."

Like so many verses in the book of Job, the author presents this verse as an answer of sorts. In the previous verse, Job declared that his sense of God's presence had kept him from sin and preserved his innocence. In this verse, Job obliquely declares that he has not been tempted by wealth.

> 31:25 If I had rejoiced because I had great wealth and possessed so much,

This verse is connected directly to the previous verse. It too presumes the answer, "No I did not." We have rendered *v'che cabir matzah yadee* (literally, "and that my hand found much") as "[I] possessed so much."

While Job tries to present himself as righteous, Rashi is not convinced. He argues that Job did not manifest his wealth in the presence of the poor simply to avoid provoking them.

> 31:26 If I had gazed at the sun as it shone on the moon, as it moved in splendor,

Here is another possible sin for which Job might deserve punishment, had he indeed committed such a sin. But he did not do so. Job did not worship the sun or the moon, both objects of veneration at the time in which he lived.

> 31:27 If my heart had been secretly seduced so that my mouth kissed my hand [as an act of worship],

We follow Ibn Ezra who suggests that the kissing of the hand was an act of idolatry. This is a continuing thought, tied to the preceding verse. In both verses, Job is claiming that he did not worship idols.

> 31:28 That indeed would have been a criminal offense, for I would have denied God on high,

Job concludes the argument that he has been making in previous verses by once again saying that had he done so, he would have deserved punishment. But he denies having done so.

> 31:29 If I had rejoiced at the misfortune of someone who hated me, if I had been happy when evil found that person,

Job continues his argument with a different set of hypothetical statements.

> 31:30 I never allowed my mouth to sin by calling out a curse against the [misfortunate] one [who hates me].

This verse clearly refers to the enemy mentioned in the previous verse. We have added words for clarity and to avoid gender specificity.

> 31:31 If my male servants never said, "Would that we had some of his meat for we are not satisfied."

The phrase *me yetain* has a literal meaning of "who will give." It is often used idiomatically to suggest a hope or as a conditional statement, that is, "would that." This is how it is used in this verse. What seems to be intended by the phrase *m'tay ohalee* (literally, "the men of my tent") are the men who work for Job, that is, his male servants. In this verse, Job is claiming that none of his servants complained that they were insufficiently or inadequately fed. Moreover, they were fed with meat, which was clearly more expensive than being fed with grains. Since Job provided so well for his servants, therefore, he should be looked upon as a good employer.

> 31:32 No stranger ever spent the night in the street. I kept my door open to the wanderer.

While we follow others who translate *orach* as wanderer, it could be translated as "way." This would then yield: I kept my door open to "the way." In any case, the clause suggests that Job invited strangers into his home.

> 31:33 If like other people, I hid my sins to conceal my guilt in my heart.

While this may be an unusual way to frame his claim, it is another hypothetical statement that assumes the same conclusion that he has offered in previous verses: "then I would have deserved to suffer, but I did not."

> 31:34 Because I feared the crowd and the contempt of the [ruling] families so terrified me, I kept quiet and would not leave the house.

In this verse, the author presents the reader with a realistic description of the effect of social pressure on an individual. Both the ruling elite and the masses reject Job. They make his appearance in society so uncomfortable that he stays at home and speaks to no one.

> 31:35 If someone would only listen to me! Here is my signature. Would that God would answer me! Let my opponent make a claim [against me] in writing.

This is a difficult verse to understand because it is long and the relationships between the different phrases are not clear. The verse seems to be written in "legalese." Job is willing to present his case in writing. He wants his opponent to do the same. While the text only implies who "would answer," the Targum suggests the Almighty. Rashi uses *ha-Makom* (the Place), another name for the Divine. As Rashi presents his view of the verse, Job says, "Would that *ha-Makom* would testify on my behalf, for there is none like God, as Perfect, as Righteous, Who could serve as a witness."

> 31:36 Surely I would carry it on my shoulder. I would put it on like a crown.

As Rashi sees it, Job says that he would carry the message of the book mentioned in the previous verse. God will then vindicate him.

> 31:37 I would tell that person every step that I took. I would approach that person like a prince.

If only Job could find someone who would accept his position and take his case. He would tell that person everything and would treat him with deference.

> 31:38 If my land would cry out against me and its furrows weep together,

Having dealt with the possible complaints of people, the poor in Job's society, as well as those who may have wandered into that society, and those who contend with him in legal and religious matters, Job now turns to the land upon which he lives as if it might also lodge a complaint against him.

> 31:39 If I have consumed its yield without paying for it, if I disappointed those who worked it.

Rashi takes "without paying" as a reference to someone who would hire day laborers and oppress them by not paying them. He presents his readers with another possible meaning of the first clause: a reference to the second tithe. It was permitted to convert the second tithe to money, and bring the money, rather than the produce, to Jerusalem. Thus according to

Rashi, Job is referring to the sin of eating second tithe produce without paying the money. (See Deuteronomy 14:24–26.)

> 31:40 Then let thornbushes grow instead of wheat and prickly weeds come up instead of barley. Here end the words of Job.

Job is once again presented as being so sure of his position that he is willing to bring a curse upon himself if he is wrong: "If I am not right in my case and correct in my argument, then let me be destroyed."

Since Job continues speaking in chapter 42, Rashi takes the last words of this chapter as Job saying: "If I have done all this, may my speech end here." There is no point in continuing his argument if his words to this point have not been accepted.

Chapter 32

> 32:1 So the three men stopped answering Job because he was innocent in his own eyes.

THE THREE "FRIENDS" FAILED to convince Job of his guilt. Since they believe that suffering is punishment for guilt, the three friends must believe that Job is guilty. On the other hand, Job looks at his deeds and knows that he has not sinned. Therefore, his suffering cannot be a punishment. What is at stake is an ancient belief and an error in logic: the ancient belief is that if one sins, then suffering is the punishment. It does not follow that if one suffers, one has necessarily sinned. One can argue that if it rains, the grass will get wet. But one cannot argue that because the grass is wet, it must have rained. There can be another explanation; perhaps, someone turned on the lawn sprinkler.

Gersonides introduces this chapter with a statement. Since Job felt that he was innocent, his three "friends" could not prove that he was not innocent. Since they believed, as was noted, that sin precipitated punishment, it was incumbent upon them to prove Job guilty in order to justify his suffering. When they failed to do so, they became silent.

> 32:2 Then Elihu, son of Barachel, the Buzite of the family of Ram, became incensed. He was angry that Job had justified himself rather than God.

It may be that the statement of Elihu's family connections is made to indicate his elite status.

> 32:3 He was also angry with the three friends for condemning Job, without being able to refute him.

The author presents the reader with a challenge: Why was Elihu angry at the three friends? Could it have perhaps been because Job was condemned for no reason? Or was it that Job's friends could not present a reason for Job's condemnation?

Rashi explains Elihu's anger and Job's condemnation differently from what might be expected. He presents the rabbinic tradition that the verse is an example of a Masoretic correction of a text that contained a problem in it. These corrections, eighteen in all, were enumerated in rabbinic midrash. According to Rashi, before this correction, the verse would have said, "By their silence, the three friends condemned, as it were, God." To avoid such an impious statement, the scribes wrote the verse in its present form.

Ibn Ezra argues that Elihu is angry because the three friends thought that Job would be condemned by his own statements. Somewhat facetiously, he notes that those who think that the Scribes made a change in the text know something which he does not know.

For Gersonides, Elihu is angry because Job has made himself more righteous than God. However, Gersonides thinks that the reason Elihu is angry with the friends can be understood in one of two ways. Either they condemned Job but could not refute his arguments or they condemned Job by accusing him of sins even though they thought he might be innocent.

> 32:4 Elihu had waited to speak to Job because the others were older than he.

Not only is Elihu presented to us as a person of good breeding, the author also demonstrates that he is a courteous person. Being younger than the three "friends," he waited his turn before speaking to Job. Nevertheless, as the next verse indicates, when he finally does speak, he speaks out of anger.

> 32:5 Seeing that the three men had no way of responding, Elihu became furious.

Elihu may be angry because his basic beliefs—virtue is rewarded through a life of ease and the doing of evil is punished through suffering—are being threatened by the case of Job, who insists that although he is suffering, he is innocent. It is important to note that challenging this view was tantamount to a challenge to all of prophetic Judaism. His anger may be a result of his waiting to speak. Or his anger could emerge from his frustration with the discussion up until now. It is also possible that Elihu's youth has played a role in his anger.

> 32:6 Elihu ben Barachel, the Buzite, began speaking: I am young and you are old. Therefore, I held back, fearful to express my opinion to you.

Elihu begins by explaining why he has taken so long to enter into the discussion and debate.

> 32:7 I said, "Age should speak and old age should teach wisdom."

A lovely notion embedded in the midst of this dialogue, perhaps a statement that emerges from the culture of the time.

> 32:8 Indeed there is a spirit in humanity. It is the inspiration of the Almighty that gives the human understanding.

We have translated this verse in a way that avoids any gender specificity. Rashi makes it clear that is it is not age which makes for wisdom. Rather, it is the "spirit of God."

> 32:9 It is not the seniors who are wise, nor the aged who understand what is justice.

According to some, the singular *rav* is a term denoting some rank, such as "superior, senior, master, teacher or captain." Following the context, we have chosen "seniors" which suggest status and age in American English. However, Maimonides, in his *Guide for the Perplexed*, takes *rabim* to mean "many," translating the phrase as "Not many are wise" (*Guide* III:54). In any case, the author is arguing something that is counterintuitive. Those whom society might think are supposed to be wise are not necessarily discerning.

> 32:10 Therefore, I say, "Listen to me. I will give you my opinion."

Having argued that age (and its implied experience) does not necessarily produce wisdom, Elihu—a young man—is emboldened to present his opinion.

> 32:11 I have been waiting for your words. I have been listening to your reasoning, while you have been looking for words.

Elihu attacks the three "friends" for being unable to present a cogent argument against Job. All they produce is (meaningless) words.

> 32:12 I paid attention to you, but not one of you could refute Job or answer his arguments.

Elihu is clearly not pleased with his friends. He is disappointed in them. Job has threatened Elihu's basic beliefs. In turn, that has threatened Elihu's sense of self. So either he or the elders have to refute Job.

> 32:13 Don't say, "We have found wisdom. Let God get rid of him rather than a human being."

This is Elihu's admonishment of the friends. He strikes out at them, "Don't you dare excuse yourself by saying, 'It is in God's hands. Let God do what God will with Job.'"

Rashi reads it as "Lest you say we have found wisdom in our silence, that we don't provoke or condemn him (Job) any more, for God will get rid of him and not a human. You should not have diminished God's honor in this way."

> 32:14 He has not directed his words against me and I will not use your arguments to answer him.

Elihu nows offers readers a fresh approach than the arguments that were offered to Job by his other friends. Elihu knows that the arguments of the friends were insufficient to convince Job of his guilt. Some commentators see the first pronoun of the verse as a reference to Job. Others do not do so. They seem to read the first part of the verse as a reference to Job's friends.

Rashi explains the first clause of this verse as Elihu's statement that he had perhaps learned of Job's pleadings by tradition.

Ibn Ezra reads the verse as Elihu's amazement that although he had not heard their precise argumentation, they were unable to persuade Job.

> 32:15 They are shocked. They can't answer. Words fail them.

The young man has surprised his elders. In the face of his negative comments, they are unable to respond. Rashi takes the world *heeteeku* (which we have translated as "fail") to mean that the old men are unable to speak. For Ibn Ezra, it either refers to their inability to speak until someone would transmit (*heeteek* [pass on]) their words or the ability to speak was taken from them. For Gersonides, it means that "speech was removed from them so that they were left as if they were mute."

> 32:16 I wait, yet they don't speak. They just stand there and don't answer.

Elihu is looking for an answer to the challenge presented by Job, which threatens to undermine his theology: how can the suffering of the innocent be explained?

> 32:17 For my part, I too will speak. Even I will express my opinion.

Elihu tells the readers that he will now take his turn to speak—implying that he will explain what happened to Job although others have failed to do so.

32:18 For I am filled with words and the wind within my gut forces me.

The sentiment of this verse is clear. Elihu feels compelled to speak out. The Hebrew of the verse is earthy and direct. The words bubble up and erupt from inside of him. He cannot control them. And they come from a deeply rooted place inside of him. The two words *ruach b'vitnee* literally mean "wind in my belly." But this is not the "hot air" of contemporary American English which would suggest "empty words." Nor does it imply "a bellyful" which means "I have had enough." While *ruach* could mean "spirit," one would hardly expect "spirit" in one's belly. Following the idiom of American English, we have rendered *b'vitnee* as "my gut."

32:19 Behold my gut is like [new] wine bottled up, like new wineskins about to burst.

Elihu presents the reader with a striking image of new wine. The gases of continuing fermentation create pressure. If such pressure is not vented, the wineskins will burst. Such is the anger of Elihu. He is "ready to burst at the seams."

32:20 Let me speak so I can find relief. Let me open my lips and respond.

This verse continues the sentiments of the previous verse. Elihu can't stand it. He wants to speak. He has something to say—and he has to say it immediately. He wants to argue with Job. He wants to enter the debate with him. He wants to prove him wrong.

32:21 I will not favor any person nor will I flatter any person.

This is Elihu's way of saying that he will only speak the truth without regard to the individual who might be slighted as a result of his words. In idiomatic American English, we might say, "he will not mince his words."

32:22 For I don't know how to flatter, else my Maker would swiftly take me away.

Although the verse consists of simple words, it is challenging to translate. The first three words, *kee lo yadatee* (for I don't know), require an object. The next word, *achaneh*, is a finite verb (I [will] flatter) and not *lachnot*, the expected infinite form of the verb. One could translate the four words of the first clause as "For I don't know. I will flatter." However, we and most translators assume that the negative particle *lo* (no, not) carries to *achaneh* to give the meaning—"For I don't know how to flatter."

We have rendered the second clause *c'maat yesaynee osenee* (literally, "quickly my Maker will lift me up") as "my Maker would swiftly take me away."

The Targum avoids a literal translation of the verse and translates: "For I don't know how to be accepted as a friend (*l'esemodaa*), would that the One who made me would speedily grant me favor (*yesovar lee apeen*)." (Literally, *yesovar lee apeen* means "lift up my face.")

Ibn Ezra thinks that *yesa'eynee* could mean "God will burn me" (rather than simply "took me away"), basing his suggestion on interpretations of a similar word in 2 Samuel 5:21. He contends that Elihu is claiming that if he were to favor Job, God would not protect him. Rather, God would "burn" him.

Chapter 33

33:1 Job, now listen to my words. Pay attention to all that I say.

Elihu wants to make sure that Job pays careful attention to what he has to say. Elihu's statement is similar to Job's words in 13:6.

33:2 Behold, I am opening my mouth so that my tongue can speak.

This is a rather obvious statement. A literal translation of the last clause of the verse, *dibrah leshonee b'cheekee*, would yield "my tongue speaks in my throat," something that really does not make sense in American English. His language is flowery and he seems to be stalling. After all, he spent nearly all of chapter 32 telling the reader why he was speaking and he has yet to make his point. The reader may feel the desire to encourage him to get to his point. Perhaps it is his youth. Perhaps it is his uncertainty.

33:3 From my sincere heart come words of knowledge. My lips will say what is plain.

Elihu continues to preface his remarks.

33:4 The spirit of God made me and the breath of the Almighty gave me life.

This statement is designed to give credence to what Elihu is about to say. Rashi thinks that it is a statement of humility.

33:5 Answer me, if you can. Confront me and take a stand.

Elihu is so sure of his position that he challenges Job to reply to it.

33:6 I am the same as you before God. I too was shaped from clay.

While this verse is designed to place Elihu on equal footing with Job, it is challenging to translate it idiomatically. The word *c'fecha* (literally, "like your mouth") has the meaning "I am like you."

33:7 Behold, fear of me should not make you afraid nor should
my hand be heavy on you.

Elihu seeks to reassure Job that the two of them should be able to speak openly without restraint.

33:8 My ears have heard what you said. I have listened to the
sound of your words.

In case there is any confusion, Elihu wants to make sure that both Job—and his readers—understand that he heard everything that Job said and understood the meaning of his words.

33:9 I am pure without transgression. I am innocent without sin.

This is an amplification of the previous verse. This is not Elihu speaking on his own behalf, as if to present his bona fides. Elihu is repeating what he has heard Job saying.

33:10 God finds complaints against me. God thinks that I am
God's enemy.

According to Elihu, this verse is a continuation of Job's argument.

33:11 God put my feet into stocks. God watches all my paths.

Elihu continues repeating what he thinks Job has been arguing. This reference to "stocks" appears only in Job. The other reference is Job 13:27.

33:12 Let me now answer you. In this, you are not correct. For
God is greater than humankind.

It seems that Job has argued (and indeed this is the main thrust of the book of Job) that although mortals cannot struggle with God nor challenge divine justice, Job still maintains his innocence. Elihu wants Job to come to understand that no mortal can comprehend divine actions. Rashi tells readers that God need not defend divine righteousness since the righteous actions of God are far greater than those of mortals.

33:13 Why do you argue with God? The Divine will not answer
anyone's words.

The intent of this verse is clear. But *devarav* (literally, "his words") is difficult to translate because it is not clear whose words are intended. The context suggests "your words." We have taken *devarav* to suggest an anonymous group, that is, anyone's words.

> 33:14 Although God may speak one way or another, mortals may not sense it.

Elihu is suggesting the oft-repeated sentiment that humans cannot fathom the reasons of the Divine for specific actions, framed in the familiar "God works in mysterious ways."

> 33:15 In a dream, in a night vision, when deep sleep falls upon humans as they slumber on their beds.

> 33:16 Then God may open the ears of humans so that God may frighten them with terrors that will befall them.

We have placed these verses together since one is required to make sense of the other. According to Maimonides (*Guide*, II:32), verse 15 indicates the mechanism for prophecy. Maimonides suggests that prophecy, for all prophets except for Moses, occurs in dreams or in visions.

Rashi thinks that the notion of a dream in verse 15 and "ears being opened" in verse 16 are exemplified by what happened to Avimelech (Genesis 20:6). He takes the end of verse 16 to refer to that which occurs to sinners who suffer is a confirmation of their punishment.

Ibn Ezra reads the last clause of the given Hebrew text to mean that the suffering of the wicked is the result of a divine judgment.

> 33:17 To keep one from doing wrong and to hide pride from a person.

Although *maaseh* (deed) has no modifier, the Targum adds *bishah* (bad) after *ovdah* (deed). This enables us to translate *maaseh* as "doing wrong."

For Rashi, it is illness that keeps a person from doing wrong. He takes *maaseh* to mean an act that the person intended to carry out. As an explanation of the second clause, Rashi tells the reader that suffering is sent to the would-be sinner in order to humble the person so that they might repent and avoid death. Rashi's complete understanding of the verse would be something like "[Illness and suffering] keeps a person from doing an intended deed and instead humbles the person to repent and avoid death."

> 33:18 To keep one's soul from the pit and one's life from falling on one's sword.

There are two words in this verse that carry some baggage of mythology with them. To die is to go into the grave. "To keep one's soul from the pit" seems to suggest preventing death.

Chapter 33

Rashi believes *bashalach* refers to a weapon and suggests that the lance or sword is the possession of the Angel of Death. As he takes the verse, God does Job a favor by bringing suffering upon him, sparing Job's soul.

> 33:19 Pain chastens the individual in bed whose bones ache continually.

What is being suggested is that suffering may have an instructive purpose, even if it does not have an immediate connection to sin.

> 33:20 Even bread disgusts the individual and the soul rejects desirable food.

Sick people are often unable to eat, whether they are offered simple food or fancy food. This verse may be seen as a description of what happens to a person who is being chastised. It may also serve as further warning by Elihu to Job.

> 33:21 One's flesh begins to shrink and one's bones now begin to stick out.

The author of Job presents the reader with a graphic picture of self-starvation caused by illness. To translate the verse idiomatically and to transcend gender specificity, we have moved from the literal translation of *yichel b'saro mayroee*, "his flesh is consumed and can't be seen"—to "the person's flesh begins to shrink."

> 33:22 The individual's soul approaches the grave and one's life to those who bring death.

This verse continues the description of the individual now under discussion from numerous previous verses. While the identity of "those who bring death" is unclear, Ibn Ezra understands *lamimitim* as angels of death.

> 33:23 Yet if there is an angel for that person, one among a thousand who might intercede to proclaim one's uprightness,

The Targum adds two Greek loanwords to amplify its translation of the verse: *peraclete* (advocate) and *kategor* (accuser, prosecutor). Thus, the Hebrew text is understood to be seeking "one advocate from a thousand prosecutors to proclaim one's uprightness."

Perhaps Rashi is following the Targum when he suggests that the thousand are those who would proclaim the person's transgressions, while there is only one who would intercede to proclaim one's uprightness.

For Ibn Ezra, the role of the angel is to speak on the person's behalf. He deduces from this verse that those angels charged with bringing death are many, while there is only one angel who is charged with safeguarding an individual.

> 33:24 Then God will be gracious to the individual and say, "Release this person from going into the grave. I have found a ransom for this person."

While it is not explicit in the verse, we have followed Rashi and identified God as the subject. God is the one who is ever willing to be convinced of a person's merits.

> 33:25 This person's skin will be smoother than that of a child. It will become again as in the days of one's youth.

In this obscure statement, Elihu seems to be promising Job that if he repents, his health will be restored.

> 33:26 Let that individual pray to God, for God will grant that person favor with joy. The individual will experience God's presence. God will return that person to a righteous state.

For both idiomatic and theological reasons, we have not translated *v'yar panav* as "he will see His face." Rather, we have chosen to transcend its gender specificity and its particular theology to "the individual will experience God's presence," something for which many of us yearn. The literal translation "he will see His face," that is, experience God's presence, assumes that the unnamed subject of the verb "see" is the human. It is conceivable that the subject could be God. If that is indeed the case, then the phrase could be "God will see the individual with joy" which would continue the sense of the previous verse.

> 33:27 The individual declares before all humanity, "I have sinned. I perverted what was right. I gained nothing from it."

Again, Elihu encourages Job as the sinner to declare his sin before witnesses and return to a righteous path. Readers may be familiar with this verse since it appears in the liturgy of the High Holidays.

> 33:28 God has saved my soul from the grave and I shall live to yet see light.

The text is written in the first person but it is traditionally read as in the third person. We have translated it in the first person. While God is not named in this verse, we assume that God is indeed being referenced. Such a declaration is what may be expected from the repentant sinner, now redeemed.

33:29 Behold such things does God do to a person, twice and even three times.

Rashi takes "twice and even three times" as a reference to the chastising of a sinner through illness, not to destroy the sinner but to move the sinner to repentance. Should the sinner continue to provoke God, then that sinner will need to worry about death and *Gehinnom*. Rashi sees a parallel to the use of "twice" and "three times" in the formulaic phrases of Amos describing "three transgressions, indeed four" and directed against Gaza, Tyre, Ammon, Moab, Judah, and Israel. (See Amos chapters 1 and 2.)

33:30 To take the person's soul out of the pit, to be illumined by the light of life.

This verse is somewhat optimistic. It follows directly on the previous verse. God can raise the person from darkness into light—perhaps even simply through a relationship with the Divine. Since *shachat* (pit) can also mean "grave," this verse may be a reference to the delivery from death in this life.

33:31 Pay attention, Job. Listen to me. Be silent and I will speak.

33:32 If you have something to say, answer me. Speak up. I want you to be cleared.

One might say that Elihu wants Job to have a fair trial or one could say that Elihu is playing "good cop" in the familiar game of "good cop, bad cop."

33:33 If not, listen to me. Be quiet and I will teach you wisdom.

In this verse, Elihu once again reveals his point of view. Elihu believes that suffering is intended to cause repentance. If a suffering person turns to God, one's suffering will be relieved. Elihu asks Job to answer this, and if not, to be silent and listen to his superior wisdom.

Chapter 34

> 34:1 Then Elihu began speaking.

ONCE AGAIN, THE AUTHOR uses the Aramaic formula *v'yaan . . . v'yomer* (literally, "he answered . . . and said") which we have translated as "[He] began speaking." Although Elihu will charge Job with denying Divine Providence, the burden of this chapter and the entire book is precisely an attack on the assumption that if one does good, one receives good (or reward) and that if one does evil, one is punished. This theme is woven throughout the entire book of Job. Job's claim, however, is that he has been good. He has been obedient. He has attempted to please God. Yet, he has suffered nonetheless. The very beginning of the book contains the notion that there is a kind of wager between Satan and God, following the conversation that they have with one another. Job has been put to a series of tests. These tests give rise to the verses that follow.

> 34:2 You who are wise, listen to my words. You who are learned, hearken to me.

Elihu makes his case to the elite of society.

> 34:3 For the ear tests words as the palate tastes food.

Elihu opens up his comments for evaluation and scrutiny.

> 34:4 Let us choose what is right for us. Let us know for ourselves what is good.

While the word *mishpat* is often translated as "justice," we have translated it as "right" to fit the context of the verse.

> 34:5 For Job has said, "I am innocent, yet God has taken away my rights."

This statement is something that readers may feel that they have already read. It certainly reflects the statements Elihu has made concerning

Job's position. Although *mishpat*, translated as "right" in the previous verse, is a singular noun, we have translated it here in the plural as "rights" for idiomatic reasons. Rashi reads *mishpatee* (which we translate "my rights") as "proof of [my] words." The force of Rashi's comment is certainly the opportunity for Job to tell his side of the story.

> 34:6 Would I lie about my rights? Though I am without transgression, my wound remains incurable.

The three words *al mishpatee achazayv* literally mean "upon my rights, I will lie." We have taken them to be Job's defense of his own position. Therefore, we have translated them as a rhetorical question that he raises.

Perhaps this verse is a free association of Job's defense—consistent with what we have heard him say in previous verses and reiterated by Elihu.

> 34:7 What kind of man is Job, drinking in derision like water?

The metaphor undertaken by the author in this verse seems to mean that Job cannot be changed by what is said to him.

> 34:8 He goes about with those who do evil. He walks with evil men.

Elihu posits that Job socializes with those who, like him, are evil. Job is both attracted to those who are evil because he is evil and he becomes evil as a result of the company that he keeps.

> 35:9 For he [Job] says that one gains nothing pleasing God.

The various tests that Job has endured could well have produced the statement attributed to Job in this verse. One could easily say that Job tried to please God and he gained nothing. In fact, he suffered even as he attempted to do what is pleasing to the Divine.

> 34:10 Therefore, you who are sensible people, listen to me. Far be it from God to do evil, for the Almighty to do wrong.

To accept Job's position, Elihu would have to condemn God's actions as evil, something that he is unable to do. Thus, Elihu, just like the other "comforters" in the book of Job, is locked into the proposition that good actions bring mortals good actions by God and bad actions by people bring punishment upon themselves. For Elihu, as for Job's other "friends," Job's suffering is proof of Job's sin. To think otherwise would involve blaming God, an incomprehensible notion for them.

> 34:11 God renders unto humans according to their actions and brings upon humans according to their behavior.

Simply put, people get what they deserve. This notion of Elihu is a continuation of what he has posted, a position from which he is unwilling to move: a righteous God rewards and punishes justly. This is similar to Abraham's question in Genesis 18:25.

> 34:12 Surely God would not condemn unjustly. The Almighty would not pervert justice.

The text contains the word *yarshea* (condemn). The context requires the addition of "unjustly." This is precisely Job's argument. He claims that he has been condemned unjustly.

> 34:13 Who appointed God over earth? Who put God in charge of the whole universe?

This is a rhetorical question asked by Elihu. God alone controls the earth and the universe. It is the divine will that controls all.

> 34:14 If that is what God intended, God would draw in the divine spirit and breath.

This verse is dependent on the following verse for meaning. Elihu links God's justice to God's maintenance of life itself. Were God wicked, then God would destroy all life.

> 34:15 All flesh at once would die and humankind would return to dust.

This verse continues the previous verse and describes what the outcome would be were God to remove spirit and soul from the world. It certainly is an echo of what we read in Genesis 2:7, "Then God formed the human of the dust of the ground, and breathed into the human's nostrils the breath of life; and the human became a living soul," and Genesis 3:19, "Dust you are and to dust you shall return."

> 34:16 If you can understand, hear this! Listen to my words.

Although the literal meaning of *l'kol melay* is "the sound of my words," we think that a better idiomatic translation is "my words." Alternatively, though with less specificity, we could employ the American English idiom, "the sound of my voice" which connotes tone over content.

> 34:17 Could one rule who hates justice? Would you condemn the righteous and mighty one?

It seems that the first clause describes God. The second clause may be describing Job if it is understood to be somewhat facetious. The "mighty" are mentioned again in 34:20 below.

> 34:18 Who can say to a sovereign ruler, "You are good for nothing," and to heirs to the throne, "You are wicked"?

The point that Elihu is making is that only God has the power to override *lèse majesté* and tell the truth about sovereign rulers and express that honestly to them. In order to avoid any gender specificity, we translated "kings" as "sovereign rulers" and "princes" as "heirs to the throne."

> 34:19 Who is not partial to heirs to the throne nor favors the rich over the poor, for they are all the work of God's hands?

If God is the source of justice for all, then God can favor no one individual. For Rashi, only God, as the Sovereign of the World, is the One who favors no one.

> 34:20 At midnight, in a moment, they die. People crumble and pass away. Untouched by a human hand, the mighty are taken away.

The Targum relates the verse to events in Jewish history. Those who "die in a moment" were the people of Sodom. Those who "die at midnight" were the Egyptians. Those who "were taken away" were the haughty sinners.

> 34:21 For God's eyes are upon the ways of humanity. God sees all their steps.

Although *eesh* (literally, "man") is in the singular in the first clause and *tzaadav* (his steps) refers to a singular person, to make this gender free and to fit the American idiom, we have translated it as "humanity" and "their steps."

> 34:22 There is no darkness, there is no gloom in which evildoers may hide.

As noted above, we have translated *tzalmavet* as "gloom" rather than the traditional "shadow of death" as in Psalm 23:4.

> 34:23 It is not for a mortal to set a time to go before God for judgment.

Our translation depends on an emendation of *od* (further) to *moayd* (time). While we understand the verb *yaseem* to mean "to set a time," Rashi understands it to mean to put a charge on someone. Thus, God does not make up additional charges over and above what the person has done. For Rashi, Elihu's statement is not a rebuttal of Job. Rather, he is in agreement with what he understands Job to be saying in Job 23:6

> 34:24 God smashes the mighty without investigation and sets up others in their places.

This verse points to the inscrutability of what happens in the world more than the justice of it. Elihu's response to Job's complaint that God acts unfairly is to stress God's justice in all divine acts. One would otherwise wonder why Elihu would declare that God smashes "without investigation."

> 34:25 Thus, God knows their deeds. God overthrows them in the night, and they are crushed.

Rashi's understanding of this verse may provide us with insight on the previous verse. For him, Elihu's argument is that since God knows all the acts of mortals, whether good or bad, God does not need to enter into contention with them. Such a view confirms our translation of *lo chayker* in as "without investigation."

> 34:26 God beats them as wicked people in a place where all can see.

The Targum offers two translations that may help us to understand this verse. The first translation is "In place of the wicked, they are beaten in a place where they are seen." The second translation is "Their punishment is in the place of the wicked where the righteous may be judged innocent."

> 34:27 For as much as they had turned away from following God and would not reflect on God's ways.

The last clause suggests that their ignorance of "God's ways" was a conscious choice of these wicked people.

> 34:28 To bring before God the cry of the poor, for God will hear the cries of the suffering.

The connection between the previous verse and this verse suggests that because hardhearted people would not attend to those who needed help, it was up to God to help them—and God would do so.

> 34:29 Whether this occurs to an individual or a nation, if God is silent, who can condemn God? If God hides God's face, who can see God?

We have moved the final clause of this verse to its beginning to make it read more easily. This verse highlights a profound theological issue. If God is really all-powerful and infinitely greater than humans, we have no way of really understanding God's response to individuals or nations or even if God responds at all. We cannot condemn God, nor can we see what God does not wish us to see.

> 34:30 So that a godless individual not reign and there be none to ensnare a people.

Rashi reads this first clause to mean that such a person would not rule over the poor. He understands this verse as Elihu's retort to Job. How dare Job deride a God who cares for the downtrodden?

> 34:31 Were one to say to God, "I have suffered, but as for me, I will not resort to violence."

Our rendering of the two verbs *nun-sin-alef* and *chet-bet-lamed* as "suffered" and "resort to violence" respectively is informed by the context suggested by the previous verses.

> 34:32 Teach me what I cannot see. If I have done wrong, I won't do it again.

It would seem that this verse is words that Elihu would put into the mouth of a sinner, particularly Job. If Job, or anyone like him, fails to see why he is being punished, let him first acknowledge that he must have done wrong, implore God to instruct him as to what sin he committed, and then promise that whatever it was, he will not do again. This verse follows Elihu's view (as well as the others of Job's "comforters") that suffering is proof of sin.

> 34:33 Should God reward you as you would have it, although you reject God? You have to choose, not me. Speak of what you know.

Elihu continues to berate Job. What does Job expect, having questioned God's justice? Does he expect something good will happen? For Elihu, only when Job acknowledges God's justice can Job expect positive change in his situation.

> 34:34 People of understanding keep saying to me as does every wise person who can hear me.

This verse requires the next verse to make its meaning clear. Rashi thinks that the first clause means that such "people" say that Job makes no sense when he speaks. This is explicitly stated in the next verse.

> 34:35 Job makes no sense when he speaks. His words have no meaning.

Elihu now claims that not only he, but also others, can see that Job has no case challenging the justice of God by claiming that he suffers without reason. Such a claim is the necessary position of those who hold the view that doing good is requited with good and that suffering is proof of evil doing.

> 34:36 Would that Job were tested to the utmost because of his responses like wicked people.

The first word in the verse, *avee*, is difficult to translate. It is an interjection, meaning "would that," with a possible etymology from the root *bet-ayin-hay* (desire). *Netzach*, often translated as "splendor" or "duration," can also have the meaning of a superlative. We have rendered it as "to the utmost."

> 34:37 Adding rebellion to sin, in front of us, he claps his hands and keeps saying things against God.

To fit into an American English idiom, we have translated *baynaynu* (among us) as "in front of us" and *v'yerev* (he multiplies words) as "he keeps saying."

Having not convinced Job, Elihu is angry that Job persists in his complaints, which threaten the theology of Elihu and other comforters of Job.

Chapter 35

35:1 Elihu then answered:

THE AUTHOR CONTINUES THE Aramaic usage of the phrase "answering and saying" to introduce a response.

35:2 Do you think that it is right [for you] to say "I am more righteous than God"?

For Elihu, it is either one way or the other. There are no other options. If Job is right, then God is wrong. For Job to consider such a notion is blasphemy, according to Elihu.

Rashi takes *mishpat* (which we have translated as "right") to mean a judgment, a judgment of mortals against their Creator. Rashi may be alluding to Isaiah 45:9. We follow Ibn Ezra in taking *tzedkee* (my righteousness) as "I am more righteous."

35:3 If you say, "What do you gain? How does this benefit me [more] than if I had sinned?"

Rashi explains the first clause in this verse as: What benefit to me are [my] upright ways? He takes the last clause to mean "[in what way] is my righteousness better than my sins?" For Ibn Ezra and Gersonides, *yiskon* means "benefit."

35:4 I will answer you and your companions with you.

Rashi's understanding of the verse is "I will answer your companions who were silent when you spoke," whose silence showed that they had no answer for you.

35:5 Look at the heavens and see. Gaze at the skies which are way above you.

Rashi writes in the singular masculine. Thus, he understands *shamayim* (heavens) as God: "Since Heaven is so high and you are so low, [God] gains benefit from neither your wickedness nor your virtue. Why then do you boast to God of your virtue?"

> 35:6 Were you to sin, how would it affect God? Were your transgressions to be many, what do you do to God?

The theology behind this verse can be difficult to understand. The basic question it poses is: Does God care about the actions of humans? Does God, the giver of Torah, care whether Jews perform *mitzvot* (sacred obligations, commandments)? This verse and the verse that follows are alluded to by Maimonides (*Guide* 3:23, 493), God ". . . does not care either for the obedience of those who obey or for the disobedience of those who obey." Precisely because Maimonides denies that these things affect God (*Guide* 1:35, p. 80, 81, and 1:36, p. 84), some readers concluded that Maimonides did not believe that God cared about the performance of *mitzvot*. Like Maimonides, Elihu asserts here that human behavior has no affect on God.

> 35:7 Were you to be virtuous, what would you give God? What would God take from your hand?

As noted above, one could conclude from this verse that God is beyond the concern for the actions of mere mortals. Such a conclusion would belie the basic notion of Judaism and its sister religions of Christianity and Islam, which both affirm a caring God. Nonetheless, Elihu is making the point that God in no way benefits from human action and therefore has no self-interest in how humans behave.

> 35:8 Your wickedness touches only people like yourself. Your virtue affects only other humans.

Virtue and vice, as Maimonides pointed out in his *Guide for the Perplexed* (3:54, p. 635) are functions of society. Were a person to live alone, virtue and vice would be irrelevant. Perhaps we also cultivate virtue in order that we might treat others correctly.

The Targum adds *cheevach* (your guilt) and *dachaya* (innocent). The Targum also changes the word order to translate the verse as "For a wicked person such as you, there will be guilt and your virtue will affect [only] an innocent person."

Rashi understands this verse to mean that only other humans are affected by one's virtue or one's vice. He connects this verse to the verse that follows by adding this phrase in his understanding of the two verses: "See how many are the wicked who oppress those who cry out."

> 35:9 Under the weight of oppression, people cry out for relief from the power of the mighty, they call for help.

We have translated *mayrov* (because of the many) and *mezroa* (because of the arm) as "under the weight" and "to avoid the power" respectively. This is not a literal translation but gives the sense of the text, which is clear. Oppression by the powerful brings a human response.

As Rashi reads this verse, those who oppress others cause their victims to cry out. The unfortunates who suffer because of the power of the mighty call out against them.

Ibn Ezra understands the verse to be Elihu's response to Job: "Do what you will, you cannot affect God. God hears the cry of the oppressed and the call of those who suffer the power of the mighty."

> 35:10 Yet no one says, "Where is God, my maker, who gives songs in the night?"

This verse is connected to the verse that follows. As we shall see from the comments of the classical commentators, the meaning of the last clause is not clear. What is the force of nocturnal songs?

For the Targum, the answer is that God orders the angels to sing praises at night.

Rashi provides readers with another answer. He takes *zimerot* (songs) to be related to the root *zayin-mem-raysh* (to prune) as in *v'carmecha lo tizmor* / You shall not prune your vineyard (Leviticus 25:4). Thus, the last clause means that God destroys (literally, "prunes") the wicked at night.

Ibn Ezra offers us two interpretations of "who gives songs in the night." Some contend that it refers to God, as in *motzay voker va'erev tarneen* / You make the outgoings of morning and evening rejoice (Psalm 65:9). While *tarneen* is understood as "rejoice," Ibn Ezra reads it as "cause to sing." Others think that the negative particle *lo* (no) in the first clause carries over to the second clause, specifically, "no one [no human] . . . gives songs in the night."

> 35:11 Teaching us from the beasts of the earth and granting us wisdom from the birds of the sky.

While this seems like a simple verse, it is actually somewhat difficult. The particle *mee* or *may* is derived from *min*. The word can mean "from" or "more than," among its many other meanings. We have chosen "from," for we think that the author wants to suggest some knowledge derived from nature.

Rashi disagrees with us. He adds *yotayr* (more than) to make clear his understanding of *mee*, *may* and *min*. As he understands the verse, God has taught us and given us wisdom more than "beasts" and "birds" and thus made us greater than them.

> 35:12 People cry out there. Yet, God does not answer, because of
> the pride of the wicked.

In reviewing this verse, a reader has to determine the force of *sham* (there). Does it refer to the earth and the sky of the previous verse, i.e., the domain which we mortals inhabit? Is the author suggesting that God is indifferent to human suffering? Second, we have to ask about the use of "pride of the wicked." Why should people of such character inhibit a divine response?

For Rashi, the verse means that although God sees the poor who are oppressed and crying out, because of the pride (perhaps arrogance) of those who oppress them, God still does not answer.

For Ibn Ezra, it is those who oppressed the poor who are now being oppressed themselves. And it is they who are now crying out for mercy. However, God does not answer their cry.

> 35:13 God will not listen to a deceitful cry. Nor will the Almighty
> pay any attention to it.

This seems to substantiate Ibn Ezra's understanding of the previous verse. The past evil of the oppressor will prevent their prayer from being heard by God. In an otherwise literal translation, the Targum translates *shav* ("deceit," hence, "deceitful cry") as *shikra* (falsity, lie).

Immediacy is the main element contained in Rashi's comment on the verse. God will not immediately respond to a "deceitful cry," because God is long-suffering and restrains anger.

> 35:14 Indeed, although you say that you pay no attention to it,
> your case is before God. You should [place your] hope in God.

While we have seen *teshureynu* from the root *shin-vav-raysh* (pay regard to) in a different form in the previous verse as *yeshurenah* ([God will] pay . . . any attention to it), the challenge is determining to what or to whom does the suffix *ehnu* refer? Is it to Job's case or is it to the Deity? Assuming that the reader would know that God could not be seen, and considering the context, we take *ehnu* to refer to Job's case.

U'techolaylu, from the root *yod-chet-lamed*, may mean either "to wait" or "to hope." Thus, the word may mean either "you should wait for God" or "you should [place your] hope in God." Following the views of the commentators, we have chosen "hope."

> 35:15 And now God does not order in divine anger nor does God know excessive words.

The word *pash* only appears in this verse and no other place in the Bible. Because its meaning is uncertain, it may have the following meanings: "high spirits, arrogance, excessive words, silliness, stupidity, or folly." We have chosen the meaning of "excessive words" because of the context of this verse and those that precede it.

> 35:16 Job opens his mouth with useless talk. Not knowing, he keeps talking.

With this verse, Elihu has rejected all of Job's arguments.

Chapter 36

36:1 Elihu continued speaking

36:2 Give me a moment and I will tell you that there is more to say for God.

WHILE WE HAVE IDIOMATICALLY rendered *cee od l'eloha milim* as "that there is more to say for God," the Targum renders the phrase as *arom tuv l'elaha maylyah* (because there are more words for God).

36:3 I get knowledge from afar and I ascribe righteousness to my Maker.

Ibn Ezra understands "from afar" as a reference to ultimate causes.

36:4 Truthfully, my words are not false. One whose ideas are correct is with you.

As part of his attack on Job's arguments and as a defense of his own, Elihu argues that his views are correct and implies that Job's views are false.

36:5 Behold God is mighty. Yet God does not despise [mortals]. God is mighty in the power of understanding.

No object is provided for the verb "despise" so it is not clear who or what is not despised by God. The Targum supplies *tzadika* (righteous) as the object of "not despise." Ibn Ezra supplies *chenam* (for no reason) as the predicate of "not despise."

Rashi takes the first "God is mighty" to refer to divine wisdom and divine compassion. He takes the second "God is mighty" as a reference to God's vengeance upon the wicked, which explains the first clause in the next verse.

36:6 God does not preserve the life of the wicked. God will give judgment to the poor.

In this verse, Elihu affirms the righteousness of God in yet another way. For Job and for the reader of the book of Job, the two affirmations do not necessarily find confirmation in the lived experience. Ecclesiastes said it another way: "For a sinner may do evil one hundred times, yet God will be patient" (8:12).

> 36:7 God does not take God's eyes off the righteous but exalts them forever by seating them with sovereign rulers on a throne.

While we have changed the order of the words in our translation for clarity, the author proclaims the reward that awaits the righteous, even if he spells it out in anthropomorphic terms. This verse is an expression of the belief that God rewards the righteous even as God punishes the wicked.

> 36:8 If they are bound in chains, tied in bonds of affliction.

This verse is linked to the next verse. The last word of the verse, which we translate as "affliction," may also mean "misery" or "poverty." The Targum identifies those in chains as *rashiayah* (the wicked). Rashi, on the other hand, thinks it is the righteous who are bound in the chains of suffering and disease.

> 36:9 God recounts to people their deeds, including their sins which they arrogantly committed.

Although *poalam* (their work) is a singular noun with a plural suffix, we have rendered it as "their deeds" for idiomatic reasons. Such a translation also allows it to parallel *pishayhem* (their sins), another plural noun with a plural suffix.

> 36:10 God opens their ears to reproof, telling them to turn away from evil.

The verse refers to those people mentioned in the previous verse. The verb *shin-vav-bet* may mean "return, repent, or turn." To fit the context, we have used the last meaning, translating it as "turn away."

> 36:11 If they obey and serve God, they will spend their days in prosperity and their years in pleasure.

Once again, Elihu presents readers with the notion: Do good and you will receive good; do bad and you will receive bad. The book of Job as a whole presents a challenge to this worldview.

> 36:12 If they do not obey, they will die by the sword and perish without knowledge.

The author seems to imply that people will die without knowing why they were punished, that is, the reason they are killed. Their deaths, according to this theology, is a result of their actions.

> 36:13 The godless store up anger. They do not cry out even when God fetters them.

This verse is a continuation of the theme established by previous verses.

> 36:14 Let them die in their youth. May their lives be like male prostitutes.

This is certainly a strong statement. It may be read either as a curse or as a statement about the future. If it is to be read in line with the sentiments of the previous verses, then it should be considered a curse.

> 36:15 God delivers those who suffer while they suffer. God opens their ears in their affliction.

There is a play on words in this verse with contradictory notions: *chet-lamed-tzadee* (deliver) and *lamed-chet-tzadee* (affliction). What is also suggested is that affliction causes people to be fully aware of their situation.

> 36:16 God drew you away from a narrow place to a broad place without restriction, to the comfort of a table laden with desserts.

In this verse, Elihu says to Job that his present suffering is an opportunity to repent. By repenting Job will be able to receive all manner of good things.

> 36:17 You have been served with the judgment due the wicked: justice. This judgment has taken hold of you.

The first clause of this verse seems to suggest that Elihu is telling Job that he, Job, has been punished sufficiently. The second clause implies that Elihu is telling Job that his punishment is indeed appropriate for his sins.

> 36:18 Don't let anger lead you astray. Nor let wealth or a large ransom mislead you.

The meaning of *b'saphek* may begin with either the Hebrew letter *samech* or *sin*. It is placed with the cantillation mark of *etnachtah*, suggesting the conclusion of a clause. The word, however, seems extraneous. Without it, the clause makes sense.

> 36:19 Will your cry for help avail you to keep you from distress or all your physical exertion?

In this verse, Rashi reads Elihu saying to Job, "You have come to cry out [to God] that no trouble befall you and none who possess power [*maamatzay koach*] should oppress you. If so, how will God collect the debt God is owed?"

> 36:20 Don't yearn for the night so that you can snatch people from their homes.

This is the only instance in which such an implication is made as to the nature of (one of) Job's sins.

> 36:21 Watch out that you don't turn to evil, for you might choose that because of affliction.

It is unclear whether the last clause suggests that Job has been tempted by "evil" rather than "affliction" as if he had a choice between the two or whether he has been tempted by "evil" because of the "affliction" he has endured. Or perhaps he would prefer evil to affliction. Maybe he has been afflicted so that he will not choose evil.

The second clause impacts the meaning of the first clause. Job is being warned against turning to evil, but he has not done so. If this is the case, one can read the verb *bacharta* (you have chosen) as being in the "prophetic perfect," that is, to be understood as "you might choose." Such an understanding of the verb would also comport with understanding *mayonee* as "rather than affliction." In either case, a warning against an action indicates that the action has not yet taken place.

> 36:22 God is supreme in power. Who can be a teacher like God?

Rashi explains this verse to mean that God is so powerful that no one can escape from God. Therefore, God is a unique teacher who can make a sinner repent and return to the Divine. Rashi differentiates between the actions of God and human beings, quoting *hineni mamter c'ayt machar barad cavayd* / Behold I am about to rain heavy hail upon you at this time in the morning (Exodus 9:18). As this text indicates, God warns sinners of impending punishment, hoping that they will repent. As for humans, if one wanted to exact revenge upon another, it would be without warning, in order to prevent the escape of the intended victim. Since there is no escape from God's punishment, God provides a warning.

> 36:23 Who has ordered God's way? Who could say to God, "You have done wrong"?

Both clauses in this verse attempt to convey the same notion: God is supreme over all things. Thus, God cannot be questioned about any one thing.

> 36:24 Remember to praise God's work that humans have observed.

The difficulty of translating this verse is a result of the various meanings understood by translators of the root *shin-yod-raysh*. Some take it as the intensive form of "to sing." Others, including our three classical commentators, derive it from *shin-vav-raysh* (to see, observe). It is their understanding that we followed in our translation.

> 36:25 Every human has seen it. Every mortal has viewed it from far away.

Rashi explains "it" as God's work, thus referring this verse to the previous verse. Ibn Ezra is very specific about his understanding of the subject of this verse. Any person of intelligence will look at God's work.

> 36:26 Behold, God is great beyond our knowing. The number of God's years is beyond our finding out.

Rashi reads this verse in connection with the previous verse. He takes the last clause as the reason why one should look "far away," that is, to ask about the ancient peoples and learn from them.

> 36:27 God draws up the drops of water, distilling rain from their mist.

To the modern reader who lives in cities and suburbs rain may be a nuisance. To the ancient Israelite dwelling in the parched wilderness, rain was life itself. While the ancients were not schooled in the modern science of meteorology, they understood that there was some relationship between evaporation and rainfall.

> 36:28 The heavens pour down rain which falls upon the multitudes of people.

The importance of rain in Jewish thought is demonstrated by the insertion of *mashiv ha-ruach umoreed ha-geshem* (Who causes the wind to blow and brings down the rain) into the Amidah, the core prayer of Jewish worship. This phrase is recited from the fall holiday of *Shemini Atzeret* through the first day of Passover in spring.

> 36:29 Who can understand the dispersion of the clouds, the thundering of God's pavilion?

The marvels of nature are taken as evidence of the powers of God.

> 36:30 Behold, God spreads light upon the sea, covering its deepest depths.

We have assumed *alav* (upon it) in the first clause is a reference to *ha-yam* (the sea), which appears in the second clause. For a smoother translation, we have moved "the sea" from the second clause into our translation of the first clause. We also understand *shorshei* (literally, "the roots of") to mean "its deepest depths."

> 36:31 God judges peoples by them. God provides them with abundant food.

As Rashi notes, the reference to "them" is "the clouds." Thus, it is rain through which God judges people. Without rain, things would be unable to grow. Famine would ensue. And with famine comes death. Since it was believed that God controlled the rain, God was both the ultimate source of food and, as a result, life. Rashi explains that by controlling the clouds, God can withhold rain and thereby punish nations by famine and other plagues. The wicked are thus judged from on high. The generation of the flood was punished when "the flood gates of the deep burst apart" (Genesis 7:11). The sinners of Sodom were punished when "All [their] land [was] devastated by sulfur and salt" (Deuteronomy 29:22). And Sisera was punished when "From heaven . . . the stars in their courses fought against [him]" (Judges 5:20).

Rashi continues. He explains further that God can provide "abundant food" from on high to those God chooses, as the Torah suggests: "Behold I will cause to rain bread from heaven for you" (Exodus 16:4).

> 36:32 God covers the light with clouds yet directs it to the one who pleads for it.

Ibn Ezra is most helpful in understanding this verse. He suggests that God covers the light by clouds. He turns to the meaning of the root *pay-gimel-ayin* (to touch) to explain *c'maphgeeha*, which he takes to mean "rain." As he explains the clause, God directs the sun to affect, that is, to touch, the moving clouds which contained the rain.

> 36:33 The thunder proclaims what is coming. Even cattle sense the approaching storm.

Rashi takes the first clause as a reference to God. The thunder, thus, means that God instructs people to examine their deeds and return in penitence to God. He takes *mikneh* in the second clause to mean "possession acquired through rainfall" rather than "cattle." Relating *oleh* to *el al* / to the heights (Hosea 11:7) and to *hukam al* / raised on high (2 Samuel 23:1), he takes it to mean "heavenward." Ibn Ezra reminds us that by observing the behavior of cattle and other animals, one can determine whether or not a storm is approaching.

Chapter 37

> 37:1 My heart trembles at this and would leap from its place.

CLEARLY DESCRIBING AN OVERWHELMING emotional state, this is an introduction for what is to follow in the verses below.

> 37:2 Listen most carefully to the roaring of God's voice, to the rumbling which comes from God's mouth.

While the text is referenced with a masculine pronoun, we have rendered it gender neutral particularly because we believe that it is indeed God whom the writer has in mind. It seems clear to us that God is the source of the sound, even as that source seems to be perceived through the medium of thunder.

> 37:3 God sends forth its sound throughout the entire heaven and divine lightning flashes to the ends of the earth.

Gersonides tells us that the thunder is directed to descend throughout the heavens so that it can be heard in every place where there are clouds.

> 37:4 A voice roars afterwards. God thunders forth with the sound of divine majesty, holding nothing back so that God's voice can be heard.

It is unclear whether the author intended to ask readers to believe that thunder was really God's voice or if thunder was simply a metaphor for God's power. While we would opt for the latter, the distance of time makes it difficult to precisely determine the author's intentions.

> 37:5 God thunders with the divine voice in a marvelous manner.
> God does great things beyond what we can know.

The Targum adds a new note to God's wonders by inserting *al perishan d'atid lemebad* (concerning events about to occur) into an otherwise literal translation of the verse.

> 37:6 God says to the snow, "Fall to the earth." And to the rain showers, [God says,] "Be torrents."

We have translated *mitrot uzo* (literally, "his powerful rains") as "torrents." It is clear that according to the author, the phenomena of nature operate by divine will.

> 37:7 God puts the divine seal on the hand of every person so that every mortal may know God's handiwork.

Rashi takes the first clause of this verse to mean that when a person sins, that person seals their own verdict for all the punishments to be meted out for those sins when that person dies. There is once again an echo here in the High Holiday liturgy, specifically the *Unetaneh Tokef* prayer (best known for its theme of: "Who will live and who will die?"). He takes the second clause to mean that God will announce the reasons for those punishments.

> 37:8 The wild animals go into hiding and stay in their dens.

The author describes the effect of heavy rain, even on wild animals. Rashi takes the verse to relate to agents of divine punishment. Not only does God have wild animals to carry out such punishment, God also has windstorms and cold to do so.

> 37:9 The storm comes out of its chamber. And cold comes with the north wind.

It may be that some ancient mythological belief is behind the notion of some "chamber" from which "the storm comes." In other words, somewhere in the heavens, there is some place from which evil emerges, at the direction of some demon.

> 37:10 Ice—and wide expanses of water that are frozen solid— comes from the breath of God.

For Ibn Ezra, *b'mutzak* is a reference to the solid earth which is like a point at the center of the spheres. For Gersonides, *mineshmat* means "God's will." He explains *mutzak* as what occurs when dew is frozen and turns to frost.

> 37:11 Indeed with plenty of water, God loads the clouds. God spreads lightning flashes through the clouds.

The first two words of this verse, *af b'ree*, are taken as the name of the angelic prince of rain in the poetic prayer for rain recited in the *musaf* (additional) service on Shemini Atzeret. We have rendered *b'ree* as "with plenty of water." We have taken *af* to mean "indeed" since it is difficult to render in English.

> 37:12 By God's design, they circle over the surface of the entire earth. They do whatever God commands.

The author is describing the seemingly circular movement of the clouds visible to the inhabitants of the settled world.

> 37:13 Whether for a particular tribe or for a particular country or as an act of steadfast love, God will bring it on.

The Targum translates the verse as "Whether there is rain as punishment, for peoples and deserts or whether there is gushing rain for trees of the mountains or valleys, or whether it is a nice rain for fields and vineyards, God will supply it for all."

> 37:14 Job, listen to this. Stop and reflect on the wonders of God.

The wonders of nature are taken to be the works of God. He is commenting directly to Job at this point.

> 37:15 Do you know how God exerts control over all and brings lightning out of a cloud?

For Rashi, the nature of *b'soom Eloha* (God exerts control) means that "God establishes a covenant dependent on a [divine] word."

> 37:16 Do you know how the clouds are suspended, those marvels of God who is perfect in knowledge?

Once again, the marvels of nature are seen as proof of the wisdom of God. There is some wordplay on this verse regarding knowledge. This verse—as well as the previous verse—begins by asking Job "Do you know?" God, on the other hand, is described as *tmim de'im* (perfect in knowledge).

> 37:17 [Do you know why] your clothes seem warm when God keeps the south wind from blowing on the land?

We think that *halo tayda* (do you know), which introduced the previous two verses, is assumed here. Job is being challenged to explain a wonder of nature. The assumption is that if Job cannot explain such wonders, he has no right to challenge the wisdom, and thereby the justice, of God.

Two questions that we need to understand in this verse are meteorological. The other question is grammatical. It seems that the south wind in some manner causes an elevation in temperature, and that this is what causes the person to be warm in their garments. Amos Hacham (1921–2012), a well-known Israeli Bible scholar, suggests this may be describing a situation in winter, when a cold front ceases, and warm weather that the text understands as coming from the south, causes a person who has bundled up against cold to be warm in their garments.

It is unclear what may be assumed by *me* (from *min* or "from") when added to *darom* (south [wind]). Perhaps we are to understand that the wind is kept from blowing and hence the rise in temperature. This is how we have translated the verse. Or perhaps we should understand *me* as suggesting that the blowing of wind from the south was the cause of the rise in temperature. The Targum's translation suggests this "by reason of" meaning of *me*.

> 37:18 Can you join with God in spreading out the skies which are as strong as a cast metal mirror?

The imagery of the sky, seemingly ethereal, being compared to a mirror, cast of metal, is striking. The contemporary Bible scholar, Avivah Zornberg, suggests that mirrors used by women are seen as powerful spiritual tools.

> 37:19 Teach us what to say to God, for we cannot present our case because of darkness.

This verse seems to be speaking to Job saying, "If you are so smart as to challenge God, why don't you tell your comforters what they should say to God. If you are enlightened, provide arguments for those you think are in darkness." Job has not claimed that he stands in the light while others are in the dark, but his "comforters" have contrived arguments he did not put forth, rather than responding to the arguments he actually made.

> 37:20 Should God be told that I wish to talk? Would one speak [to God] and be swallowed up?

The Targum expands this verse: "Is it possible that I would speak? For if a human would speak, that human would be accused."

> 37:21 Now no one can see the sun in the skies until the wind passes and clears [the clouds].

An idiomatic translation of the verse requires some adjustments to the text. We take *ohr bahir* (literally, "bright light") to mean "the sun." We have also made an addition of "the clouds" which is not in the Hebrew text but it is suggested by the suffix *aym* (them) in the verb *va't'haraym* (and clears them).

What seems suggested by the verse is the existence of a natural order. Thus, the sun can be blotted out by the clouds. However, when the clouds are moved by the wind, the sun can be seen.

> 37:22 God comes in fearsome majesty out of the north in golden splendor.

Rashi sees this verse as a continuation of the previous verse. Thus, it is also a continuation of the attack made by Elihu on the other three comforters.

> 37:23 The Almighty whom we do not comprehend is magnificent in power. In God's great justice and righteousness, God does not oppress.

Rashi takes *lo metzanuhu* (literally, "we cannot find Him"), which we have rendered as "we do not comprehend," to mean that we cannot object to any divine judgment on humans because of the greatness of divine power. This power, argues Rashi, affords humans the ability to achieve atonement through something as small as a handful of grain of limited monetary value or through the sacrifice of a pair of doves, something less than the value of an ox, ram, or donkey. Since he takes *mishpat* (justice) to refer to suffering, Rashi thinks that God does not afflict anyone more than is necessary and certainly does not afflict an innocent person. Rashi quotes the expression *ish kematnat yado* / each man according to the gift of his hands (Deuteronomy 16:17), understanding from it that God judges each person according to their ability, accepts each person based on what they have to offer and does not expect more from a person than they have to give.

> 37:24 Therefore, people revere God. God pays no heed to those who think that they are wise.

Elihu presented his case to Job and against Job: God is righteous and does not punish those who are innocent. Job, who claims that he is innocent and yet has been punished, simply does not or will not understand that if God is righteous, then Job cannot be righteous. (Otherwise, he would not have been punished.) To think differently is to pretend to have the capacity for knowledge of which humans are incapable.

Chapter 38

38:1 Then Adonai answered Job out of the whirlwind:

THIS IS PROBABLY THE most quoted verse in the entire book of Job. Job now finds himself in direct contact with the Creator of the universe. The term "whirlwind" implies a radical change and signifies a deep challenge. It also suggests a relationship between God as Creator and the divine plan to show Job the beauty of the world even amidst his suffering. Even so, there is a problem with the nature of the argument which will occupy chapters 38–41. All of these chapters contrast divine power and understanding with human attributes, in particular, Job's power and ability to understand. Of course, God is more powerful than men or women. And yes, the marvels of the universe test the limits of human understanding. Nonetheless, the argument from divine capacity does not answer Job's questioning the relation of virtue to suffering and vice to enjoyment. However, at the conclusion of the discussion (in chapter 42), Job will submit. The brave statement Job made in an earlier chapter still stands out: *hayn yektelaynee lo ayachayl ach derachay el panav ocheeach* / Were God to kill me, for that I might hope. Yet I will argue my position in front of God (Job 13:15). God has power over Job. God can kill Job. Nevertheless, God cannot win the argument thereby. Job insists on his innocence and demands that God prove him wrong.

38:2 Who is the one who would darken counsel with senseless words?

God challenges Job by saying, "Who is Job to challenge God?" Yet, the book of Job in its entirety is actually a challenge to God.

38:3 Act like a man. I will question you and you will answer me.

We have moved from the literal translation of *ezor-na c'gever chalatzecha* (gird up your loins [for battle]) to a more idiomatic translation, "act like a man," because, although this translation, like the verse, is gender specific, it will mean more to the modern reader.

> 38:4 Where were you when I laid out the foundations of the earth? Tell me if you understand.

God treats Job as a "Johnny come lately." In other words, God implies that the divine perspective on the world has depth and perception that Job could never achieve. One may argue that such a question does not meet Job's objections. It is true that we may not know the origins of the universe, but such ignorance does not touch the question of whether there is a moral dimension to the universe. What Job seems to understand, even if his "comforters" do not, is that he, although innocent, has suffered as if he were guilty. That suffering seems to belie the notion that virtue is rewarded and vice is punished. It also seems to undermine the idea of a just God ruling the universe.

> 38:5 Do you know who set its dimensions? Or who stretched out a measuring line on it?

This verse reflects an early understanding of science and the dimensions and boundaries of the earth. But its purpose is to establish God as the architect and builder of the universe. In our era, modern technology affords us the unprecedented opportunity to understand the world's dimensions. The great explorers set out on their courses precisely to discover this, as did the great astronomers such as Galileo and Copernicus. It is no accident that scientists such as Galileo and Darwin came into conflict with the religion of their time. While our relatively modern capacity to measure and understand may cause us to think we have greater power than the ancients, we are still subject to human limitations, illness, natural and human made disasters. Perhaps we can now measure the earth, but we are still minute in comparison to the One who conceived and created it.

> 38:6 On what were the pillars set? And who laid the cornerstone?

Once again, Job is being challenged. He is being questioned about his knowledge of the origins of the world. But such a challenge is insufficient to counter the argument that Job has made: although he is innocent, he has suffered. The notion of God as Creator does not adequately address the problem of evil although this is the traditional Jewish response to it. The presumption is that the grandeur of the universe as described in Psalm 90:1–3, for example, will cause the individual to rethink one's stance on personal suffering. It is supposed to take the individual out of one's own selfishness to contemplate one's place in the larger world. Nonetheless, such a perspective does not provide ease nor does suffering prove guilt.

> 38:7 When the stars of morning sang together and the angels shouted for joy.

Although the Hebrew text has *b'nai elohim* (literally, "sons/children of God"), we follow the Targum and translate it as "angels."

> 38:8 Who closed in the sea with doors when it broke out of the womb?

It seems clear that a remnant of ancient cosmology is retained in this verse, including the notion that the creation of the world is in some way mirrored in the birth of humans. Echoes of the notion that the creation of the world involved God conquering waters are found in many other biblical sources including Genesis 1, Psalm 24 and Psalm 104.

> 38:9 When I made a cloud its garment and thick darkness its wrapping.

This verse describes more of the cosmology of creation. Following the imagery of the womb in the preceding verse, this verse describes how the oceans are wrapped like a baby.

> 38:10 When I fixed its boundaries and set its bars and doors.

This continues the theme from the previous verses. God created the world and Job did not. This claim allows God to establish authority over the decisions that impact upon Job.

> 38:11 I have said, "This far shall you come but no further. And here your swells stop."

Again, for the author of Job, God is the master of all nature.

> 38:12 Have you ever commanded the morning [to appear] or informed the dawn?

In this verse, the rhetorical questioning continues, comparing divine power to human power. Does God's power answer the challenge Job has posed to God's justice? Does might make right? Just because God is Creator of the world, need God's justice not be evident to God's creatures?

> 38:13 To grasp the edges of the earth so that the wicked are shaken from it.

According to this verse, creation has a moral purpose. The world is as it is to keep the wicked out of it. However, the wicked are indeed included in it.

> 38:14 Like clay under a seal, the earth is molded. Like a garment, humans stand on it.

What seems to be under discussion by both the Targum and Rashi is the resurrection of the dead. According to Rashi, the first clause tells readers that the bodies of the dead will revert to their appearance at the time of death. During resurrection, the individual will be revived and will rise up in their clothing.

> 38:15 Light will be kept from the wicked. Their arrogant arm will be broken.

A midrash on this verse appears in several places, including the following from the Babylonian Talmud (*Chagigah* 12a): The light which the Holy One of Blessing created on the first day, Adam saw through it from one end of the world to the other. When the Holy One of Blessing peered at the generation of the flood and the generation of the Dispersion, and saw that their actions were destructive, the Holy One stood up and hid it from them, as it is said (Job 38:15), "Light will be kept from the wicked."

Rashi and Ibn Ezra both seem to see this as a continuing reference to the resurrection of the dead. It is important to note that "arm" generally refers to "right arm," which is a reference to strength.

> 38:16 Have you ever gone into the sources of the sea? Have you ever walked into its deepest depths?

Once again, we are presented with the contrast of divine power and human strength. The author is engaging in repetition and hyperbole as part of a literary style rather than actually adding anything new or significant to the argument that Job has been treated in an unjust manner. It is true that modern science has demonstrated that the oceans are one of the least known and understood areas in our time. Approximately 95 percent of the oceans have not been explored. Perhaps it is this vast unknown to which the author is alluding.

> 38:17 Have the gates of death been shown to you? Have you seen the gates of the shadow of death?

So little we know about death. We even avoid talking about it. How unknowable it is for those still living. And we have a reasonable fear of death—the gates of death have not been revealed to us. Even were they to be revealed, would that mean that we were not dying? Can a living human being really come close to seeing or understanding death?

We have already noted that while "the shadow of death" is the traditional translation of the word *tzalmavet*, it is may be better translated as "gloom." Nevertheless, the context here suggests the more traditional translation.

> 38:18 Have you ever thought how enormous are the dimensions of the earth? If you know all about it, tell [me].

This verse is a comment on Job's finitude and God's infinite power. The message of the text is that contemplation of one's own finitude should bring about humility. The text continues to be written in the form of a rhetorical challenge to Job, almost a taunt.

> 38:19 Which is the way to where light dwells? And where is the place of darkness?

This verse continues the questioning of the previous verse. Does Job have insight into the knowledge that God possesses as Creator?

> 38:20 Could you take them to their territory? Do you know the way to their houses?

Although the suffixes of the verbs and nouns are singular, the context that is indicated by the previous verse, specifically light and darkness, suggests the plural translation that we have adopted.

> 38:21 Because your days are many and you were born at that time, you surely would know.

This verse is a sarcastic statement. Were Job to claim that he knew something about creation, he would need to have been alive at the time of creation. This verse is about human limitation in the face of divine creative energy. If we cannot fathom God's creative power, can we really fathom how God runs the world? The author's argument is that there is so much that appears to us unjust, yet it is clear we see such a limited part of the picture.

> 38:22 Have you ever come into where snow is stored? Have you ever seen where hail is kept?

This is a continuation of the challenges that God is placing before Job. The content may be a little different, but the basic argument remains the same. We have rendered *otzrot* (treasuries, storehouses) as "is stored" and "is kept," to maintain an idiomatic sense to the verse.

> 38:23 Which I stored up for times of trouble, for the days of battle and war.

This verse follows directly on the previous verse. The notion of bad weather as a means of war is included in the Song of Deborah (Judges 5:4 and 5:20–21).

> 38:24 In what way is light dispersed? How is the east wind spread upon the earth?

This verse appears to be the same argument that we have seen before. The focus is somewhat different, but it is still about the power of the Divine.

> 38:25 Who cut a channel for a flood or made a path for a thunderstorm?

The author is cataloguing the natural phenomena of the world which are beyond human power to create. The list is long and includes many things we may take for granted. The power of nature, of God's creation, is spelled out at length, in this chapter and in the following chapters.

> 38:26 To cause it to rain on a land where no one is, upon a wilderness where no one lives.

Readers may wonder about the force of the statement. The preceding verses suggested a divine purpose which Job could neither understand nor fathom. In this verse, the author has included a description of an event without purpose: falling rain that provides no human benefit. Perhaps the author is hinting at the notion that sometimes things just happen. If this is the case, then Job is justified. His suffering would not be suffering. It could just be attributed to bad luck. A more traditional read might be that the author is hinting at the possibility that humans are not the center of the universe. There is a natural world outside of human existence and habitation. If Job can look at himself as a small part of a much larger universe, he may have a different perspective on his suffering.

> 38:27 To satisfy the desert and wilderness and causes it to bud with grass.

The word *shoah*, which appears in this verse, has come to only refer to the Holocaust. However, it has many other meanings in the Bible. It can mean "what breaks out suddenly" or "a storm which breaks out violently." When joined with *meshoah* (as it is here), it can mean "dreariness and desolation, trouble and ruin, or desert and wilderness." We believe that the last option best fits the context of this verse.

> 38:28 Does rain have a parent? Who begot the drops of dew?

The questions presented in this verse assume that God is the cause of all. In this verse, the author paints beautiful images of God as father of nature. But they still lead back to Job's questioning whether such is the source of morality.

> 38:29 From whose womb did ice come out? Who bore the heaven's frost?

And in this verse, the author paints God as the mother of nature, trying to bolster the argument without addressing Job's plaint.

> 38:30 When water becomes hard as a rock and the surface of the ocean is frozen.

The wonders of nature are described in this verse. Water, a liquid, becomes a solid. The very substance in which we can swim becomes a surface on which we can walk. Again, Job is being challenged that he is a human of limited power and God is all powerful. As a result, he should forgo his questioning of divine justice.

> 38:31 Can you bind the chains of the Pleiades or loose the bonds of the Orion?

The configuration of the stars are set. No human can change them. Thus, like many of the previous verses, this verse describes the order of nature. This reflects, according to traditional belief, the power of God and the lack of power of the human being.

> 38:32 Can you lead out the constellations in their seasons? Can you guide the bear and her cubs?

The word *mazarot* is difficult to translate. It is used here and nowhere else in the Bible. Various scholars have proposed different meanings for this word: constellations, stars, Venus appearing as the morning star and the evening star, the Hyades, Arcturus, and those constellations in the southern Zodiac. We have chosen "constellations" since its general sense seems to fit the verse. While there may be some debate among astronomers and scholars as to the exact technical aspects of this verse, they provide a poetic rather than scientific perspective, following similar challenges that have been made to Job in previous verses.

> 38:33 Do you know the laws of heaven? Can you set its rule upon the earth?

It is not clear as to what the possessive suffix *-o* (his/its) of *mishtaro* (his/its rule) refers. The context suggests either "its" or possibly "God's."

Although *shemayim* is a plural noun, the Targum and our three classical commentators understand the -*o* ending to refer to heaven's.

> 38:34 Could you raise your voice to the clouds that a flood of water might cover you?

Again, it is obvious that Job could not do what is being asked of him. The author describes the power of God to do so.

> 38:35 Can you dispatch lightning? Do they report, "Here we are"?

The argument continues.

> 38:36 Who put wisdom into our hearts or gave understanding to our minds?

The author now focuses on wisdom and the implantation of wisdom in the human mind, rather than simply the control of nature that was argued in previous verses. Our translation is made difficult by two uncommon words in the verse, *teechot* and *sechvee*. Since they seem to be parallel, the meaning of one should suggest the meaning of the other. Since wisdom is that which is being inserted, and one might think that the inner parts are somehow the receptacle, "hearts" would fit the American English idiom. We have added "our."

The word *sechvee* is a *hapax legomenon*, that is, it appears only once in the entire Bible. It reflects the meaning as a cock or rooster as it is used in the morning blessings. However, the Targum, Rashi, and Ibn Ezra take the word to mean "heart," in the sense of "mind."

> 38:37 Who can accurately count the clouds? Who can pour out the heavenly jars?

This section is describing the grandeur of the created world.

This is yet another set of questions which contrast human and divine knowledge, the intent of which is to poetically describe God's powers as creator and manager of the world. The question of how this relates to divine justice if answered, is answered only implicitly and imperfectly.

> 38:38 When dust hardens and clods stick together.

The previous verse dealt with rain. This verse seems to describe what happens without rain. In many places in North America, what occurs appears to be different. Dust does not "harden" nor do clods congeal when drought comes. Rather, the dust is carried away by wind and clods of earth become dust. In turn, this is carried away by the wind.

> 38:39 Will you hunt prey for a lioness? Will you satisfy the hunger of young lions?

The choice of lions, as Gersonides suggests, is probably due to their huge appetites. Therefore, it takes a great deal of effort to feed them, even more than human beings. This verse challenges the ability of humans like Job to provide sustenance for all creatures who inhabit the earth, as God their creator is responsible for doing. See Psalm 145:16, Psalm 147:9, Psalm 104:10–14, Psalm 136:25, for descriptions of God's role in providing food for all creatures.

> 38:40 When they crouch in their lairs and when they lie in wait in a thicket?

This continues the previous verse. Obviously, neither Job nor anyone else can provide for the food chain of wild carnivores. Once again, the author presents the order of nature as something out of the control of humans. The implicit argument underlying such control is simple. If humans cannot do so, then who is capable of doing so? The only answer is God.

> 38:41 Who provides food for the raven when its young cry out to God and wander about for food?

The author presents a striking image in this verse. The chirping of the raven's hungry chicks is taken as a prayer to God. This is directly echoed in Psalm 147:9 as mentioned above.

Chapter 39

> 39:1 Do you know when mountain goats give birth? Have you noted when they bear their young?

RASHI OFFERS A TROUBLING explanation for this verse. In doing so, he quotes the Babylonian Talmud (*Bava Batra* 16a–b), which suggests that mountain goats hate their offspring. As soon as they are about to give birth, they go up on high rocks so that the baby goat, upon emerging from the birth canal, will fall to earth and die. To prevent this from happening, God prepares an eagle to catch the baby goat in its wings and save it.

Gersonides acknowledges the Talmudic source that Rashi cites. He contends that if it is not true, then he believes the verse was intended to simply suggest that animals bear offspring with great difficulty. This puts their offspring in danger. Hence, divine providence insures that such offspring be in the best possible condition in order to survive birth. This seems to be the intent of the author of the verse.

> 39:2 Do you know how many months it takes until they bear?
> Do you know when they will give birth?

The verse continues the same argument as the previous verse, as well as those in the previous chapter.

> 39:3 They crouch down. Their wombs split open. They send out their young.

The imperfect forms of all three verbs suggest the rapid succession of one stage of delivery to the next.

> 39:4 Their young grow strong. They increase out in the open. When they leave, they don't return.

The sense of this verse is that the offspring whose birth was described in the previous verse grow into healthy adulthood. They reproduce and form families that require new pasture land and hunting grounds. The cycle of life is then continued. All of this is under divine guidance and direction, something beyond the control and understanding of human beings.

> 39:5 Who let the donkey go free? Who untied the ropes of the wild ass?

The text returns to the form of rhetorical questions that has characterized God's speech since the beginning of chapter 38.

> 39:6 I have made the desert its home and the salt land its dwelling place.

This verse is a reference to the wild donkeys of the last verse. It is difficult, nonetheless, to determine the precise meaning of *aravah* here. It is not necessarily always sandy and waterless. To fit the context of the verse, we have translated it as "desert."

> 39:7 It mocks at the roar of the city. It does not hear the shouts of the driver.

With poetic anthropomorphism, the author attributes human feelings to a donkey, one that lives in the wilderness, far from the human habitation of the city and its resulting turmoil, away from the control of humans over animals.

> 39:8 It scours the hills for its pasture, seeking anything that is green.

The freedom of wild animals is balanced by their need to search for food. For good or ill, the domestication of certain animals carries with it an easier source for food. At this point, the direction that the author is taking the argument is not clear. However, it seems that the animal world is complicated, beyond the ability of humans, such as Job, to control.

> 39:9 Will the wild ox be willing to serve you? Will it bed down at your feeding trough?

This rhetorical question reminds Job and the reader that wild animals will not serve any human master. God has power over wild and domestic animals, while humans control only a small portion of the animal population. This perspective is relevant in our time when habitat loss due to humans threatens many of the earth's species.

> 39:10 Could you bind the wild ox to the furrow by its bridle? Will it harrow the valleys after you?

This verse once again posits that certain animals cannot be used for agricultural work.

> 39:11 Would you depend on its great strength and leave your hard work to them?

The question in this verse is the same as in the previous verse: can a wild ox be domesticated? Can it be trained to do the work that other animals have been trained to do? The question, like all the questions in this section, is rhetorical. It serves as a reminder that the natural world is far greater than human designs or needs, and that not everything serves human purposes.

> 39:12 Do you believe that it will bring home your seed or gather the grain to your threshing floor?

This verse assumes a further degree of domestication. The animal "knows" its pen and "knows" where the "threshing floor" is and what is to be done there.

> 39:13 The wings of the female ostrich beat wildly, but are they like the wings and feathers of a stork?

Although an ostrich may have wings and it may even beat them, it cannot fly. However, the ungainly stork can indeed fly. Perhaps in line with what has been written previously, the point is that some animals can do things which others cannot, even if they have the same kind of limbs.

> 39:14 For it lays its eggs on the ground and warms them in the dust.

Apparently, this is referring to the ostrich of the previous verse.

> 39:15 It forgets that some foot may smash them, that some wild animal may tread on them.

To the human eye, the actions of the ostrich seem to lack foresight. The author describes the bird as "forgetting" though it is unlikely that this human trait is what is at issue in the ostrich's behavior.

> 39:16 It treats its children harshly, as if they were not hers. It does not fear that her labor would be in vain.

Eggs that are left on the ground, not placed in a nest, nor warmed by the body heat of the mother may suggest that the mother does not care about her young. On other hand, perhaps she doesn't mind if the effort she spent in producing the eggs is wasted. This verse seems to reflect some natural history of ostriches. They have a very high rate of predation, and males are highly involved in the care of hatchlings.

> 39:17 For God has not granted her wisdom nor apportioned her understanding.

This verse implies the difference between animals—or at least these specific birds—and human beings.

> 39:18 But when it takes off into the heights, it mocks the horse and its rider.

This verse deals with the particular talents of the bird described in previous verses. One can expect that each animal has its own unique talent. But one should not expect one animal to do what another animal can do—even if it looks equipped to do so. This is part of the mystery of God's creation.

> 39:19 Did you give the horse its strength? Did you garb its neck with a mane?

In this verse and the six that follow, the author turns our attention from a bird to a horse.

> 39:20 Can you make it roar like a locust? The power of its snorting causes terror.

This verse suggests that the horse approximates the noise and the terror of an advancing cloud of locusts or humans on the attack. Thinking about the sound of an advancing cloud of locusts or the sound of an advancing group of horse riders suggests the terror of an imminent attack of locusts about to consume everything. It could also suggest the terror of an imminent attack of human enemies about to kill all before them.

> 39:21 It paws the ground, rejoicing in its power. It goes out for battle.

For Rashi, it seems that the horses are happy to engage in battle. And attacking horsemen travel through the valleys. Ibn Ezra explains that "the horses dig their feet [hooves] into the ground."

> 39:22 It [the warhorse] scorns fear and is not afraid. It does not turn away from the sword.

Ibn Ezra explains that "scorns fear" means that the horse would not fear what would frighten a human being. He takes the last phrase to mean that such a horse would not retreat from the sight of a sword.

> 39:23 The quiver rattles upon it as well as the flashing spear and sword.

Although it is difficult to gaze back over the course of history and determine the precise armament of warriors of the past, translators must make certain choices. There are a number of choices for the last word in this verse: "javelin, short sword, hunting knife, or scimitar." We have chosen "sword."

The Targum provides a different list of weapons carried on the horse, *aloyee teshray zayna* (upon it rests weapons): *charbah shennah* (a sharp sword), *morneeta v'romcha* (a lance and a spear). However, "quiver," which would suggest a bow and arrows, is not included in the Targum's list.

Rashi explains the rattle to his readers. The quiver is apparently so full of arrows that the galloping movement of the horse causes them to knock against each other and make a great deal of noise. The "flashing [of the spear]" is due to the spearhead (*lahav*) being made of iron.

> 39:24 With a roar and with rage, it swallows the earth. It pays no attention to the call of the shofar.

The author describes the onslaught of a warhorse, neighing, with bloodshot eyes, rushing toward the enemy, refusing to be held back by the *shofar*'s signal to retreat.

> 39:25 On hearing the horn, it answers "hurrah!" Even at a distance it can smell a battle and hear the shouts of the commanders and the battle cries.

Again, the warhorse is described as if it were its rider. Since *shofar* (the usual word choice in the verse rather than "horn") carries a specific connotation and what is being described is the anticipation of military action, we have chosen "horn" to better fit the context. As in many an army, the sound of the horn calls soldiers to attention, to which their response, depending on the particular army, may be *he'ach* or "here" or "present." We have rendered it as "hurrah" since it seems to be more than just a count-off or roll-call. Sounds and smells evoke a battlefield, even at a distance. War, like a musical dance, has its own steps. Its "music" includes the shouted orders of officers and the cries and alarms of war. The onomatopoetic word *teruah* can refer to both the sounds of war and to the sounds of religious worship (as when the *shofar* is used during the High Holidays).

> 39:26 Does the falcon fly high due to your understanding or stretch its wings toward the south?

We have returned to birds. Specifically, here and in the next verse, birds of prey.

> 39:27 Does the vulture ascend at your command and build its nest on high?

We have chosen to translate *nesher* as "vulture" although it is often mistranslated as "eagle." We also recognize the connotations surrounding "vulture" but the Griffon vulture is a beautiful bird that soars the skies above Israel.

> 39:28 The vulture makes its home upon a rock and spends the night there. A rocky crag is its stronghold.

This seems to be a continuation of the previous verse's discussion of vultures.

> 39:29 The vulture seeks its food from there. Its eyes can see it at a distance.

The place of the vulture's nest in a high crag is advantageous: the vulture can see its prey before its prey can see the vulture. The vulture, a scavenger, searches the landscape from on high to find carrion.

> 39:30 Wherever are the slain, there is the vulture. Its chicks lick up the blood there.

To avoid determining who does the hunting and who cares for the young, we have inserted "the vulture" into the text. It is clear that the author is graphically describing the details of the natural habitat of vultures in order to emphasize the complicated aspects of nature.

Chapter 40

40:1 God answered Job.

WHILE THIS VERSE APPEARS to be a simple literary device to introduce God's response in this ongoing dialogue, Gersonides suggests that when God saw that Job was unable to answer, God responded (as the next verse indicates) that one can gain instruction from impending evil. One could not challenge God without incurring a penalty. Job would answer, as the third verse indicates, that he henceforth would be silent.

40:2 Will the one who argues with the Almighty correct God?
Let the one who contends with God answer the Almighty.

In Rashi's understanding of the first clause, it reads "Is a human God that a human should rule?" Then Rashi follows with "Regarding the one who comes to argue with God, God will answer that person."

Ibn Ezra understands the statement a bit differently. He suggests a read of the first clause as "Is it ethical that a person would argue with the Almighty?" Then Ibn Ezra follows with "If Job would reprove God, why won't Job answer God?"

For Gersonides, the first clause is God's irritated response to Job: "[God says,] I have gone beyond what is required by law to deal with him. Why won't he answer?" Gersonides thinks that the second clause may mean, "the one whom God reproves should respond to that reproof."

40:3 Job then answered Adonai

The author uses the formulaic phrase that we have seen several times before in the text, *va'yaan . . . va'yomar* (literally, "he answered and said") which we render simply as "answered."

40:4 I am insignificant. How can I respond? I shall put my hand to my mouth.

If the thrust of the argument against Job is that he is nothing compared to God, then a (perhaps unintended) consequence of that argument is that

Job should not be challenged to contend with God since there is such a disparity in power between him and God. Job here decides to be silent because of this disparity. It might have been easy (or easier) for him to question God before, but now that he is confronted with God, perhaps he realizes that he cannot speak.

> 40:5 I spoke once but will not answer again. Twice, but not again.

This reads like a formulaic response, as if Job were pleading his case in a courtroom. Rashi contends that Job has made his case. He has actually spoken a little, but he will not speak again, that is, he will no longer plead his case.

> 40:6 Then God answered Job out of a whirlwind.

What seems intended by *sa'arah* is the sound of the wind, which becomes unintelligible to Job.

> 40:7 Prepare yourself. I will ask and you will answer.

To avoid gender specificity and to be more idiomatic, we translated *ezar na cagever halatzecha* (literally, "gird up your loins like a man") as "prepare yourself."

> 40:8 Will you impugn my justice? Will you condemn Me so that you can be acquitted.

Although it is clear that *tarsheeaynee* (condemn Me) and *titzdak* (you can be acquitted) are legal terms, a more idiomatic translation of the second clause would read, "Would you make me look bad, so you can look good?"

> 40:9 Do you have an arm like God? Can your voice thunder like the Divine?

The author of Job has no fear of anthropomorphic statements when referencing God's power. The reference to God's arm is really a metaphor for God's strength. This verse returns to the kind of comparative, rhetorical question we have seen in chapters 38 and 39.

> 40:10 Adorn yourself with power and majesty and dress yourself in glory and splendor.

If Job wants to claim that he cannot enter into contention with God because he is worthless, then God says to him caustically, "Then cover over that worthlessness with the appearances of worth, that is, if you think that you are nothing, pretend to be something." This verse seems related to the verses that follow it. The adornments that Job is told to put on are those that are needed in order to subdue the wicked.

> 40:11 Let loose the fury of your anger. Bring low any proud person that You see.

This is God's invitation to Job: if you don't like how I am dealing with evildoers (and the problem that evildoers sometimes prosper), then you see what you can do with them. You should take on the task of humbling the prideful. This could also be seen in our day as a kind of psychological displacement. Job, who is angry at God, because of what he perceives as unfair treatment, is being advised to direct his anger elsewhere, at other human beings who may have done nothing to him.

> 40:12 Humble every person. Trample down the wicked where they stand.

This verse continues the advice given by God to Job in the previous verse.

> 40:13 Hide them all in the dust. Cover their faces in secret.

In this verse, it seems that the author has placed his own feelings into the mouth of God, speaking against those in his own society who lord over him. It is also possible that God is asking Job to deal with the evildoers and giving him instructions on how to do so. This verse is part of a section that spans from verses 9–14. Verse 9 is about "Do you have power?" Verse 10 says, "If so, adorn yourself with Godly qualities." Then 40:11–13: "Punish the prideful and the wicked." Next 40:14 will follow with "I will acknowledge your saving power."

> 40:14 Then I will acknowledge to you that you can be saved by your own right hand.

This language is once again reminiscent of court proceedings. But it is also the language of salvation. It is the kind of language found in Psalm 98:1, Psalm 118:15–16, and Exodus 15:6. This language said that God, the God of the Torah and of the Psalms, is a God who redeems and saves. If Job can smite evildoers, then God will acknowledge Job's power. Since Job cannot do so then Job is forced to acknowledge God's power. This is not in opposition to God being a God of justice. However, if one does not have might, how can one enact or enforce justice? This verse is another contrast between Job and God, but the contrast is about more than simply power, and yet highlights the importance of power.

> 40:15 Behold the Behemoth that I have made along with you. It eats grass like cattle.

It is not clear what a behemoth is. According to rabbinic tradition, the Leviathan and the Behemoth were created at the same time as Adam. Whenever it was created, we are dealing with a mythic beast here, which is mentioned in the book of Enoch, as well as other post-biblical traditions and in various works of midrash.

> 40:16 Behold the strength it has in its loins. Look what power it has in the muscles of its body.

No matter what animal this is, it is clearly a large, powerful—and complicated—creature.

> 40:17 Stiff as a cedar, it holds its tail. The sinews of its thighs are interwoven.

This description could fit a crocodile. It does not seem to reflect an elephant. And it would be more difficult for it to be a description of some kind of sea animal. The description seems to indicate that the author is dealing with a mythically large and powerful creature.

> 40:18 Its bones are tubes of bronze. Its bones are rods of iron.

This is a strong and solid animal.

> 40:19 It is the first of the ways of God. Yet the God who made it can bring the sword to it.

What is being suggested by the author is that the God who creates is also the God who can destroy. There are creatures on earth so strong and powerful that only God, who has power over them, can subdue and control them. The author is using mythic language to describe mythic creatures: God has power over all creation, even the largest, strongest beast that exists.

> 40:20 For the mountains bring its food and all the beasts of the field play there.

The mighty animal seems to be both a herbivore and a carnivore. It eats plants that grow on the mountains. The beasts of the field provide the animal with an abundant prey.

> 40:21 It lies beneath the shady trees, hidden in the marsh by reeds.

This is a large animal that can still be stealthy in pursuit of its prey but it is not a predator.

> 40:22 The shady trees cover it with their shadow. The willows of the brook surround it.

The animal is hidden by the plants of its watery habitat. As a result, this verse seems to imply that the animal might be a crocodile.

> 40:23 Were the river to surge, it would not flee. Were the Jordan to rise up to its mouth, it would be at ease.

The author describes an animal that is assisted by its natural environment and is untroubled by changes in it. This is indeed a very powerful animal.

> 40:24 Can anyone capture it by its eyes or make a hole in its nose with a snare?

How does one capture an animal by its eyes? Perhaps it means to mislead an animal by appearance and then entrap it. But how would one do so with such a powerful—perhaps mythical—animal?

> 40:25 Can you pull up the Leviathan with a hook? Can you press down on its tongue with a rope?

The text continues with another comparison of divine power with human power. The implicit answer to these rhetorical questions is "no." Note that many Christian Bibles start chapter 41 here, eight verses earlier than the traditional text of the Hebrew Bible.

> 40:26 Can you put a rope through its nose or pierce its jaw with a hook?

This is a reference to some sort of hook that may be bent like a reed and is used to draw the fish from the sea.

> 40:27 Will it keep pleading with you for mercy? Will it speak to you softly?

The anthropomorphism is easy to understand in this verse. It implies that the Leviathan is able to speak and communicate its desires. In this case, the animal pleads for mercy, for its life, or at least to be released from the hook. The author is mocking in this verse. The idea that such an animal would plead or speak softly is preposterous for such a fearsome beast, as is the idea that Job could catch it, and as is the idea that Job should or could question God's justice.

> 40:28 Would it agree [to a covenant] to be your servant for life?

Although an idiomatic translation of this verse is difficult, its anthropomorphism is even more troubling. Can a sea animal make a covenant? Can one take such an animal as a "servant" or "slave?" It seems that this verse is simply another attempt by the author to compare divine power with human power. But it is more than just another attempt. It is poetry that presents Job and the reader with a challenge: mythic language and folktales. This creature is beyond human understanding. Thus, can it be contained through a legal instrument, be subdued through the means that humans use to subjugate one another? Will the world of wild beasts, of divine creative energy that God inhabits, ever be brought into submission by our human means of social organization? Leviathan, the force of the deep, is far more powerful than any human institution that uses a covenant to bring about servitude. The mythic power of Leviathan cannot be subdued by anything other than a greater power from a similar realm, that is, God.

> 40:29 Would you play with it like a bird? Would you put a leash on it for your children?

In this verse we follow Rashi, who sees it as describing the tying of a cord around the neck of an animal so that children can walk with it (much like we do with a leash and a dog).

> 40:30 Will tradespeople barter it? Will merchants divide it?

Chabareem means "guildsmen," that is, those who belong to the same professional association. Because "guildsmen" reflects a medieval situation, we have chosen the gender-free "tradespeople." While it is unclear whether the author is writing about business or a meal, we have assumed that the first clause parallels the second clause. Thus, we have translated it as "barter."

> 40:31 Would you fill its hide with harpoons? Would you stick fish spears into its head?

In this verse, once again, we see the implicit argument of human incapacity in the face of divine power.

> 40:32 Put your hand on it? That battle you would remember and would never do it again!

Rashi understands the first clause as a charge: "Will you be strong enough to fight it and use your hand to smite it?" But Ibn Ezra reads the verse quite differently. For him, the verse is advice: "Put your hand on it if you can, because if you could, you would not battle with it. If you tried, you would not live. Who then would think of putting a hand on it?"

Chapter 41

> 41:1 Such a hope is false. The very sight of it [the Leviathan] will send one hurling down.

WHO OR WHAT IS referred to by *toachalto* (its/his hope)? This verse seems to continue to discuss the Leviathan and its apparent invulnerability. If so, perhaps the hope is that the Leviathan can be captured or killed. Note that some Bibles start chapter 41 eight verses earlier, making this verse the ninth.

Similarly, *yootal* (will be hurled down) raises the question as to what or who will be hurled down. Perhaps it is the aforementioned "hope." Or is it the person who has seen the beast? What can be said about the verse is the sense that "hope is false" and the sight of the Leviathan is terrifying.

> 41:2 No one is so fierce as to rouse it. How then could anyone stand up to me?

The logic of this verse is as follows: if the Leviathan is so dangerous that no one will challenge it, how much more dangerous is it to challenge the Source of all life and the Creator of the Leviathan?

> 41:3 Who has given something beforehand that I should repay that person? Everything beneath the heavens belongs to me.

On the basis of *ashalaym* (I will repay), as well as what is suggested by the rest of the verse, we have chosen to translate *hekdeemanee* as "Who has given me something beforehand."

> 41:4 I will not be silent while it boasts or speaks of victories or the brilliance of its plan.

We take *badav* to mean "its boasting," which we have rendered as "while it boasts." Accordingly, we have translated *cheen erco* as "the brilliance of the plan." Were we to consider *badav* as deriving from "pole," then it could refer to the dimensions of the Leviathan. In that case, *cheen erco* might mean "the grace of its shape."

Since the nouns *badav* (its/his boasting) and *erco* (its/his plan) have masculine suffixes, and since Hebrew lacks gender neutral suffixes, it is not clear what or who is being described. It may be the Leviathan. Perhaps it is a subtle attack on Job, who has been in a debate with God and thinks he is winning.

Basing his teaching on a Midrash found in Genesis Rabbah 49:10, Rashi understands this difficult verse to mean that God will not be silent before the children of a righteous person. Following the Midrash, Rashi understands *bad* as branch, thus *badav* is "his branches," meaning his children. They will receive the reward due to their parent and they will find merit in remembering their parent. Rashi takes "victories" to refer to the struggles of that person to do what is right and good. Because of the gracious qualities of that person, God will reward those children.

> 41:5 Who can uncover the surface of its garment? Who can come with its double bit?

An animal is being described in this verse. "Its garment" seems to be its hide. That hide is covered with something which seems different from other elements of its hide but they can't be separated into two distinct elements.

The implication of *cefel risno* (double bit) is that this creature is so powerful that the means of control must be doubled.

> 41:6 Who would open up the doors of its face? Terror surrounds its teeth.

The implicit question in this verse is who would be stupid enough to provoke a beast to open its mouth.

> 41:7 Its pride is its scales, closely joined to each other.

Rashi explains the animal's pride. Because of its scales, it is protected as if it were surrounded by shields. He also explains "closely joined." The scales act like armor. It seems that they overlap one another so that the animal is protected from any attack.

> 41:8 Each is so close to the next that no air can pass between them.

This continues the description of the beast's scales.

> 41:9 Each is joined to the other. They adhere together. They cannot be separated.

The scales make the beast impervious to attack.

> 41:10 Its snortings flash out light. Its eyes are like the rays of dawn.

A mythical animal is treated in a mythical manner. Rashi suggests that *ateshavav* (snorting) is actually "sneezing." Whenever the animal sneezes, there is a flash of light that emanates from its eyes. The intensity of the flash is similar to the first rays of sun at dawn.

> 41:11 Flaming torches come out of its mouth. Sparks of fire spew forth.

As with other mythological beasts, such as dragons, the ability to project fire is part of its arsenal.

> 41:12 Smoke pours out of its nostrils, like a pot boiling on smoking reeds.

What is exuded by the nostrils of the beast is a mixture of steam and fumes like those that emerge from the burning of reeds.

> 41:13 Its breath will ignite coals even as flame comes out of its mouth.

Further evidence of the incendiary nature of the beast.

> 41:14 Strength rests in its neck. Its power skips before it.

This is a powerful, fire-breathing, frightening beast. But the precise intent of the verse is unclear. Perhaps it means that the beast's appearance manifests its strength. Or maybe it means that its appearance terrifies all who see it.

> 41:15 The folds of its flesh are compressed. They are rigid and immovable.

The advantage of such a bodily configuration is that it is firm, unshakable, enduring. Nonetheless, the author is trying to describe a frighteningly powerful creature. Rashi wants to make sure that the reader understands the import of such a description. So he tells his readers that what is being described is flesh beneath the scales of the beast. Similarly, when fish are caught and their scales are removed, one can see flesh beneath the scales. (The scales of the Leviathan were described in 41:7–9.)

> 41:16 Its heart is firm as stone, as hard as the lower millstone.

The various meanings of heart in Hebrew and English seem to be intended by the author here. The beast's courage, determination, and resolve are being described. For Rashi, the heart of the beast is as strong as the foundation stone of a building.

> 41:17 When it rises up, the mighty are terrified. Being defeated, they retreat.

Shevarim can mean "disasters" or "defeats," and thus *mishevarim* could mean "because of being defeated." We have translated it as "being defeated" in order to fit the context.

> 41:18 Neither sword nor spear nor dart nor any other weapon has any effect on it.

To describe the mythical power of the mythical animal, the author tells us that it is invulnerable to any known weapon. *Masa* is a reference to a weapon without specification.

> 41:19 It regards iron as if it were straw and brass as if it were rotten wood.

Since there is no weapon that can harm the beast, it has no regard for the strong metals from which they were made.

> 41:20 No arrow can make it flee. For it, slingshot stones become stubble.

Once again, the verse includes a description of ineffective weapons that indicate the invulnerable quality of the beast. Rashi upgrades the "slingshot stones" into the rocks hurled by a ballista. In any case, nothing can disturb the beast.

> 41:21 A cudgel is thought of as a piece of straw. It laughs at the rattle of a javelin.

The word *totach* (cudgel, club) occurs only here. In Modern Hebrew, it means a "cannon."

> 41:22 Its belly is covered with sharp scales, leaving a trail in the mud like a threshing sledge.

Although the literal meaning of *chaduday chares* is "sharp potsherds," what is meant by the author are the sharp protuberances created by nature rather than articles crafted by humans. Hence, we have rendered it as "sharp scales."

> 41:23 It makes the deep boil like a cooking pot. It churns the sea like a pot of ointment being made.

The imagery of both clauses is clear. By its movements, the beast stirs up the sea so that its waves resemble a pot being cooked, either to make a meal or to make medicine.

> 41:24 It leaves a shining track, so that one might think that the sea had grey hair.

In this verse, we are witness to the author's poetic description of the Leviathan once again. When it moves, it leaves a "shining track" in the sea. The color of the foam of the track is contrasted with the color of the rest of the sea.

> 41:25 Nothing on earth is like it, a creature without fear.

For Ibn Ezra, the rule which the Leviathan manifests is in the sea and not on the earth. He takes the second clause to indicate that no other creature is as fearless as it. Ibn Ezra even suggests that some interpret the uncommon form *heasu* (which we have translated "a creature") as lacking a letter *hay* which would make the word *asahu*, meaning that God made it fearless.

> 41:26 It looks down on all who are haughty. It rules over all who are proud.

The last word in this verse, *shachatz* (proud), is key to its understanding. It also gives us the moral meaning behind a series of verses that seem to be irrelevant to the author's argument.

Chapter 42

> 42:1 Job then replied to God,

WHILE THE STYLISTIC FORM "He answered and said" is used, we have rendered it simply as "replied." This is Job's final opportunity to make a cogent argument defending his position and his innocence. He has already spoken in his own defense through the end of chapter 31, when the text told us his words ended. Thus we might even expect that what we are about to hear is not his defense, but a new point of view, based on what he has heard from God. If one of us were to be so privileged as to have God speak to us directly from out of a whirlwind, is it not likely that we too, would be changed and change our point of view?

> 42:2 I know that You can do everything. Nothing can prevent You from carrying out your plans.

Job admits that he is nothing compared to God. Not only can God do everything in the present, God can also do everything in the future.

> 42:3 [God asked,] "Who, without knowledge, conceals [My] plan?" [Job answers,] "Therefore, I declare that I did not understand. I did not comprehend what was beyond me."

Rashi reads the first clause as a question directed to Job, "Who is the person who would hide and obscure the wonders of the Holy One?" Job admits that he knows that all things are in God's hands, saying, "I declared some of God's wonders, the ones I knew. But there are still hidden things [a play on *maaleem*] which I do not comprehend."

Ibn Ezra understands the first clause as Job's question, "Seeing that all power and all wisdom belong to God, who would deny God's plan?" Ibn Ezra adds, "Only someone without sense and without knowledge would do so." He takes *lo hegaditee* to be Job's statement that "Something which was not right came from my mouth, for I had entered into things too wonderful for me which I did not understand and which one could say that I could not understand. I can only understand that which You make known to me."

> 42:4 [Job continues:] Hear now, please, and I will speak. I will ask and you will make known to me.

It is not clear who is speaking but we assume, based on the preceding verse, that it is Job who is speaking. Gersonides combines this verse and the verse that follows into Job's statement: "At first, I had understood divine providence as something of which I had heard but had not properly proved it. Now my eyes see God's control of the universe. God's providence over every existing individual has been properly proven."

> 42:5 My ears have heard You and now my eyes have seen You.

According to Rashi, this is Job's statement that although he has heard about God many times before, this is the first time that he has seen God's Presence, the *Shechinah*. Rashi goes on to explain the next verse (42:6) in light of this one: having merited seeing God's Presence, Job now rejects his life and would be comforted were he to go to his grave, to the dust and ashes from which he came.

> 42:6 Therefore, I reject what I have said and repent, being just dust and ashes.

We have rendered this verse idiomatically. The text has two verbs, *emas* (I will reject) and *v'nechamtee* (I repented). We understand that what Job rejects is what he has said. Hence we add "what I have said" for the verse to make sense. The phrase *al afer v'eyefer* (upon dust and ashes) is challenging. While sitting on ashes or lying on ashes as a means of repentance is attested in Jonah 3:6 and Esther 4:3, neither sitting or lying is mentioned here. Moreover, dust is not mentioned in these verses from Jonah and Esther, but dust is mentioned here. Both dust and ashes are mentioned in *v'anochee afer v'eyefer* / I am only dust and ashes (Genesis 18:27). This is also an indicator of humility and contrition. Thus, it seemed fitting to add "being just" before these three words, which conclude Job's speech.

The Targum transforms Job's final words into a statement of resignation: "This is just the same as my rejecting my wealth and being consoled for the death of my children, who were but dust and ashes."

Gersonides offers a surprisingly spiritual statement. He understands the statement to mean that Job's pain departed when he properly cleaved to the Holy One.

> 42:7 After Adonai had said these things to Job, God said to Eliphaz, the Temanite, "I am angry with you and with your two friends because you have not spoken to me correctly, as did my servant Job."

This verse and those that follow seem to have been written by a different hand. The tone and message is different than most of the rest of the book. But we have been bequeathed this book as a whole unit and have to understand it within the context of its other chapters and verses. The issue of God's justice which Job and the author raised has not been sufficiently resolved. The "comforters" of Job, one of whom was Eliphaz, offered standard answers that reflected the theology of his age. But this verse seems to begin to justify Job's complaints.

> 42:8 Now take for yourselves seven bullocks and seven rams and go to my servant Job. Offer them up on your behalf as a burnt offering. My servant Job will pray for you and since I favor him, I will not treat you badly even though you did not speak of me in a proper way, as did my servant Job.

Rashi explains the sacrifice of the bullocks and rams as a means by which the three "comforters" of Job can be once again acceptable to God and gain favor from the Divine. Only if Job prays for Zophar, Bildad, and Eliphaz will their sins be forgiven and their transgressions no longer be remembered. Because God favors Job, God will accept his prayers.

> 42:9 So Eliphaz the Temanite, Bildad the Shuchite, and Zophar the Naamanite went and did what Adonai had instructed them. Adonai favored Job [and accepted Job's prayer on their behalf].

In this verse and the previous verse, the notion of "finding favor" indicates the acceptance of prayer. We added the bracketed phrase to the end of the verse to relate this verse to the previous verse. Divine favor was granted to Job in response to his prayers on behalf of his companions.

> 42:10 After Job prayed for his friends, Adonai returned to Job what had been snatched from him. God actually gave him twice what he had before.

While nothing can replace what Job lost or what he went through, God seems to be trying to recompense Job for what he has been forced to undergo at God's behest. The Hebrew uses *shav et sheveet* (literally, "to return a captivity"). We have rendered it as "return what had been snatched." Wealth, children, and health were suddenly taken from Job like a conquering and rampaging enemy army.

> 42:11 All his brothers and sisters and all of those who had known him before came and had a meal with Job in his house. They comforted him and consoled him concerning all of the evil which God had brought upon him. Each person gave a silver coin and a gold ring.

Now that Job has been accepted once again into society, he is no longer a person to avoid. One can now go to his house and join him for a meal. Rashi assumes that all of the people mentioned in this verse had been close to Job before Job encountered all his troubles. Then they kept away from him, assuming that Job's problems were a direct result of his sinning.

> 42:12 Adonai blessed the last part of Job's life more than the first part. He had 14,000 sheep, 6,000 camels, 1,000 yoke of oxen, and 1,000 female donkeys.

Ibn Ezra reminds us that while Job's animals were doubled, the number of years he might live were not under his control and are therefore not stated here.

> 42:13 Job had seven sons and three daughters.

Job's family was replaced but it was not returned to him. While he might appear to be better off, nothing can replace the pain and loss that he felt.

> 42:14 Job named his first daughter Yemimah, his second daughter Ketziah, and his third daughter Keren Ha-puch.

Each daughter's name had meaning, although it is difficult to ascertain why he chose these particular names. Yemimah meant "turtle dove." Ketziah meant either "cassia" or "bow-shaped." Keren Ha-Puch meant "little make-up box."

Rashi explains that the names of Job's daughters reflected their beauty. Yemimah was as bright and clear as the dawn. Ketziah wafted perfume as a cassia bush wafts its scent. Keren Ha-Puch was named after the container in which eye shadow is placed. (This suggests that Keren Ha-Puch had beautiful eyes.)

> 42:15 Nowhere in the land were there women as beautiful as Job's daughters and their father bestowed an inheritance on them along with their brothers.

While Rashi spoke of the physical beauty of Job's daughters in his comment on the previous verse, he indicates that this verse refers to the beauty of their actions. Apparently, it was the goodness of such acts that motivated Job to provide them with an inheritance equal to their brothers.

> 42:16 After this, Job lived 145 years. He saw his children and his grandchildren, even to the fourth generation.

It should be noted that Job and his children and grandchildren comprise three generations. Thus, the author's intent must have been to include his great-grandchildren in describing Job's new fortune.

> 42:17 Job died, old and full of years.

Gersonides concludes his commentary on Job by quoting Exodus 23:20: "Behold I am sending you an angel before you to guard you." Gersonides implies that the angel brings with it the argument that the order of the world, as well as the various beings in it, were for the sake of human beings. Moreover, the angel comes with proofs from reason and from the order of nature, as well as with words of the prophets. They all agree on the same thing. When Job heard what was said and he understood such order, he changed his mind, renounced what he has said, and ended with correct words.

For Further Reading

Eisen, Robert. *The Book of Job in Medieval Jewish Philosophy*. New York: Oxford University Press, 2004.
Frankl, Viktor E. *Man's Search for Meaning*. Boston: Beacon, 1959.
Jaffe, Hirshel, James Rudin, and Marcia Rudin. *Why Me? Why Anyone?* Northvale, NJ: Aronson, 1994.
Kushner, Harold. *When Bad Things Happen to Good People*. New York: Avon, 1981.
MacLeish, Archibald. *J.B.* Boston: Houghton Mifflin, 1956.

Printed in Dunstable, United Kingdom